3rd International Conference on Natural Language and Speech Processing (ICNLSP 2019)

Trento, Italy
12-13 September 2019

ISBN: 978-1-5108-9245-3

ICNLSP 2019

Proceedings of the 3rd International Conference on Natural Language and Speech Processing

12–13 September, 2019
University of Trento
Trento, Italy

 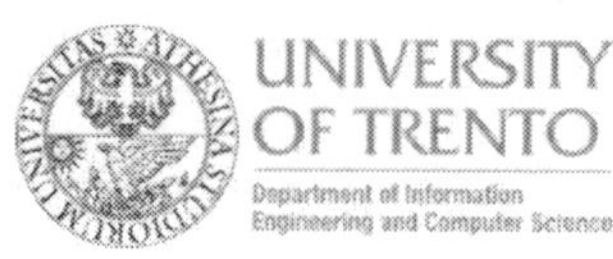 

Introduction

Welcome to ICNLSP 2019, the third edition of the International Conference on Natural Language and Speech Processing, held on September 12th, 13th 2019, and hosted at the univeristy of Trento in Italy.

ICNLSP is an opportunity and a forum for researchers and students to exchange ideas and discuss research and trends in the field of Natural Language Processing and Speech Processing.

The 46 papers submitted to ICNLSP 2019 have been reviewed by 3 reviewers. The program committee decided to accept 20 of them with an acceptance rate of 43 %. The papers will be presented orally. They cover various topics dealing with both speech and text: building resources, text summarization, spoken language understanding, etc.

The program includes also two keynotes. The first one, entitled "Detecting the fake news before they were even written", will be presented by Dr. Preslav Nakov from Qatar Computing Research Institute (QCRI), Qatar. The second keynote "One world - seven thousand languages" will be presented by Prof. Fausto Giunchiglia from University of Trento, Italy.

The conference is preceded by the workshop on NLP Solutions for Under Resourced Languages (NSURL). The workshop is intended as a forum for solving NLP problems for low-resourced languages.

We would like to acknowledge the support provided by University of Trento and DataScientia. We would like also to express our gratitude to the organizing and the program committees for the hard and valuable contributions.

We hope that ICNLSP 2019 will be highly positive scientific event. We wish a happy time for all the participants.

Mourad Abbas, and Abed Alhakim Freihat

Trento, September 2019

Organizers:

General Chair: Mourad Abbas
Chair: Abed Alhakim Freihat

Program Committee:

Mourad Abbas, CRSTDLA, Algeria
Ahmed Abdelali, QCRI, Qatar
Mohamed Afify, Microsoft, Egypt
Mansour Alghamdi, KACST, Saudi Arabia
Messaoud Bengherabi, CDTA, Algeria
Djamel Bouchaffra, CDTA, Algeria
Fayssal Bouarourou, University of Strasbourg, France
Markus Brückl, TU Berlin, Germany
Hadda Cherroun, Amar Telidji University, Algeria
Gérard Chollet, CNRS, France
Najim Dehak, Johns Hopkins University, USA
Mohamed Elfeky, Google Inc., USA
Mahmoud El-Haj, Lancaster University, UK
Abed Alhakim Freihat, University of Trento, Italy
Neil Glackin, Intelligent Voice, UK
Ahmed Guessoum, USTHB, Algeria
Mahmoud Gzawi, university of Lyon 2, France
Valia Kordoni, Humboldt University, Germany
Tomi Kinnunen, University of Eastern Finland, Finland
Eric Laporte, UPEM, France
Shang-Wen Li, Apple Inc., USA
Georges Linarès, University of Avignon, France
Walid Magdy, University of Edinburgh, UK
Shervin Malmasi, Harvard University, USA
Lluis Marquez, Amazon, Spain
Mohammed Mediani, University of Adrar, Algeria
Fatiha Merazka, USTHB, Algeria
Hamdy Mubarak, QCRI, Qatar
Preslav Nakov, QCRI, Qatar
Alexis Neme, UPEM, France
Mourad Ouzzani, QCRI, Qatar
Ahmed Rafea, American University in Cairo, Egypt
Abdelmounaam Rezgui, New Mexico Tech, USA
Younes Samih, Universität Düsseldorf, Germany
Violetta Cavalli Sforza, Al Akhawayn University, Morocco
Tim Schlippe, Silicon Surfer, Germany
Khaled Shaalan, The British University in Dubai, UAE

Otakar Smrz, Džám-e Džam Language Institute, Czech Republic
Rudolph Sock, Professor, University of Strasbourg, France
Irina Temnikova, QCRI, Qatar
Jan Trmal, Johns Hopkins University, USA
Stephan Vogel, QCRI, Qatar
Marcos Zampieri, University of Wolverhampton, UK
Hasna Zaouali, University of Strasbourg, France

Additional reviewers:

Mohamed Azzaz, EMP, Algeria
Riadh Belkebir, USTHB, Algeria
Mohamed Lichouri, CRSTDLA, Algeria
Mhamed Mataoui, EMP, Algeria
Attia Nehar, Ziane Achour University, Algeria
Said Sadoudi, EMP, Algeria
Fayçal Ykhlef, CDTA, Algeria

Organizing committee:

Gabor Bella, Univeristy of Trento.
Mattia Fumagalli, Univeristy of Trento.
Nandu C Naird, Univeristy of Trento.
Olha Vozna, University of Trento.
Mohammad Gharib, University of Florence.
Moaz Reyad, University of Genoa.
Osama Hamed, University of Duisburg-Essen.
Mohamed Lichouri, CRSTDLA.

Invited Speakers:

Prof. Fausto Giunchiglia, University of Trento, Italy.
Dr. Preslav Nakov, Qatar Computing Research Institute (QCRI), Qatar.

Invited Talks

Detecting the "Fake News" before they were even written
Preslav Nakov

Given the recent proliferation of disinformation online, there has been also growing research interest in automatically debunking rumors, false claims, and "fake news". A number of fact-checking initiatives have been launched so far, both manual and automatic, but the whole enterprise remains in a state of crisis: by the time a claim is finally fact-checked, it could have reached millions of users, and the harm caused could hardly be undone. An arguably more promising direction is to focus on fact-checking entire news outlets, which can be done in advance. Then, we could fact-check the news before they were even written: by checking how trustworthy the outlets that published them are.

We will show how we do this in the Tanbih news aggregator (http://www.tanbih.org/), which makes users aware of what they are reading. In particular, we develop media profiles that show the general factuality of reporting, the degree of propagandistic content, hyper-partisanship, leading political ideology, general frame of reporting, stance with respect to various claims and topics, as well as audience reach and audience bias in social media.

One world - seven thousand languages
Fausto Giunchiglia

We present a large scale multilingual lexical resource, the Universal Knowledge Core (UKC), which is organized like a Wordnet with, however, a major design difference. In the UKC, the meaning of words is represented not only with synsets, but also using language independent concepts which cluster together the synsets which, in different languages, codify the same meaning. In the UKC, it is concepts and not synsets, as it is the case in the Wordnets, which are connected in a semantic network. The use of language independent concepts allows for the native integrability, analysis and use of any number of languages, with important applications in, e.g., multilingual language processing, reasoning (as needed, for instance, in data and knowledge integration) and image understanding.

Table of Contents

Twitter Bot Detection using Diversity Measures

Dijana Kosmajac
Faculty of Computer Science
Dalhousie University
Halifax, NS, Canada
dijana.kosmajac@dal.ca

Vlado Keselj
Faculty of Computer Science
Dalhousie University
Halifax, NS, Canada
vlado@dnlp.ca

Abstract

Social bots are autonomous entities that generate a significant amount of social media content. The content being created can be harmless or even contain beneficial information. On the other hand, it may target a certain audience to influence opinions, often politically motivated, or to promote individuals to appear more popular than they really are. In this work we present a simple method for bot detection on Twitter platform relying on user activity fingerprint, complemented with a set of well-known statistical diversity measures. We demonstrate the benefits of the method on two datasets used in a couple of previous studies by various researchers.

1   Introduction

Automated user (bot) is a program that emulates a real person's behavior on social media. A bot can operate based on a simple set of behavioral instructions, such as tweeting, retweeting, "liking" posts, or following other users. In general, there are two types of bots based on their purpose: non-malicious and malicious. The non-malicious bots are transparent, with no intent of mimicking real Twitter users. Often, they share motivational quotes or images, tweet news headlines and other useful information, or help companies to respond to users. On the other hand, malicious ones may generate spam, try to access private account information, trick users into following them or subscribing to scams, suppress or enhance political opinions, create trending hashtags for financial gain, support political candidates during elections (Bessi and Ferrara, 2016), or create offensive material to troll users. Additionally, some influencers may use bots to boost their audience size.

At first, automated users sharing random bits of information across Twitter may not seem like a threat, but bots can potentially jeopardize online user security. Bots on social media platforms generate spam content and degrade overall user experience. With the growth of social networks and their influence in news and information sharing, bots have become a serious threat to democracies. The "foreign actors" use bots to share politically polarizing content in the form of fake news in order to increase its influence or intentionally promote certain people and their agenda. Countermeasures are needed to combat these coordinated influence campaigns. Bots are constantly evolving and adapting their behaviour to mimic real users. Nevertheless, many of these bots are coordinated (Chavoshi et al., 2016), which means that they can show similar behaviour. This characteristic can be used to develop models for bot detection.

We explore bot detection techniques using users' temporal behaviour. Additionally, we apply a set of statistical diversity measures to describe how diverse the user behaviour is over extended period of time. Using datasets from two different researchers (Cresci et al., 2016; Varol et al., 2017) we examine if automated accounts have less diverse behaviour than genuine user accounts and if these measures can help in detecting automated behaviour without diving into language-specific analyses. Second, we explore if the way the dataset is collected affects the ability of the measures to capture the difference between bot and human accounts.

The rest of the paper is organized as follows. Related work is discussed in Section 2. Dataset used in the study is described in Section 3. Section 4 describes method we used to extract and encode features in the form of digital fingerprint. In Section 5 we describe a set of statistical diversity measures used for user fingerprint profiling. In Section 6 we present experimental setup. Section 7 is dedicated to the discussion of the results.

Finally, in Section 8 we give the conclusions and briefly discuss about future work.

2 Related Work

One of the most prominent tasks in recent social media analysis is detection of automated user accounts (bots). Research on this topic is very active (Messias et al., 2013; Yang et al., 2014; Gilani et al., 2016), because bots pose a big threat if they're intentionally steered to target important events across the globe, such as political elections (Bessi and Ferrara, 2016; Varol et al., 2017; Howard et al., 2018; Guess et al., 2019; Stella et al., 2018; Hjouji et al., 2018). Paper by (Messias et al., 2013) explore strategies how bot can interact with real users to increase their influence. They show that a simple strategy can trick influence scoring systems. BotOrNot (Davis et al., 2016) is openly accessible solution available as API for the machine learning system for bot detection. Authors (Davis et al., 2016; Varol et al., 2017) show that the system is accurate in detecting social bots. Authors (Shu et al., 2018) explore methods for fake news detection on social media, which is closely related to the problem of automated accounts. They state that the performance of detecting fake news only from content in general doesn't show good results, and they suggest to use user social interactions as auxiliary information to improve the detection. Ferrara et al. (Ferrara et al., 2016) use extensive set of features (tweet timing, tweet interaction network, content, language, sentiment) to detect the online campaigning as early as possible. Another recent work on bot detection by Cresci et al. (Cresci et al., 2016) is based on DNA inspired fingerprinting of temporal user behaviour. They define a vocabulary B^n, where n is the dimension. An element represents a label for a tweet. User activity is represented as a sequence of tweets labels. They found that bots share longer common substrings (LCSs) than regular users. The point where LCS has the biggest difference is used as a cut-off value to separate bots from genuine users. Framework by Ahmed et al. (Ahmed and Abulaish, 2013) for bot detection uses the Euclidean distance between feature vectors to build a similarity graph of the accounts. After the graph is built, they perform clustering and community detection algorithms to identify groups of similar accounts in the graph.

Bot problem on social media platforms inspired

	Total	Genuine	Bots
Original	2,573	1,747	826
Used in study	2,115	1,421	694

Table 1: Varol 2017 dataset.

	Users	Tweets
Genuine	3,474	8,377,522
Spambots #1	991	1,610,176
Spambots #2	3,457	428,542
Spambots #3	464	1,418,626
Total	8,386	11,834,866

Table 2: Cresci 2017 dataset.

many competitions and evaluation campaigns such as DARPA (Subrahmanian et al., 2016) and PAN[1].

3 Datasets

3.1 Varol dataset

The dataset used in this study is made available by Varol et al. (Varol et al., 2017) on the website[2]. The dataset, in the original study consisting of 3,000 user accounts was manually annotated by four volunteers. At the time of download of the labeled user ids, the dataset consisted of 2,573 annotated samples. However, when we crawled the bot accounts, some of the users were banned or had protected profile. The final dataset in this study consists of 2,115 accounts. In Table 1 is shown how many accounts were lost per class.

The dataset was crawled on January 5th, 2019 and it contains 5,261,940 tweets. Number of tweets per user ranges from 20 to 3,250 (we filtered out accounts that have fewer than 20 tweets). Data imbalance is evident in the original annotated dataset, as well as the reduced one.

3.2 Cresci dataset

The dataset was obtained from Cresci et al. (Cresci et al., 2017) in the form that was used in the original study. The Twitter dataset constitutes of the real-world data used in our experiments. Table 2 reports the number of accounts and tweets they feature. According to the study (Cresci et al., 2017) the genuine accounts are a random sample of genuine (human-operated) accounts. The social

---

[1]https://pan.webis.de/publications.html
[2]https://botometer.iuni.iu.edu/bot-repository/datasets.html

spambots 1 dataset was crawled from Twitter during the Mayoral election in Rome 2014. Spambots 2 dataset is a group of bots who spent several months promoting a specific hashtag. Spambots 3 group advertised products on sale on Amazon.com. The deceitful activity was carried out by spamming URLs pointing to the advertised products.

4 Digital fingerprint of user online behaviour

DNA sequences have been exploited in different areas such as forensics, anthropology, biomedical science and similar. Cresci (Cresci et al., 2016) used the idea of DNA coding to describe social media user behaviour in temporal dimension. The same idea was used in this study, with a slightly modified way of coding. We define a set of codes A_n with length $n = 6$. The meaning of each code is given in (1).

$$A_n = \begin{cases} 0, & \text{plain} \\ 8, & \text{retweet} \\ 16, & \text{reply} \\ 1, & \text{has hastags} \\ 2, & \text{has mentions} \\ 4, & \text{has URLs} \end{cases} \tag{1}$$

Vocabulary, given the code set A, consists of $3 * 2^3 = 24$ unique characters. Each character, which describes a tweet is constructed by adding up codes for tweet features. First three codes describe the type of the tweet (retweet, reply, or plain) and the rest describe content of the tweet. For example, if a tweet is neither retweet nor reply, it is plain (with the $code = 0$). If the tweet contains hashtags, then $code = code + 1$, If the same tweet contains URLs, then $code = code + 4$. Final tweet code is 5. We transform it to a character label by using ASCII table character indexes: $ASCII\_tbl[65 + 5] = F$. The number of tweets with attributes encoded with characters determines the length of the sequence. The sequence, in our case, is simply the length of a user timeline, that is, actions in chronological order with the appropriate character encoding.

The example of a user fingerprint generated from their timeline looks like:

$$fp_{user} = (ACBCASSCCAFFADADF...)$$

4.1 Fingerprint segmentation using n-gram technique

To calculate data statistics, we extracted n-grams of different length (we conducted the experiments with n=1,2,3 length combinations). Fig. 1 shows the example on 3-gram extraction of sample user fingerprint. N-gram segments are used to calculate

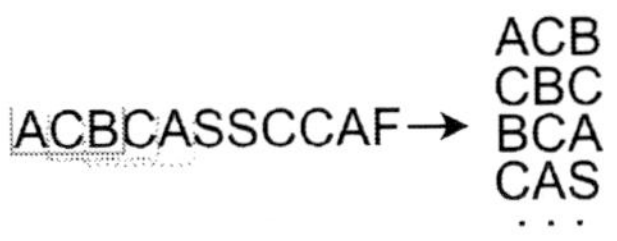

Figure 1: 3-gram extraction example from user fingerprint.

richness and diversity measures, which may unveil the difference between genuine user and bot online behaviour.

5 Statistical Measures for Text Richness and Diversity

Statistical measures for diversity have long history and wide area of application (Tweedie and Baayen, 1998). The most prominent use is in ecological domain (Morris et al., 2014) for measuring biodiversity. Diversity measures for a natural language texts are used in stylometry and authorship attribution (Stamatatos, 2009). As text statistics they are defined as computational measures that converge to a value for a certain amount of text and remain invariant for any larger size. Because such a measure exhibits the same value for any size of text larger than a certain amount, its value could be considered as a text characteristic. The intuition for using diversity measures in this work is that measures should show the differences between the observed classes. In the next couple of paragraphs we briefly describe which measures are used in this study. The following notation is used: N is the total number of words in a text, $V(N)$ is the number of distinct words, $V(m, N)$ is the number of words appearing m times in the text, and m_{max} is the largest frequency of a word.

5.1 Yule's K Index

Yule's original intention for K use is for author attribution task, assuming that it would differ for texts written by different authors.

$$K = C\frac{S_2 - S_1}{S_1^2} = C\left[-\frac{1}{N} + \sum_{m=1}^{m_{max}} V(m, N)(\frac{m}{N})^2\right]$$

3

To simplify, $S_1 = N = \sum_m V(m, N)$, and $S_2 = \sum_m m^2 V(m, N)$. C is a constant originally determined by Yule, and it is 10^4.

5.2 Shannon's H Index

The Shannon's diversity index (H) is a measure that is commonly used to characterize species diversity in a community. Shannon's index accounts for both abundance and evenness of the species present. The proportion of species i relative to the total number of species (p_i) is calculated, and then multiplied by the natural logarithm of this proportion ($ln(p_i)$). The resulting product is summed across species, and multiplied by -1.

$$H = -\sum_{i=1}^{V(N)} p_i ln(p_i)$$

$V(N)$ is the number of distinct species.

5.3 Simpson's D Index

Simpson's diversity index (D) is a mathematical measure that characterizes species diversity in a community. The proportion of species i relative to the total number of species (p_i) is calculated and squared. The squared proportions for all the species are summed, and the reciprocal is taken.

$$D = \frac{1}{\sum_{i=1}^{V(N)} p_i^2}$$

5.4 Honoré's R Statistic

Honoré (Honoré, 1979) proposed a measure which assumes that the ratio of *hapax legomena* $V(1, N)$ is constant with respect to the logarithm of the text size:

$$R = 100 \frac{log(N)}{1 - \frac{V(1,N)}{V(N)}}$$

5.5 Sichel's S Statistic

Sichel (Sichel, 1975) observed that the ratio of *hapax dis legomena* (number of n-grams that occur once in a sample) $V(2, N)$ to the vocabulary size is roughly constant across a wide range of sample sizes.

$$S = \frac{V(2, N)}{N}$$

We use this measure to express the constancy of n-gram hapax dis legomena (number of n-grams that occur twice in a sample) which we show to be distinct for genuine and bot accounts.

On the Fig. 3 we show the comparison of density plots of all measures of bot accounts versus genuine users.

6 Experiments

6.1 Data Visualizations

For visualizing the datasets in 2d space we used t-SNE (Maaten and Hinton, 2008), an enhanced method based on stochastic neighbour embedding. Fig. 2 shows the visualisations. Features used for the visualization are same as for the classifiers (diversity measures of fingerprint n-grams, in this case combination n=1,2,3). Varol dataset (the figure on the left *(a)*) appears to have more confusion between genuine and bot samples, but the separation is still visible. The right hand figure *(b)* shows Cresci dataset where we coloured separately three types of spambots and the genuine accounts. It is interesting to notice that three types of bots appear to be distinct groups in the feature space. The reason for this is likely the way how the dataset was collected. Each spambot group was collected separately around a specific event in relatively short period of time. For the opposite reason, Varol dataset is a collection of accounts that may or may not be connected by the same background event or topic.

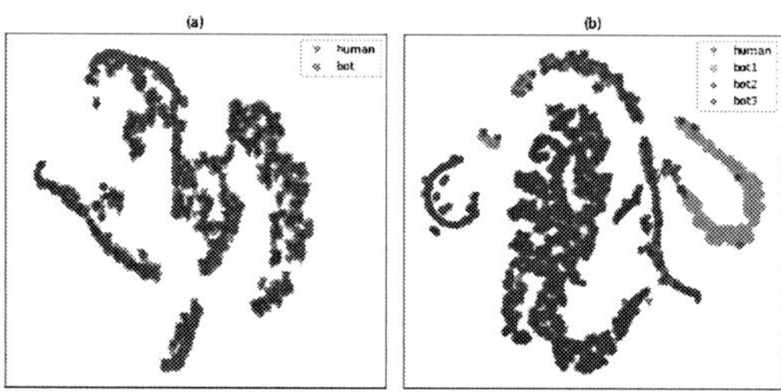

Figure 2: t-SNE representation: (a) Varol dataset and (b) Cresci dataset.

Feature extraction consists of user behaviour fingerprint generation, n-gram segmentation (where n is 1, 2 and 3), and finally, diversity measures calculation on n-gram population per sample. Fig. 3 illustrates the density differences of each measure for all n-grams. Top row consisting of 5 diagrams shows the values for Varol dataset, while bottom row refers to Cresci dataset. The figure shows that the selected measures uncover the difference between automated and genuine users. In the bottom row, Shannon's and Simpson's indices were able to capture the differences between bot networks (spambot 1, spambot 2 and spambot 3), besides the difference from genuine accounts. The last two measures mentioned in Section 5, Honoré's and Sichel's measures, as already mentioned, were originally developed for natural language text constancy measure. Both of them try to measure features that naturally occur in texts - *hapax legomena* and *hapax dis legomena*. The differences are not as prominent as for Shannon and Simpson indices. Furthermore, the feature importance discussed later will show that these two measures (Shannon and Simpson) contribute most to the classifier.

6.2 Classifiers

We conducted the experiments with five different algorithms: Gaussian Naïve Bayes, Support Vector Machines, Logistic regression, K Nearest Neighbours and two ensemble methods – Random Forest and Gradient Boosting. The implementation was done using *scikit-learn* machine learning package in python. For hyper-parameter tuning we used grid search cross validation method for every classifier. Extensive grid search didn't show significant improvement for the classifiers from using the default parameters provided in the library. The only improvement was observed with SVM classifier, where we found that it performed best with the polynomial kernel of 4th degree. We applied all classifiers on different number of n-grams (1-3), where combinations were: 1, 1+2, and 1+2+3. We run three experiments on all classifiers. The first is 10-fold cross validation on Cresci dataset, second is 10-fold cross validation on Varol dataset, and third is the experiment on classifiers with entire Cresci dataset training and entire Varol dataset validation. With the first and second experiments the aim was to explore how important it is for a dataset to be collected in a shorter time frame versus extended period of time, which is the case with the observed datasets. The third experiment is designed to test if the dataset with better results can improve the performance of the second dataset.

7 Results and Discussion

In Table 3 we report the results of the experiments using the F1 measure. The values represent average of 10-fold validation scores. First, we analyze the use of statistical diversity of n-grams as features for the set of different classifiers and the effect of increasing the n-gram order on the performance of the models. Training the Random Forest classifier on n-grams shows an increase in the performance for both datasets. However, the increase is slight with the increase of number of n-

Feat.	Classif.	C'17	V'17	V'17.v2*
1-gram	GB	0.9518	0.7229	0.6852
	SVM	0.9554	0.6920	**0.7398**
	LR	0.9494	0.6800	0.7080
	KNN	0.9552	0.6644	0.7053
	RF	0.9574	0.6919	0.7179
1+2-gram	GB	0.9578	0.7255	0.7278
	SVM	0.9651	0.7101	0.7242
	LR	0.9583	0.7044	0.7225
	KNN	0.9643	0.6989	0.7264
	RF	0.9643	0.7140	0.7138
1+2+3-gram	GB	0.9514	0.6866	0.6855
	SVM	0.9587	0.7119	0.7131
	LR	0.9608	0.6939	0.7260
	KNN	0.9633	0.7057	0.7232
	RF	**0.9667**	**0.7306**	0.7311

Table 3: 10-fold validation on datasets, F1 measure shown. *V'17.v2 results are using entire Varol dataset as test for Cresci trained classifiers. (C'17 - Cresci dataset, V'17 - varol dataset)

grams from 1 to 3. Random Forest classifier has the best performance with the F1 average 0.9667 for experiment 1, and 0.7306 for the experiment 2. Second, we can observe the dramatic difference in performance between two datasets. In the data visualizations (Fig. 2 and Fig. 3) the data separation in Varol dataset is somewhat worse than in Cresci dataset, and this is reflected in the classifiers' performance. Our argument is that this is due to a different data collection techniques. As mentioned earlier, Cresci dataset was collected around specific events and using keywords, so the users, especially bots have correlated behaviour. On the other hand, Varol dataset was collected (directly from Twitter, given the provided labeled ids) two years after the first study performed by the original researcher (Varol et al., 2017). The differences between human and bot accounts are less distinguished, but still show significant difference according to the diversity measures. In our third experiment, we used entire Cresci dataset to train the models (we used best parameters from experiment 1 for each model setup) and tested it on entire Varol dataset. The results obtained were very similar to the ones in experiment 2, and we did not gain much of an improvement. Best classifier performance was obtained with SVM, and unigram feature setting reaching average F1 0.7398.

On Fig. 4 we show a pruned estimator from

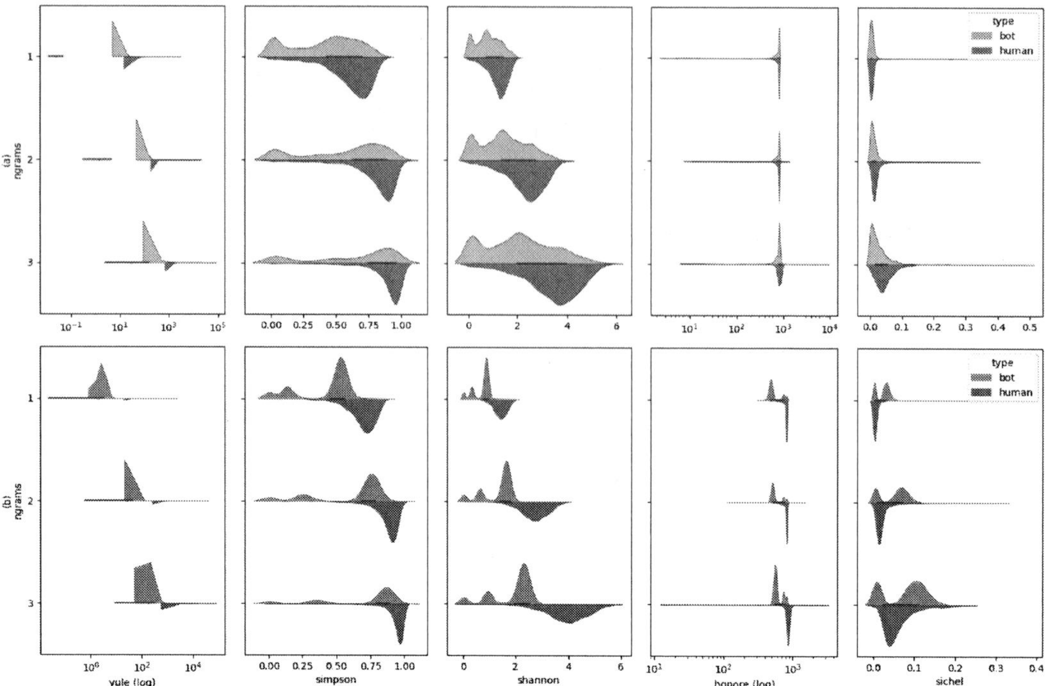

Figure 3: Diversity measures distributions for Varol (a) (top row) and Cresci (b) (bottom row) datasets.

Random Forest classifier trained on Cresci dataset with diversity measures on unigrams. The most influential feature for this classifier is Simpson's diversity measure (root). The separation between bot and human is on 2.79 value. The accounts which have less or equal the value are more likely to be bots. Other measures, such as Shannon on the second level, separate accounts further. To note, this is pruned classifier with maximum depth of 3, while in the Table 3 we did not have depth constraint. This classifier has average F1 measure of 0.9548 (+/- 0.0508) using 10-fold validation.

8 Conclusions and Future Work

In this paper we conducted a set of experiments to find a simple, yet effective bot detection method on Twitter social media platform. We show that it is possible to detect automated users by using a fingerprint of user behaviour and a set of statistical measures that describe different aspects of that behaviour. The measures describe "constancy" or "diversity" of the pattern. The hypothesis was that the automated users show lower diversity, and tend to use smaller set of types of messages over extended period of time. Through visual analysis, discussion and classification results

we showed that assumption did hold under our experimental setup. Additionally, we conducted the experiments on two different datasets used earlier in the research community to examine if the time-span of user behaviour has impact on the ability to detect bots. We showed that the dataset which was collected focused around specific topics and shorter time-span generally performed better than the dataset where users diverge. The strength of this approach lies in the fact that it is language independent.

The main drawback of our approach is that a classifier needs at least 20 tweets per user to generate a fingerprint. The number 20 was empirically picked based on our experiments (keeping the fingerprints shorter than 20 worsened the results of all classifiers). Another point is that social bots evolve over time, and they tend to be more difficult to identify with established machine learning methods. Bot creators can take advantage of the present ML knowledge and enhance their algorithms, so they stay longer undetected.

And last, to further verify our results and perform more thorough study, we plan to apply our approach to more datasets such as Russian trolls dataset collected around 2016 US presidential

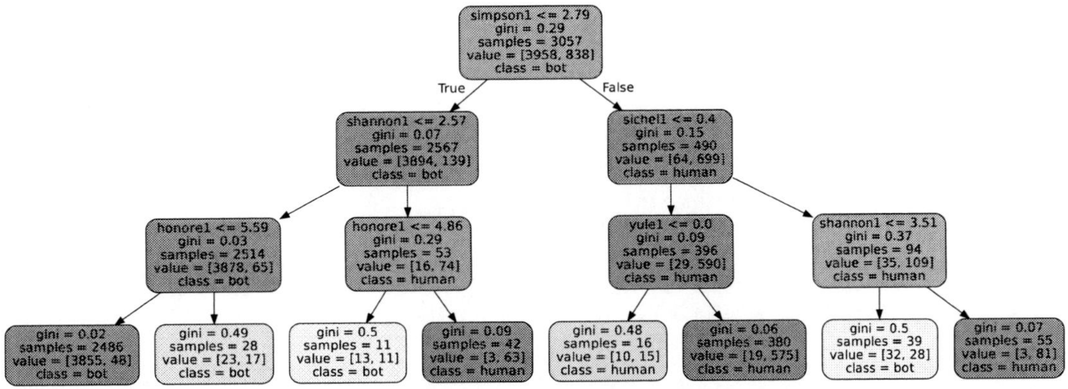

Figure 4: Example decision tree estimator from Random Forest classifier. Cresci dataset.

elections (Boatwright et al., 2018). Next, we plan to develop an unsupervised method for bot detection on the same set of features using clustering techniques.

References

Faraz Ahmed and Muhammad Abulaish. 2013. A generic statistical approach for spam detection in online social networks. *Computer Communications*, 36(10-11):1120–1129.

Alessandro Bessi and Emilio Ferrara. 2016. Social bots distort the 2016 us presidential election online discussion.

Brandon C Boatwright, Darren L Linvill, and Patrick L Warren. 2018. Troll factories: The internet research agency and state-sponsored agenda building. *Resource Centre on Media Freedom in Europe*.

Nikan Chavoshi, Hossein Hamooni, and Abdullah Mueen. 2016. Identifying correlated bots in twitter. In *Social Informatics*, pages 14–21, Cham. Springer International Publishing.

Stefano Cresci, Roberto Di Pietro, Marinella Petrocchi, Angelo Spognardi, and Maurizio Tesconi. 2016. Dna-inspired online behavioral modeling and its application to spambot detection. *IEEE Intelligent Systems*, 31(5):58–64.

Stefano Cresci, Roberto Di Pietro, Marinella Petrocchi, Angelo Spognardi, and Maurizio Tesconi. 2017. The paradigm-shift of social spambots: Evidence, theories, and tools for the arms race. *CoRR*, abs/1701.03017.

Clayton Allen Davis, Onur Varol, Emilio Ferrara, Alessandro Flammini, and Filippo Menczer. 2016. Botornot: A system to evaluate social bots. In *Proceedings of the 25th International Conference Companion on World Wide Web*, pages 273–274. International World Wide Web Conferences Steering Committee.

Emilio Ferrara, Onur Varol, Filippo Menczer, and Alessandro Flammini. 2016. Detection of promoted social media campaigns. In *tenth international AAAI conference on web and social media*.

Zafar Gilani, Liang Wang, Jon Crowcroft, Mario Almeida, and Reza Farahbakhsh. 2016. Stweeler: A framework for twitter bot analysis. In *Proceedings of the 25th International Conference Companion on World Wide Web*, pages 37–38. International World Wide Web Conferences Steering Committee.

Andrew Guess, Jonathan Nagler, and Joshua Tucker. 2019. Less than you think: Prevalence and predictors of fake news dissemination on facebook. *Science advances*, 5(1):eaau4586.

Zakaria el Hjouji, D Scott Hunter, Nicolas Guenon des Mesnards, and Tauhid Zaman. 2018. The impact of bots on opinions in social networks. *arXiv preprint arXiv:1810.12398*.

Efstathios Honoré. 1979. Some simple measures of richness of vocabulary. *Association for Literary and Linguistic Computing Bulletin*, 7:172–177.

Philip N. Howard, Samuel Woolley, and Ryan Calo. 2018. Algorithms, bots, and political communication in the us 2016 election: The challenge of automated political communication for election law and administration. *Journal of Information Technology & Politics*, 15(2):81–93.

Laurens van der Maaten and Geoffrey Hinton. 2008. Visualizing data using t-sne. *Journal of machine learning research*, 9(Nov):2579–2605.

Johnnatan Messias, Lucas Schmidt, Ricardo Augusto Rabelo de Oliveira, and Fabrício Benevenuto de Souza. 2013. You followed my bot! transforming robots into influential users in twitter.

E Kathryn Morris, Tancredi Caruso, François Buscot, Markus Fischer, Christine Hancock, Tanja S Maier,

Torsten Meiners, Caroline Müller, Elisabeth Obermaier, Daniel Prati, et al. 2014. Choosing and using diversity indices: insights for ecological applications from the german biodiversity exploratories. *Ecology and evolution*, 4(18):3514–3524.

Kai Shu, Suhang Wang, and Huan Liu. 2018. Understanding user profiles on social media for fake news detection. In *2018 IEEE Conference on Multimedia Information Processing and Retrieval (MIPR)*, pages 430–435. IEEE.

H. S. Sichel. 1975. On a distribution law for word frequencies. *Journal of the American Statistical Association*, 70(351a):542–547.

Efstathios Stamatatos. 2009. A survey of modern authorship attribution methods. *Journal of the American Society for information Science and Technology*, 60(3):538–556.

Massimo Stella, Emilio Ferrara, and Manlio De Domenico. 2018. Bots increase exposure to negative and inflammatory content in online social systems. *Proceedings of the National Academy of Sciences*, 115(49):12435–12440.

VS Subrahmanian, Amos Azaria, Skylar Durst, Vadim Kagan, Aram Galstyan, Kristina Lerman, Linhong Zhu, Emilio Ferrara, Alessandro Flammini, and Filippo Menczer. 2016. The darpa twitter bot challenge. *Computer*, 49(6):38–46.

Fiona J Tweedie and R Harald Baayen. 1998. How variable may a constant be? measures of lexical richness in perspective. *Computers and the Humanities*, 32(5):323–352.

Onur Varol, Emilio Ferrara, Clayton A Davis, Filippo Menczer, and Alessandro Flammini. 2017. Online human-bot interactions: Detection, estimation, and characterization. In *Eleventh international AAAI conference on web and social media*.

Zhi Yang, Christo Wilson, Xiao Wang, Tingting Gao, Ben Y Zhao, and Yafei Dai. 2014. Uncovering social network sybils in the wild. *ACM Transactions on Knowledge Discovery from Data (TKDD)*, 8(1):2.

Aligning the IndoWordNet with the Princeton WordNet

Nandu Chandran Nair
DISI
University of Trento
Trento,Italy
nandu.chandrannair
@unitn.it

Rajendran S Velayuthan
CEN
Amrita Vishwa Vidyapeetham
Coimbatore,India
rajushush@gmail.com

Khuyagbaatar Batsuren
DISI
University of Trento
Trento,Italy
k.batsuren@unitn.it

Abstract

The IndoWordNet is an Indian language lexical resource. The project started with Hindi WordNet, which was manually built from various resources with the preference for culture-specific synsets. Other languages were added later. The development approach used in IndoWordNet is very similar to that used in Princeton WordNet (PWN). PWN is a semantic network where English synsets are nodes, and semantic relations are edges connecting them. Due to the popularity of PWN, IndoWordNet also connected Hindi and English languages through direct (synonymy) and hypernymy linkages between their synsets. Due to the diversity of the languages, these linkages generate three types of mappings between IndoWordNet and PWN which generate the misalignment. This paper proposes to align the IndoWordNet with PWN using a large scale lexical-semantic resource called Universal Knowledge Core (UKC), which forms a semantic network where nodes are language-independent concepts. In the UKC semantic relations connect concepts and not synsets.

1 Introduction

Studies are in progress to make language resource development process cheap and quick, but even now, the process demands considerable resources and expert support. The generation of a language resource is influenced by many factors such as large global speaker population, high economic power, or high political interests (Stüker, 2009). As a result the majority of languages are under-resourced (Besacier et al., 2014). Even in 2019, if we use google translator for one of the official Indian languages, Malayalam, we can notice how a few words remain unrecognized (Figure 1). Consider the sample Malayalam sentence: "രാമു ചമ്മന്തി കഴിക്കില്ല(*Ramu chammanthy kazhikkilla*), translated as "Ramu will not eat". Here, "Chammanthy" is an Indian dish, and the translator has

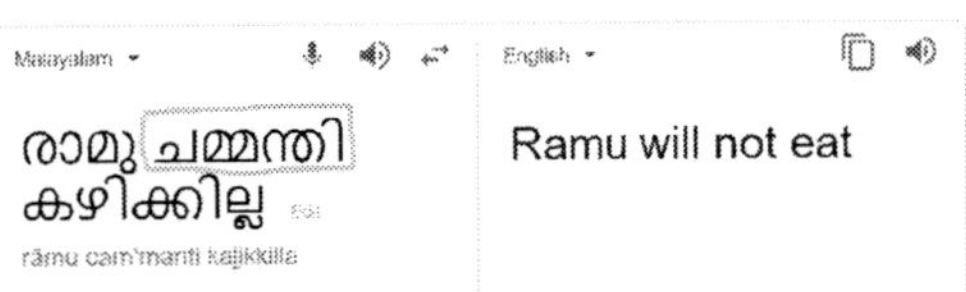

Figure 1: Missing term in translator

failed to find an appropriate translation for this word. A language resource that allows culture-specific words should have the missing term in the target translation.

Back in 2006, the joint efforts of different universities and research groups across India made it possible to develop the IndoWordNet(Bhattacharyya, 2010) - the first wordnet for Indian languages. IndoWordNet was developed to capture the cultures of India in length and breadth by including 18 languages out of 22 official languages(Bhattacharyya et al., 2010). Hindi WordNet(Narayan et al., 2002)developed at IIT Bombay, India was used as the source wordnet for IndoWordNet. Other WordNets in IndoWordNet were extended from Hindi WordNet with culture-specific and language-specific synsets. In this paper, we use the notation "IndoWordNet" to refer to the project and notation "IWN" to refer to on the Hindi WordNet. The IndoWordNet team followed Princeton WordNet(PWN)(Fellbaum, 2012) principles at a minimum level during the development.

The IndoWordNet team also focused on the translation(Chakrabarti and Bhattacharyya, 2004) across Indian languages and English and they identified the challenges for linking Hindi with English(Saraswati et al., 2010). Based on this, IndoWordNet team proposed direct (synonymy) and hypernymy linkages. These types of linkages eventually cause different types of associations between the synsets of IWN and PWN. Our challenge is to align IWN with PWN. This could allow to generate automatic dictionary across terms and also highlight the diversity among languages (Giunchiglia et al., 2017).

Our approach involves the usage of a large scale lexical-semantic resource called Universal Knowledge Core (UKC)(Tawfik et al., 2014). UKC forms a semantic network of language-independent concepts, which are linked with semantic relations. In our approach, we group the IWN synsets into three groups. We process each group of synsets in such a way to make them in a single group where one IWN synset has a concept in UKC. We have aligned IWN with PWN and find around 20K new concepts for PWN. Also, we identified around 3K synsets from IWN, which have no hypernym relations with other synsets.

The structure of the paper is as follows. Section II briefly describes IWN, PWN, and other multilingual resources like EuroWordNet, Global WordNet Grid and UKC. Section III describes the issues in the mapping of IWN with PWN. The detailed description of our approach is provided in section IV. In section V, the results obtained from the project are given. Finally, our conclusions and directions for future work are presented in section VI.

2 Background

Many multilingual wordnets such as EuroWord-Net (Vossen, 1998), MultiWordNet (Pianta et al., 2002), and Global WordNet Grid (Pease et al., 2008) have been built based on PWN. EuroWord-Net (EWN) languages are linked to a list of unstructured English word meaning. EWN has wordnets with the same structure as PWN. By translating words from PWN, MultiWordNet is adapted to the hierarchical structure of PWN and concepts of western culture. Global WordNet Grid combines wordnets and connects them to an ontology that contains core concepts of PWN like "person". Hence, concepts from many languages are defined using English in Global WordNet Grid aligned with the ontology of PWN, and in this paper, we focus on wordnet from India generated based on Hindi.

India is very diverse in many ways: religion, cultures, languages, etc. As many as 880 languages are spoken in India, and 22 official languages are adopted by different states and union territories. Hindi is one of the official languages of India. Hindi belongs to the Indo-Aryan language family, a sub group of Indo-European language family. Hindi, like any language, is enriched with concepts that are cultural manifestations. These concepts are avail-

able as lexical items in Hindi but may not be available in other languages. For example, the case of kinship terms in English. Figure 2 shows the eight words used for "cousin" based on maternal and paternal relationships.

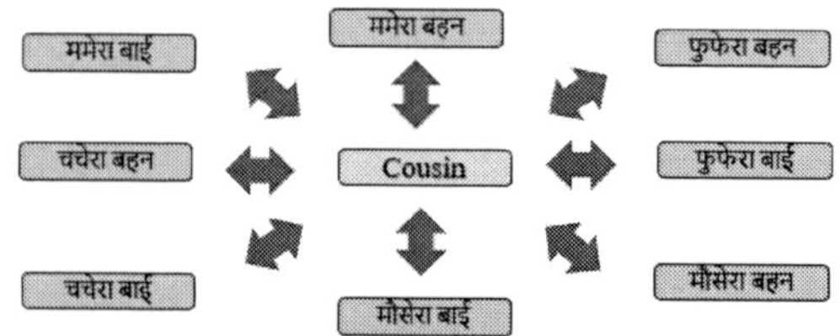

Figure 2: "Cousin" in English and Hindi

A project to develop a linked lexical knowledge base of Indian languages from Indo-Aryan, Dravidian and Sino-Tibetan language families is known as IndoWordNet. It was coordinated by IIT Bombay, India with the assistance of research groups from different parts of India. Universities in various parts of India were responsible for the development of each language wordnet. Other languages were translated from Hindi WordNet to generate the IndoWordNet's respective wordnets. Synsets are linked by relations such as hypernymy or meronymy or troponymy. The same synset identifier maintained across the languages. IndoWordNet were used in the following projects conducted at India: Indian Language to Indian Language Machine Translation (ILILMT), Cross-Lingual Information Access (CLIA) and Indian language sentiment analysis (Dash et al., 2017).

One of the challenges of IndoWordNet team was the term translation from the Indian languages to English (Chakrabarti and Bhattacharyya, 2004). The study (Saraswati et al., 2010) lists the challenges faced when linking IWN and English synsets. The work proposed two types of linkages for connecting IndoWordNet synsets with English synsets: direct and hypernymy. The direct linkage occurs if synsets from IWN have synonyms in English and hypernymy linkages occur if synsets from IWN have no equivalents in English WordNet but only are general synsets. Possible areas of hypernymy linkages can be: kinship relations, musical instruments, kitchen utensils, tools, species and grains(Saraswati et al., 2010). Hence we can argue that PWN and IWN have different hierarchy between synsets. Figure 3 shows that in the PWN, the word "chair" has parent "seat" and "seat" has parent "furniture". In IWN, "chair" has four parents,"artifact","thing","being" and "seat". And "seat" does not have "furniture" as a parent but "artifact","thing", and "being" as parents.

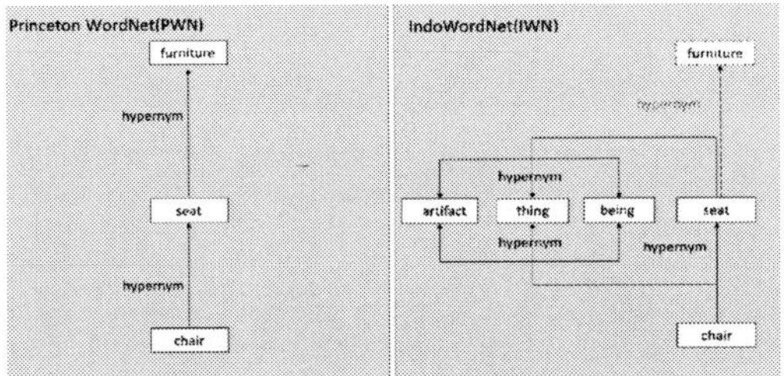

Figure 3: Ontology in PWN and IWN

Two methods are usually used to develop wordnets: merge (Snow et al., 2007) and expansion (Balkova et al., 2004). The merge approach uses the available language resources such as corpora, dictionary, or wordnet to create unique language-dependent wordnet. The merge approach relies entirely on language experts, and the resources being available. Also, the resultant wordnet from merge approach will have concepts that do not exist in PWN. For example, Dutch WordNet from EWN. The expansion approach translates a set of synsets from wordnet into a target language. The expansion has the advantage of extending semantic relations of the source wordnet and the disadvantage of being biased towards the source wordnet with less consideration towards finding the target wordnet's novel concepts. This means that the wordnet resulting from expansion approach has extensive coverage of concepts from the PWN, if PWN is used for translation. One such example is the Spanish Word-Net from EWN.

Here we follow a third, somewhat different approach. We take two available wordnets, namely PWN and IWN, and we align them using the UKC so that the synsets in IWN and PWN which have the same meaning are put in correspondence. Hence our approach avoids the biasing towards any language, especially English, and hence finding the missing concepts is less hard than EWN. Also, our approach belongs on top of the previous approaches since we use existing wordnets, and saves time by not to focus on generating wordnet.

The UKC is also a multilingual lexical database based on the WordNet principles, but in the UKC the meaning is represented using lexical concepts. The UKC considers a concept as a mental representation of what is perceive. As such it is language independent(Giunchiglia et al., 2018). The UKC has been designed in such a way that there is no bias towards any language and culture which makes the UKC extendable and open. UKC contains the lexicons and lexico-semantic relations for 338 languages, containing 1,717,735 words and 2,512,704 language-specific word meanings along with 107,196 lexical concepts excluding named entities (Batsuren et al., 2019).

UKC has two components: Language Core (LC) and Concept Core (CC). In LC, each synset is associated with one language and at least one word within that language. The synsets are linked with concepts, satisfying the condition that each synset is linked with only one concept. CC is a semantic network where nodes are language-independent concepts. Each concept has a unique id which differentiates it from any other concept. The CC has a set of semantic relations between the nodes that relate the meanings of the concepts.

In addition to this, UKC also handles the lexicalized missing concept known as lexical gaps for a language by adding a new concept for that language along with a gloss. This gloss considers a local language description of the missing synset. UKC handles the languages independently and is capable of performing language similarity and diversity studies(Giunchiglia et al., 2017). UKC was used as the core source for finding cross-lingual evidence in a multilingual task (Batsuren et al., 2019). The studies (Bella et al., 2017) and (Bella et al., 2016) explain some applications of UKC. Figure 4 shows how the synsets of English and Italian are concepts aligned in UKC. LC has the vocabularies for the concepts "chair", "seat" and "furniture" in English and Italian languages.

3 Problem Definition

Indian languages and English derive from different cultures and show language specific phenomena such as complex predicate structure(Chakrabarti et al., 2007). The linkages between IWN and English mentioned above cause three types of mappings between the IWN and PWN synsets: one to one mapping, many to one mapping, and one to zero mapping.

In this paper, we take mapping in the sense of "adding an equivalence relation for each synset in IWN to the closest synset in PWN". Such types of mappings vary upon the languages. For exam-

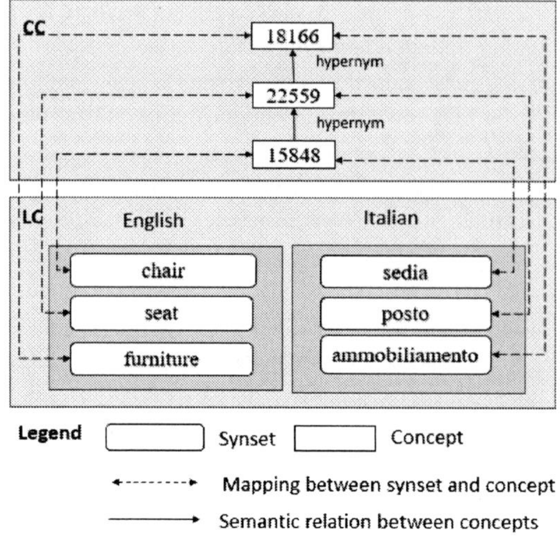

Figure 4: UKC conceptual mappings between English and Italian

ple, the study in (Cristea et al., 2004) highlights the alignment problems between PWN and the Romanian wordnet. Let us consider the three groups of mapping we have identified,

- One to one mapping:

  A synset from IWN has a corresponding synset in PWN and these synsets has one meaning. In Figure 5, the gloss from IWN "जिसने जन्म न लिया हो " (*jisne janm na liya ho*) which means "Who didn't born yet" has one corresponding synset "[unborn]" in PWN. Such type of synsets are those common in both cultures, like "chair".

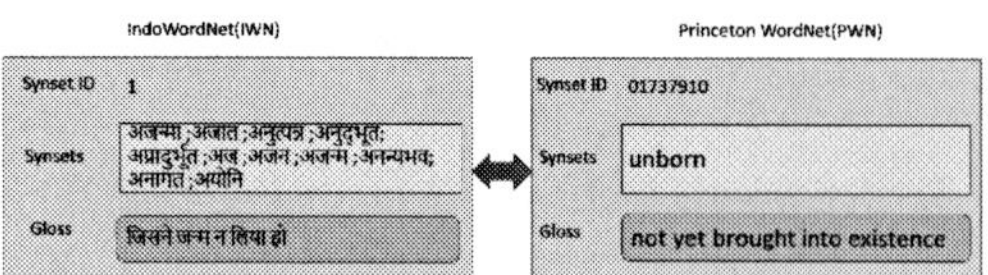

Figure 5: Example for one to one mapping

- Many to one mapping:

  Many synsets from IWN has a corresponding single synset in PWN that has the same meaning. In Figure 6, the glosses "वह स्थान जो पवि-त्र माना जाता हो " (*vah sthan joh pavitrh mana jatha ho*) and "देव स्थान या पुण्य स्थान " (*dev sthan ya puny sthan*) which mean "A place which is sacred " and "A place which is holy

or divine " respectively, have only one corresponding synset "[holy place; sanctum; holy]" in PWN. It means that the two specific concepts in one language are mapped to a general concept in another language.

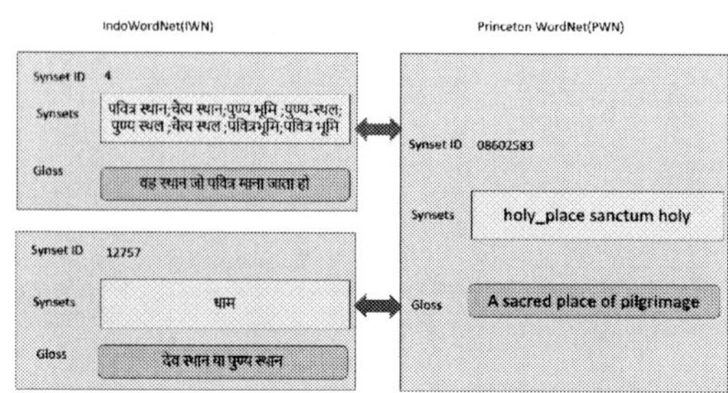

Figure 6: Example for many to one mapping

- One to zero mapping:

  One synset from IWN does not has a corresponding synset in PWN that has the same meaning. In Figure 7 the gloss "मनुष्य के जीवन में अलग–अलग ग्रहों के निश्चित भोगकाल " (*manushy ke jeevan mem alagu-alagu grahom ke nishchith fogkaal*) has no corresponding synset in PWN. The meaning of the gloss is "The period of definite companionship in many planets in human life". This word use when someone having a bad time period in their life and is related to planets in Indian astrology.

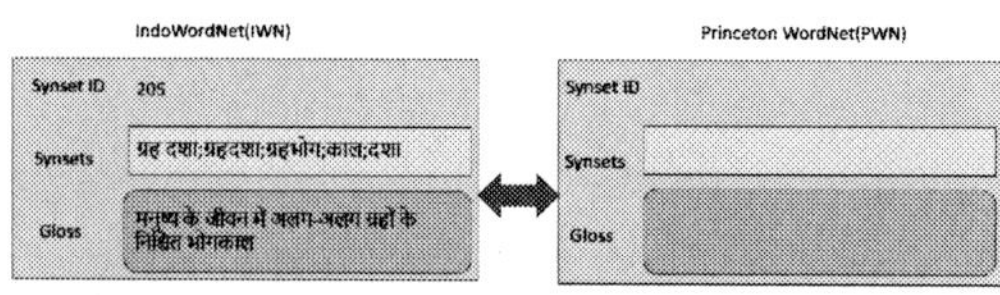

Figure 7: Example for one to zero mapping

The mappings limit IWN to be part of multilingual wordnets. We propose an approach that focuses on concepts that allows to link the languages independently which forms a single resource.

4 Aligning IWN with PWN

Our solution described below can be applied to wordnets of any language. We use the UKC to map the synsets between IWN and PWN that correspond to a single concept. While doing this we define three types of associations between the synsets of IWN and UKC. They are:

- Group A
  One synset from IWN has a corresponding single concept in UKC. These are the IWN synsets that have one to one mapping with PWN.

- Group B
  Many synsets from IWN have a corresponding single concept in UKC. These are the IWN synsets that have many to one mapping with PWN.

- Group C
  One synset from IWN does not have a concept in UKC. These are the IWN synsets that have one to zero mapping with PWN.

Our proposed approach for aligning IWN with PWN is explained below,

1. Set up the UKC
   This step focuses on preparing the UKC for the alignment of IWN with PWN. To take advantage of the PWN hierarchy, the UKC uses synsets from PWN as the concepts. This in turn makes sure the IWN synset aligned with the UKC concepts will associate the corresponding PWN synset. Also, it helps the UKC generating new UKC ids for those IWN synsets which do not correspond to UKC (and therefore) to PWN.

2. Classify the IWN synsets
   Classify the total synsets of IWN based on the association types (A, B and C) mentioned above. This step allows us to know the nature of concepts between IWN and PWN.

3. Process group A synsets
   The group A synsets of IWN are aligned with PWN. Hence it can be imported into the UKC. So the rest of the synsets from IWN could be new concepts for PWN.

4. Process group B synsets
   We analyzed the group B synsets and we found that it is a collection of 454 sub trees. The root element of each sub tree has a corresponding concept in the UKC. An interesting observation is that width and depth of the sub trees could be used to study the nature of lexical gaps between Indian languages and English.

5. Process group C synsets
   We checked to find any synset from group C

can be the child to group A synsets. Hence, we found 9,174 synsets are new synsets for PWN and 3021 synsets have no connection with other synsets of IWN.

5   Results

Table I presents the conceptual mappings between IWN and PWN using UKC based on the groups A, B and C. The final alignment between the IWN and the PWN are validated by the linguists. Let us consider the results in detail below,

- Group A
  There are 11,212 group A synsets in IWN and the UKC has corresponding 11,212 concepts. So IWN is imported into the UKC as a new language, Hindi. Figure 8 shows the alignment of the concept "unborn" in UKC. Here, there is a one to one mapping between synset and concept. The concept is linked with synsets of each languages.

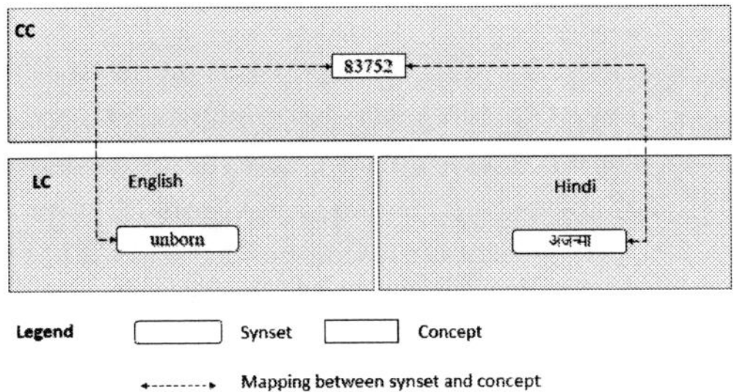

Figure 8: Group A synsets alignment

- Group B
  There are 12,048 group B synsets in IWN. The UKC has corresponding 454 concepts. The remaining 11,594 concepts are new concepts for the UKC. And also these 11,594 synsets are new synsets in the PWN. The research question here is to investigate whether the new identified synsets are lexical gaps or not. We are hoping to study the 454 sub trees and identify the areas resulting the lexical gaps. Figure 9 shows the alignment of the concept "holy place" in the UKC, one concept in CC is linked with one synset from each language. The UKC solves the many to one mapping by adding a new concept which has id -11111.

Table 1: Conceptual mappings between IWN and PWN using UKC

| | IWN | UKC | | PWN |
Groups	#synsets	#concepts	#new concepts	#new synsets
A	11,212	11,212	0	0
B	12,048	454	11,594	11,594
C	12,195	0	9,174	9,174
total	35,455	11,666	20,768	24,290

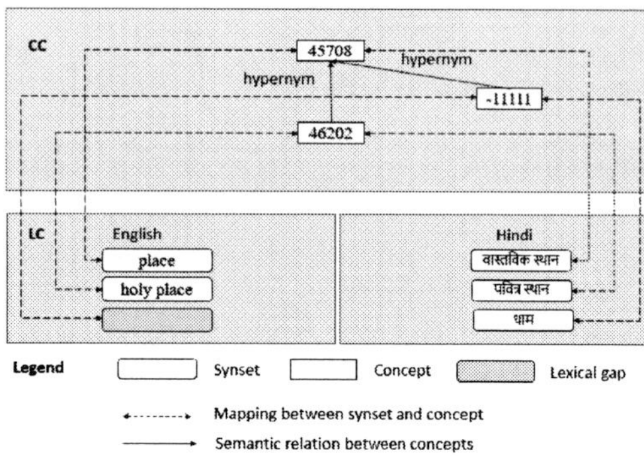

Figure 9: Group B synsets alignment

- Group C
  There are 12,195 group C synsets in IWN. The UKC has no corresponding concepts. So the 9,174 concepts are new for the UKC. Out of these concepts 3021 concepts have no hypernym relations with other 32,434 IWN concepts. Hence, 9,174 synsets are new for the PWN and need to investigate whether they are lexical gaps for the PWN. Figure 10 shows the alignment of a culture specific concept in the UKC. The UKC added a new concept in CC without the hypernymy relation and linked with the languages.

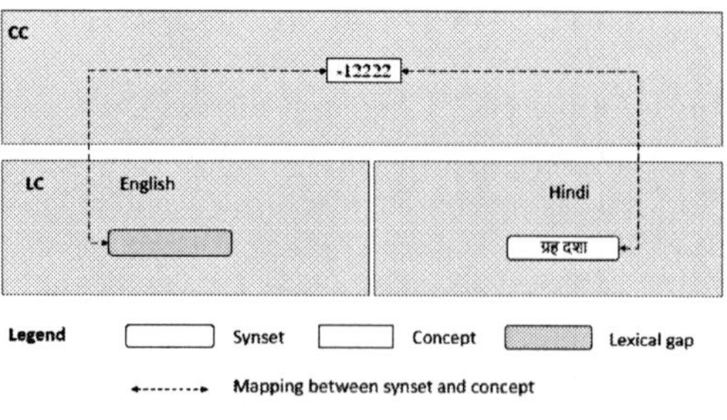

Figure 10: Group C synsets alignment

Like PWN, also in the IWN, various cases of polysemy have been found out(Peters and Peters,

2000). The polysemous 4906 synsets can be either homonymy, specialization polysemy, metonymy, metaphoric polysemy, or compound polysemy (Freihat et al., 2016). However, since this was out of the scope of the project we did not work on this further.

6 Conclusion and Future Work

This paper describes the initial stage of the generation of multilingual resources in a cheaper and faster way. We proposed an approach to align the IndoWordNet, which is the first lexical resource in Indian languages, with the PWN by taking advantage of existing linkages between the IWN and the PWN synsets.However, rather than focusing on the lexicalization problems and polysemy in IWN, we gave full attention to map one synset from IWN to one concept in UKC. The alignment of IWN with the PWN helps to connect more languages. We could integrate as many languages since the UKC forms a semantic network between concepts rather than between synsets of a language. We plan to integrate more Indian languages from IndoWordNet. Fig. 11 sample diagram of expected alignment. In Figure 11, concepts are linked with synsets from languages English and two Indian languages, Malayalam and Hindi.

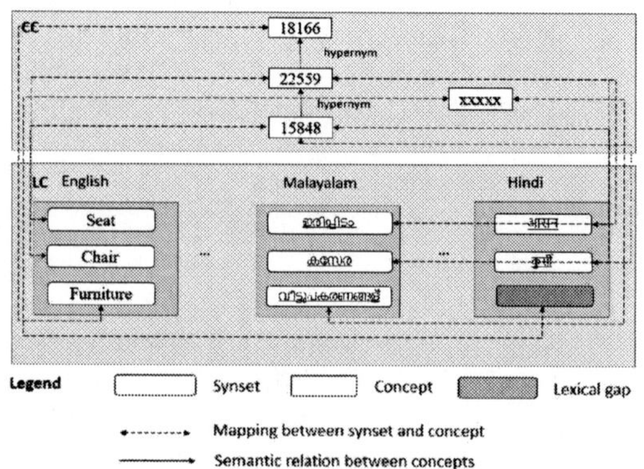

Figure 11: Alignment of the IndoWordNet with the PWN using UKC

Acknowledgments

We thank the University of Trento, Italy for allowing us to be involved in this project and for providing the facilities and full support for the successful completion.

Our heartfelt thanks to Professor Fausto Giunchiglia who gave us his continuous guidance and valuable comments during the project.

The team from Amrita Vishwa Vidyapeetham, India showed full dedication towards participation in the project.

This work has been supported by the European Union's Horizon 2020 research and innovation programme under grant agreement No. 810105 (Cy-CAT)

Our project is a sample work which we hope will motivate many people to take part in the development of under-resourced languages.

References

Valentina Balkova, Andrey Sukhonogov, and Sergey Yablonsky. 2004. Russian wordnet. In *Proceedings of the Second Global Wordnet Conference*.

Khuyagbaatar Batsuren, Gábor Bella, and Fausto Giunchiglia. 2019. Cognet: a large-scale cognate database. In *Proceedings of ACL 2019, Florence, Italy*.

Gabor Bella, Fausto Giunchiglia, and Fiona McNeill. 2017. Language and domain aware lightweight ontology matching. *Journal of Web Semantics*, 43:1–17.

Gábor Bella, Alessio Zamboni, and Fausto Giunchiglia. 2016. Domain-based sense disambiguation in multilingual structured data. In *The Diversity Workshop at the European Conference on Artificial Intelligence (ECAI)*.

Laurent Besacier, Etienne Barnard, Alexey Karpov, and Tanja Schultz. 2014. Automatic speech recognition for under-resourced languages: A survey. *Speech Communication*, 56:85–100.

Pushpak Bhattacharyya. 2010. Indowordnet. In *In Proc. of LREC-10*. Citeseer.

Pushpak Bhattacharyya, Christiane Fellbaum, and Piek Vossen. 2010. Principles, construction and application of multilingual wordnets. In *Proceedings of the 5th Global Word Net Conference (Mumbai-India)*.

Debasri Chakrabarti and Pushpak Bhattacharyya. 2004. Creation of english and hindi verb hierarchies and their application to hindi wordnet building and english-hindi mt. In *Proceedings of the Second Global Wordnet Conference, Brno, Czech Republic*. Citeseer.

Debasri Chakrabarti, Vaijayanthi Sarma, and Pushpak Bhattacharyya. 2007. Complex predicates in indian language wordnets. *Lexical Resources and Evaluation Journal*, 40(3-4).

Dan Cristea, Catalin Mihaila, Corina Forascu, Diana Trandabat, Maria Husarciuc, Gabriela Haja, and Oana Postolache. 2004. Mapping princeton wordnet synsets onto romanian wordnet synsets. *Romanian Journal of Information Science and Technology*, 7(1-2):125–145.

Niladri Sekhar Dash, Pushpak Bhattacharyya, and Jyoti D Pawar. 2017. *The WordNet in Indian Languages*. Springer.

Christiane Fellbaum. 2012. Wordnet. *The Encyclopedia of Applied Linguistics*.

Abed Alhakim Freihat, Fausto Giunchiglia, and Biswanath Dutta. 2016. A taxonomic classification of wordnet polysemy types. In *8th Global WordNet conference*, pages 105–113.

Fausto Giunchiglia, Khuyagbaatar Batsuren, and Gabor Bella. 2017. Understanding and exploiting language diversity. In *IJCAI*, pages 4009–4017.

Fausto Giunchiglia, Khuyagbaatar Batsuren, and Abed Alhakim Freihat. 2018. One world–seven thousand languages. In *Proceedings 19th International Conference on Computational Linguistics and Intelligent Text Processing, CiCling2018, 18-24 March 2018*.

Dipak Narayan, Debasri Chakrabarti, Prabhakar Pande, and Pushpak Bhattacharyya. 2002. An experience in building the indo wordnet-a wordnet for hindi. In *First International Conference on Global WordNet, Mysore, India*.

Adam Pease, Christiane Fellbaum, and Piek Vossen. 2008. Building the global wordnet grid. *CIL18*.

Wim Peters and Ivonne Peters. 2000. Lexicalised systematic polysemy in wordnet. In *LREC*.

Emanuele Pianta, Luisa Bentivogli, and Christian Girardi. 2002. Multiwordnet: developing an aligned multilingual database. In *First international conference on global WordNet*, pages 293–302.

Jaya Saraswati, Rajita Shukla, Ripple P Goyal, and Pushpak Bhattacharyya. 2010. Hindi to english wordnet linkage: Challenges and solutions. In *Proceedings of 3rd IndoWordNet Workshop, International Conference on Natural Language Processing 2010 (ICON 2010)*.

Rion Snow, Sushant Prakash, Daniel Jurafsky, and Andrew Y Ng. 2007. Learning to merge word senses. In *Proceedings of the 2007 joint conference on empirical methods in natural language processing and computational natural language learning (emnlp-conll)*, pages 1005–1014.

Sebastian Stüker. 2009. *Acoustic modelling for under-resourced languages*. Ph.D. thesis, Karlsruhe Institute of Technology.

Ahmed Tawfik, Fausto Giunchiglia, and Vincenzo Maltese. 2014. A collaborative platform for multilingual ontology development. *World Academy of Science, Engineering and Technology*, 8(12):1.

Piek Vossen. 1998. Introduction to eurowordnet. In *EuroWordNet: A multilingual database with lexical semantic networks*, pages 1–17. Springer.

Automatic Data-Driven Approaches for Evaluating the Phonemic Verbal Fluency Task with Healthy Adults

Hali Lindsay, Nicklas Linz
German Research Center for
Artificial Intelligence (DFKI),
Saarbrücken, Germany
hali.lindsay@dfki.de
nicklas.linz@dfki.de

Johannes Tröger, Jan Alexandersson
German Research Center for
Artificial Intelligence (DFKI),
Saarbrücken, Germany
johannes.troeger@dfki.de
jan.alexandersson@dfki.de

Josef Van Genabith
German Research Center for
Artificial Intelligence (DFKI),
Saarbrücken, Germany
jan.alexandersson@dfki.de

Christoph Kaller
Faculty of Medicine,
Freiburg Brain Imaging Center,
University of Freiburg,
Freiburg, Germany
christoph.kaller@uniklinik-freiburg.de

Abstract

Phonemic Verbal Fluency (PVF) is a cognitive assessment task where a patient is asked to produce words constrained to a given alphabetical letter for a specified time duration. Patient productions are later evaluated based on strategies to reveal crucial diagnostic information by manually scoring results according to predetermined clinical criteria. In this paper, we propose four alternative similarity metrics and evaluate them in a two-fold argument, using the clinical criteria as a baseline. First, we consider the capacity of each metric to model PVF production using a rank-based approach, and then consider the metrics ability to compute finer resolution clinical measures that are indicative of the underlying strategy. Automation of the clinical criteria and proposed metrics are evaluated on PVF performances for 16 letters from 32 healthy German students (n=512). Weighted phonemic edit distance performed best overall for modelling both production and strategy.

1 Introduction

Phonemic Verbal Fluency (PVF) is a standard neuropsychological test that is used to assess cognitive abilities. During this task, a person is asked to produce as many words as possible starting with a given letter in a specified amount of time. Classically, the PVF performance is then scored by counting the total number of unique words produced, however more fine-grained measures of performance (i.e. strategy) have been established to differentiate between multiple pathologies (Gruenewald and Lockhead, 1980). Troyer et al. (Troyer et al., 1997) first proposed a framework for assessing the strategy of a PVF performance: a rule-based system to determine phonemic clusters by manually defining criteria for phonemic similarity (Vonberg et al., 2014). According to this criteria, consecutive words in a production are lumped into categories if they share common first letters (e.g. *arm* & *art*), rhyme (e.g. *stand* & *sand*), share first and last sounds (e.g. *sat*, *seat* & *soot*) or are homonyms (e.g. *some* & *sum*).

While modelling production strategy (i.e., clustering and switching measures) is crucial for clinical cognitive considerations, the traditional manual approach is subjective and time consuming. There is a clear need for a data-driven automatic approach that addresses these limitations. Novel computational approaches to the analysis of *semantic verbal fluency* (SVF), where patients are asked to produce words based on a semantic cue (e.g. *animals*), could help to overcome the current limitations in PVF analysis (Woods et al., 2016; Linz et al., 2017; Clark et al., 2016; Troeger et al., 2019). The underlying rationale is to use a global similarity metric that is learned from data to derive a notion of relatedness between produced words, which can later be used to determine structures of related clusters as proxy for production strategy.

In the case of SVF, the similarity metric is semantically motivated.

Given the sparse body of research on automatic PVF analysis schemes modelling both production and strategy, further investigation on more sophisticated data-driven modelling approaches to PVF is needed. The goal of this paper is two-fold:

(1) First, we aim to introduce and compare the performance of five different similarity metrics for modelling production of PVF–in cognitively healthy participants–across sixteen letter categories, including an automated version of the current clinical criteria.

(2) Second, we propose a data-driven clustering scheme for determining phonemic clusters as a means of evaluating production strategy. In both experimental conditions, we compare the novel metrics to an implementation of the classic clinical Troyer baseline, described previously, to evaluate performance.

2 Related Work

Little previous research has proposed similar data-driven approaches for PVF evaluation which requires a phonemic similarity metric, respectively. Ryan et al. (Ryan et al., 2013) determined phonemic clusters in PVF tasks using a *phonemic similarity score*, based on edit-distance between phoneme representations from a pronunciation dictionary, and a *common biphone score*, a binary variable encoding the presence of a common initial and/or final biphone. They compared PVF performances (letter F) of martial arts fighters with high and low exposures (according to number of fights) and found significant differences in the groups mean and maximum cluster length for both biphone and phonemic similarity score approaches, and significant differences for the mean pairwise phonemic similarity provided by the common biphone method. This exploratory result demonstrates the potential of automated qualitative PVF analysis in the context of neurocognitive syndromes.

However, this approach does not capture the effect that phonemic properties might influence strategy, e.g. that some phonemes are closer in articulation than others. Previously, authors have proposed methods to weight *edit*-distance between phonemic representations with features reflective of the similarity between phonemes. Fontan et al.(Fontan et al., 2016) used Leven-

shtein (Levenshtein, 1966) distance between different phonemes, weighted by common features shared between them. Through this, they propose a new metric to evaluate automatic speech recognition systems, that seem to be consistent with human perception. Zampieri et al. (Zampieri and de Amorim, 2014) proposed a metric to enhance target word recovery for spell checking in English where they combined two weighted instances of Levenshtein distance. First, between the edit distance between two words normal spelling is calculated and then between the four digit Soundex code representations, where the Soundex algorithm represents similar sounding words as the same representation. This was combined with clustering techniques to improve spell checking. Similar methods have been used to measure pronunciation differences of dialects in Norwegian where weighted Levenshtein distance using phonetic representations and acoustic features were used with clustering techniques (Heeringa, 2005).

Given this, there is a substantial gap in advancing the state of the art in data-driven modelling of PVF speech output that can be leveraged for clinical applications.

3 Methods

Closing this gap, this section describes four proposed distance metrics for measuring similarity as well as the clinical baseline and details a *rank-cost* evaluation criteria to compare all metrics' ability to model PVF productions. Furthermore, this methodology is used in a second performance evaluation of each metric for modelling clinical clustering and switching strategy based on clusters defined by the affinity propagation clustering algorithm (Frey and Dueck, 2007).

3.1 Modelling Production

3.1.1 Metrics

Levenshtein distance (Levenshtein, 1966) is computed as the number of insertions, deletions and substitutions that are necessary to transform one word into another word. Let d, i and s represent the cost of deletions, insertions and substitutions respectively.

1. *LD*: The Levenshtein distance between the orthographic representation of words

2. *phon*: the Levenshtein distance between phonetic representations, weighted for pho-

netic similarity. Phonological feature vectors are obtained from Epitran using Panphon's database of International Phonetic Alphabet (IPA) symbol features (Mortensen et al., 2016). Each phonetic symbol is represented by a fixed-length vector of integers between -1 and 1 representing the presence (+1), absence (0), or lack (-1) of 21 phonological features. The weighted similarity score for s is the hamming distance between the phonetic vector representations. d and i are held constant at 1.

3. *pos*: Levenshtein distance between phonetic representations, weighted for position in word, d, i and s are set as q, where q is drawn from the exponential distribution at position i, with $\lambda = 0.5$.

4. *sem*: The semantic distance between word vector representation. Semantic representations of word vectors were obtained from the German fastText model (Grave et al., 2018; ?) and similarity is approximated as the cosine distance between the vectors.

5. *Troyer*: Implementation of Troyer clinical criteria for phonemic clustering (Troyer et al., 1997). Values were calculated by (1) string matching the first or last 2 letters, (2) matching the first two sounds of phonetically transcribed words, (3) for rhyming, matching the last two sounds of phonetically transcribed words and (4) for homophones, matching phonetic transcriptions of the whole word. Each criteria was weighted as 1 and the sum of criteria present was used as a score. The max score was a 4 and the lowest 0. Words with equivalent scores where sorted alphabetically.

Phonetic transcriptions were obtained with Epitran, a python library that translates orthographic to phonetic representations (Mortensen et al., 2018).

For each letter category, c, in our data set a vocabulary of the set of all words produced, V_c, is constructed. The vocabulary V_c has length N. For each of the described similarity metrics f, a table of size NxN is created where the similarity between every word in vocabulary is calculated. The result is a square, symmetric similarity matrix, S_c, for each metric.

3.1.2 Evaluation

Difference of scale for each of the metrics renders direct comparison impossible, therefore performance of the metrics is evaluated via ranking tables.

For each similarity matrix of a letter category S_c, a list is generated for every word in the vocabulary, V_c, of the most similar to the least similar as determined by the metric f. To formalize this, a rank table T is created for every word w in each letter vocabulary V_c.

Once all tables are populated, the rank cost of the PVF samples RC_f are calculated by c for each f. Given a production $P = w_1...w_n$, a metric f and ranking tables for each word $T_{w_1}^f...T_{w_n}^f$ the rank cost of P, given f, is determined as

$$RC_f(P) = \frac{\sum_{j=1}^{n-1} T_{w_j}^f[w_{j+1}]}{n-1}$$

Using rank based comparison is motivated by a two arguments. First, ranking makes different similarity metrics comparable, by rendering issues of scale irrelevant while preserving the individual metrics outcome. Second, the resulting RC_f can be interpreted directly as the offset of the mean rank, when used for predicting the next word from our vocabulary. The similarity metric f which is better at modelling production will have a lower RC_f.

3.2 Modelling Strategy

3.2.1 Metrics

After modelling production, it is crucial to consider that the clinical *Troyer* metric is not a method of modelling production, but rather a clustering strategy to explore the underlying cognitive process of this clinical task. Taking this into account, the following methodology aims to compare each metric's ability to model the underlying strategies of the PVF task.

Affinity Propagation Clustering (AP clustering) is a clustering algorithm based on each point in a data set—in this application, the similarity matrix S_c for each metric f—passing messages simultaneously through two matrices, representing either responsibility or availability. The end result is an emergence of data points—or words from V_c—that are considered exemplars, having high responsibility, while remaining points are then grouped around the exemplars to create clusters,

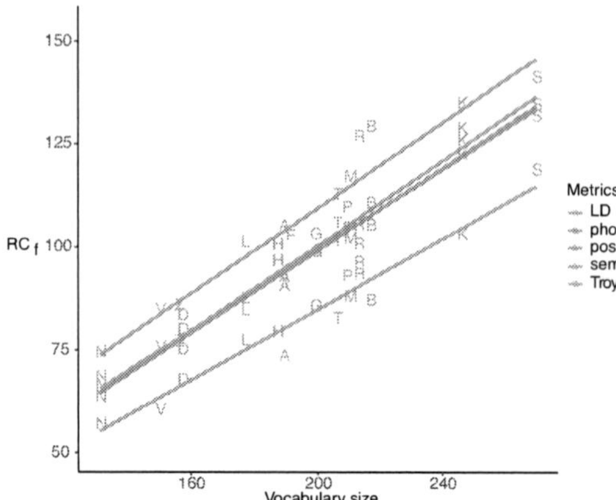

Figure 1: Median RC_f for each letter and method f as a function of vocabulary size. Different f are indicated by color. Lines indicate fit of a linear model.

or better suited by availability (Frey and Dueck, 2007). A unique point of AP clustering is that the number of clusters is not predefined, but emerges from the data. This concept lends itself naturally to the idea of clustering in PVF, as exemplars can be seen as the general topic that is being searched for during the production.

To apply this to the data, for every letter category c, the generated similarity matrix S_c for each metric f is used to create a set of clusters as determined by AP clustering algorithm. The resulting clusters are then saved and applied to each production in the data set to consider the strategy estimated by each metric. Consecutive words in each participant production are compared to see if they belong in a cluster as determined by each similarity metric.

For example, if a participant was given the letter category C, they might produce the following:

cat, crab, crawl, crib, cash, cache

The clusters generated from a selection of the similarity metrics using the AP clustering algorithm to cluster the PVF performance would yield the following, where words within a set of brackets indicate a computed cluster:

Troyer: [cat], [crab, crawl, crib], [cash, cache]
sem: [cat, crab], [crawl, crib], [cash], [cache]

3.2.2 Evaluation

The quality of the AP clustering technique on this task is evaluated using the silhouette coefficient. This measure is ideal as it does not require a ground truth. This measure looks at the fit of a cluster by considering if every point is in its closest cluster, or if another cluster would be more suitable. Each point in the dataset is considered. First, the average distance between the chosen point and all points in its own cluster ($distance_{cohesion}$) is calculated. Then, the average distance between the same point and all points in next nearest cluster is calculated ($distance_{separation}$).

$$\frac{distance_{separation} - distance_{cohesion}}{max(distance_{separation}, distance_{cohesion})}$$

The silhouette coefficient is bounded from -1 to 1, where positive values indicate higher quality clusters and negative values typically indicate that a point has been incorrectly clustered (Rousseeuw, 1987).

The ability of the metrics to model strategy is evaluated by looking at the average rank cost within clusters as well as the average rank cost between clusters, or switches. The rank cost tables created previously are used to calculate this respectively.

The average rank cost of clusters is calculated by looking at the rank cost of transitions between words in each cluster and normalized by the number of transitions in a cluster.

The average rank cost of switches in a production is calculated by summing the rank costs of transitions between cluster boundaries and normalizing by the number of switch transitions.

Metrics with a lower average rank cost within clusters and higher average rank cost of switching are seen to better model strategy.

4 Experiment 1: Modelling Production

For the first experiment, one minute PVF performances of 32 German students (9 male, 23 female; Age 22.88) from 16 different letter categories (i.e. *A, B, D, F, G, H, K, L, M, N, P, R, S, T, V, Z*) were collected. These were manually transcribed on a word level into sequences of correct responses. Words were converted into phoneme (IPA) representations using the python *epitran*[1] package. For each letter category c, a vocabulary V_c was constructed to calculate the RC_f of each sample as described in Section 4.

Statistical analysis was performed using R (software version 3.4.0). Performance of metrics over all letters was examined with a linear mixed

---

[1] https://github.com/dmort27/epitran

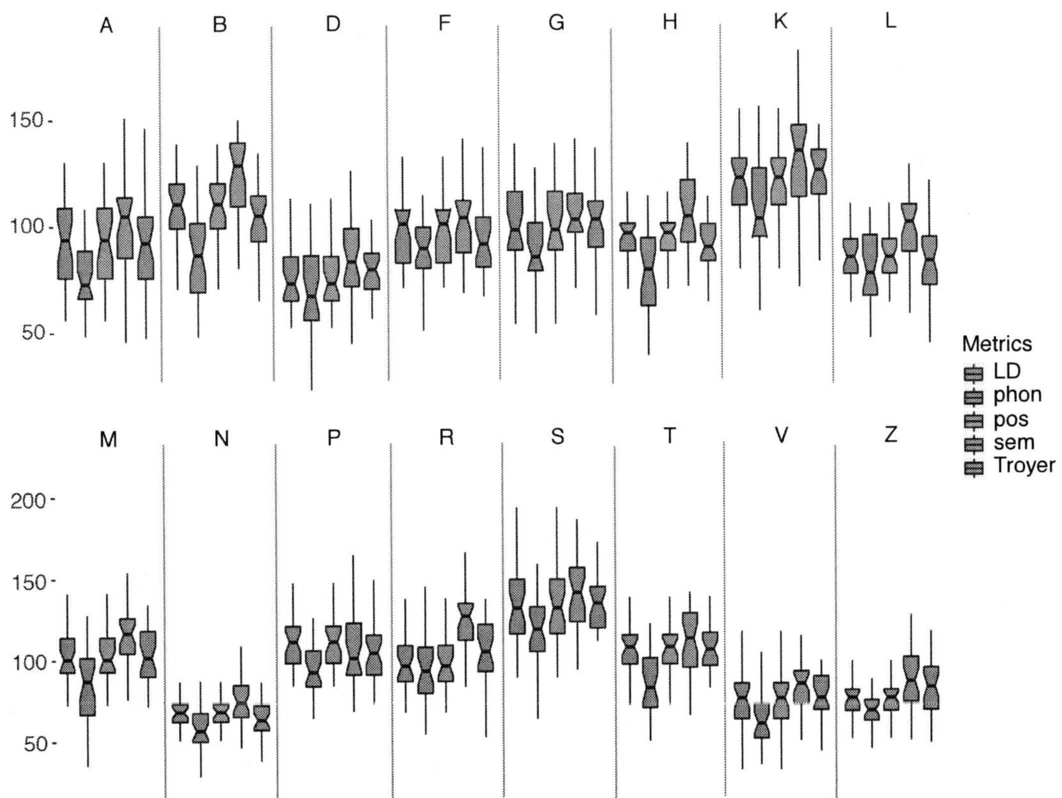

Figure 2: Comparison of RC_f values for distance metrics f and letter categories. Each boxplot represents one letter category and contains results from the five distance metrics defined in Section 3.1. In the case of black and white prints, metrics for each letter category match the legend from top to bottom as left to right.

effects analysis using the *lme4* (Bates et al., 2014) package. Each RC_f was modelled as a single data point and letter and metric were represented as fixed effects. The participant identifier was modelled as a random intercept.

5 Experiment 2: Modelling Strategy

The affinity propagation clustering algorithm was implemented in python from *scikit-learn* framework (Pedregosa et al., 2011). The same parameters were used to determine all models. The preference parameter serves as an indicator of how fit a word in the vocabulary is to be an exemplar, higher values indicate that it is more likely where as lower values indicate that it is less likely. This also influences the number of clusters produced, where higher preference values lead to more clusters and lower preference values lead to fewer cluster. The preference parameter was set for each word in the vocabulary as the Zipf word frequency as de-

termined by the python wordfreq package (Speer et al., 2018). The zipf word frequency represents the frequency of the word in a large, in this case German, corpus on a 'human-friendly' scale. The result is a value between 1.0 and 8.0, where the larger the value, the more frequent the word is in the language. The goal of using the word frequency during clustering is to give a high exemplar weight to more frequent words to make the clusters relevant to the PVF production task. The remaining parameters were left at their default values; the damping factor was set to 0.5 and convergence iteration rate at 200. Each previously computed similarity matrix S_c was used as an input to generate clusters for each metric f.

The average rank cost of clusters in a production was computed as described in 3.2.2.

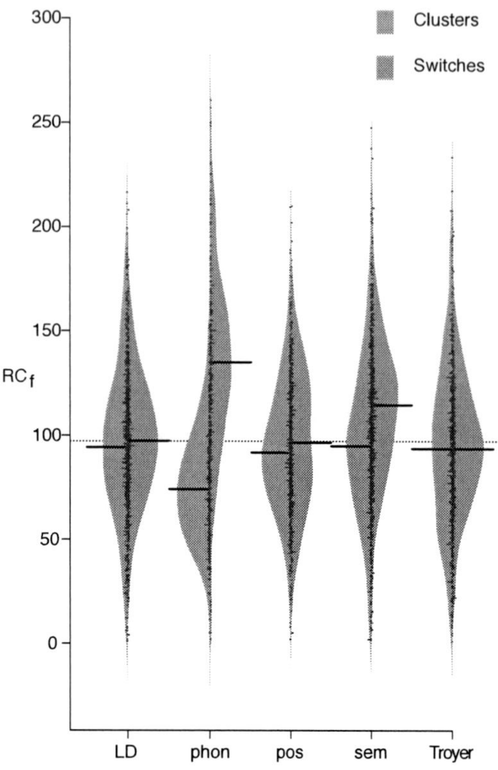

Figure 3: Beanplots comparing the distribution of average rank cost of clustering and switching across all letter categories, by metric. The left distribution is for clustering and the right distribution is for switching. The long bar in the distribution represents the median.

6 Results

6.1 Experiment 1

Results are displayed in Figure 2, where a better fit is indicated by lower RC_f. One boxplot is shown for each letter category. The threshold for rejecting a null hypothesis and determining statistical significance is set at 0.05 for all tests performed.

The linear models were created as described in 3.1.2 and revealed that RC_f values were significantly lower for the *phon* and significantly greater for the *sem* metric. Performances varied across letter categories with the lowest overall RC_f values being observed for the letter N and the highest for S.

6.2 Experiment 2

Evaluation of cluster quality as produced by the AP clustering algorithm is monitored via their silhouette coefficients as described in section 3.2.2

and are shown in Table 1.

The highest quality clusters were produced by the *phon* metric. The *pos* metric had the second highest quality on average. The remaining metrics all produced relatively close values for all letter categories with *Troyer* performing slightly better than *LD* and *sem*. Overall, all metrics on average produced positive cluster values.

LD	phon	pos	sem	Troyer
0.025	0.738	0.330	0.083	0.170

Table 1: silhouette coefficients

Figure 3 uses beanplots to compare each metric by the distribution of average rank cost within a cluster and the average rank cost of switches. *Phon* had a much lower average rank cost within clusters where as all other metrics were relatively equal, with *Troyer* having slightly lower than LD. Sem had the highest average cluster rank cost.

For each metric, a paired-samples t-test was conducted to compare average RC_f, aggregated across letter categories, between clustering and switching conditions. There were significant differences in average rank cost for clustering and switching for *phon* (t(222)=-20.17, p<0.05), *sem* (t(222)=3.69, p<0.05) and *pos* (t(222)=-2.372, p<0.05). No significant differences were found for the metrics LD or Troyer.

7 Discussion

For modelling the entire production, *phon* outperformed the *troyer* and *LD* metrics in every letter category, showing an improvement from our baseline measurements. Overall, the metric that best modeled the data based on the ranked cost evaluation was *phon*. The semantic similarity measure *sem* had the highest average rank cost across all letter categories, leading us to believe that the task as a whole is not semantically motivated.

For modelling strategy based on clustering and switching, the phonetically weight edit distance *phon* continued to have the highest quality clusters as indicated by a low rank cost across all letter categories. This metric also best modelled the switching procedure between clusters as indicated by a high rank cost. In addition,

While the semantically motivated *sem* metric performed poorly on modelling the overall production it was able to capture the relationship of clustering strategy, albeit not as well as *phon*. This could be due to the lower quality of clusters produced by the *sem* metric, as determined by the silhouette coefficient, however the overall score is within a reasonable range. Another consideration is that the phonemic task has little semantic underlying notions for producing clusters and phonemically derived measures are more suited to the task. There is also a possibility that within phonemic verbal fluency there are phonemic and semantic strategies that motivate clustering and switching. For example, a cluster of the words "grandmother", "grandfather", and "grandstand" would be both semantically and phonemically motivated.

8   Conclusion

This paper compared different similarity metrics for their ability to model production in PVF for multiple letter categories. The proposed *phon* approaches significantly outperformed the simple *LD* baseline and automated *troyer* methods for both modelling production and strategy. Surprisingly, the *scm* metric performed poorly in comparison to all other metrics when modelling the entire production sequence, but was able to capture the notion of underlying strategies of clustering and switching.

Further development of the newly proposed metrics should be continued by tuning parameters for AP clustering per evaluated metric to achieve higher quality clusters rather than the uniform configurations demonstrated in this paper. Further investigations could also combine semantic and phonemic methods by classifying clusters as being either semantically motivated or phonemically motivated. The next step in this line of research would be to apply these new PVF techniques in a clinical application and evaluate the effectiveness of these features to distinguish between different pathological groups. Similar evaluations should be conducted for other languages, since results may vary due to phonemic differences.

References

Douglas Bates, Martin Mächler, Ben Bolker, and Steve Walker. 2014. Fitting linear mixed-effects models using lme4. *arXiv preprint arXiv:1406.5823*.

D. G. Clark, P. M. McLaughlin, E. Woo, K. Hwang, S. Hurtz, L. Ramirez, J. Eastman, R. M. Dukes, P. Kapur, T. P. DeRamus, and L. G. Apostolova. 2016. Novel verbal fluency scores and structural brain imaging for prediction of cognitive outcome in mild cognitive impairment. *Alzheimers Dement (Amst)*, 2:113–122.

Lionel Fontan, Isabelle Ferrané, Jérôme Farinas, Julien Pinquier, and Xavier Aumont. 2016. Using phonologically weighted levenshtein distances for the prediction of microscopic intelligibility.

Brendan J. Frey and Delbert Dueck. 2007. Clustering by passing messages between data points. *Science*, 315(5814):972–976.

Edouard Grave, Piotr Bojanowski, Prakhar Gupta, Armand Joulin, and Tomas Mikolov. 2018. Learning word vectors for 157 languages. In *Proceedings of the International Conference on Language Resources and Evaluation (LREC 2018)*.

Paul J Gruenewald and Gregory R Lockhead. 1980. The Free Recall of Category Examples. *Journal of Experimental Psychology: Human Learning and Memory*, 6:225–240.

Wilbert Heeringa. 2005. Measuring dialect pronunciation differences using levenshtein distance. *Zeitschrift fr Dialektologie und Linguistik*, pages 205–208.

Vladimir I Levenshtein. 1966. Binary codes capable of correcting deletions, insertions, and reversals.

Nicklas Linz, Johannes Tröger, Jan Alexandersson, and Alexandra König. 2017. Using Neural Word Embeddings in the Analysis of the Clinical Semantic Verbal Fluency Task. In *Proceedings of the 12th International Conference on Computational Semantics (IWCS)*.

David R. Mortensen, Siddharth Dalmia, and Patrick Littell. 2018. Epitran: Precision G2P for many languages. In *Proceedings of the Eleventh International Conference on Language Resources and Evaluation (LREC 2018)*, Paris, France. European Language Resources Association (ELRA).

David R. Mortensen, Patrick Littell, Akash Bharadwaj, Kartik Goyal, Chris Dyer, and Lori S. Levin. 2016. Panphon: A resource for mapping IPA segments to articulatory feature vectors. In *Proceedings of COLING 2016, the 26th International Conference on Computational Linguistics: Technical Papers*, pages 3475–3484. ACL.

F. Pedregosa, G. Varoquaux, A. Gramfort, V. Michel, B. Thirion, O. Grisel, M. Blondel, P. Prettenhofer, R. Weiss, V. Dubourg, J. Vanderplas, A. Passos, D. Cournapeau, M. Brucher, M. Perrot, and E. Duchesnay. 2011. Scikit-learn: Machine Learning in Python. *Journal of Machine Learning Research*, 12:2825–2830.

Peter Rousseeuw. 1987. Silhouettes: a graphical aid to the interpretation and validation of cluster analysis.

James O Ryan, Serguei VS Pakhomov, Susan E Marino, Charles Bernick, and Sarah Banks. 2013. Computerized analysis of a verbal fluency test. In *Proceedings of ACL*, pages 884–889.

Robyn Speer, Joshua Chin, Andrew Lin, Sara Jewett, and Lance Nathan. 2018. Luminosoinsight/wordfreq: v2.2.

Johannes Troeger, Nicklas Linz, Alexandra Knig, Philippe Robert, Jan Alexandersson, Jessica Peter, and Jutta Kray. 2019. Exploitation vs. explorationcomputational temporal and semantic analysis explains semantic verbal fluency impairment in alzheimer's disease. *Neuropsychologia*.

Angela K Troyer, Morris Moscovitch, and Gordon Winocur. 1997. Clustering and Switching as Two Components of Verbal Fluency: Evidence From Younger and Older Healthy Adults. *Neuropsychology*, 11(1):138–146.

Isabelle Vonberg, Felicitas Ehlen, Ortwin Fromm, and Fabian Klostermann. 2014. The absoluteness of semantic processing: Lessons from the analysis of temporal clusters in phonemic verbal fluency. 9:e115846.

David L. Woods, John M. Wyma, Timothy J. Herron, and E. William Yund. 2016. Computerized Analysis of Verbal Fluency: Normative Data and the Effects of Repeated Testing, Simulated Malingering, and Traumatic Brain Injury. *PLOS ONE*, 11(12):1–37.

Marcos Zampieri and Renato Cordeiro de Amorim. 2014. Between sound and spelling: Combining phonetics and clustering algorithms to improve target word recovery. In *PolTAL*.

Automatic Detection and Classification of Argument Components using Multi-task Deep Neural Network

Jean-Christophe Mensonides, Sébastien Harispe, Jacky Montmain
LGI2P, IMT Mines Ales,
Ales, France
`firstname.lastname@mines-ales.fr`

Véronique Thireau
CHROME, Université de Nîmes,
Nîmes, France
`veronique.thireau@unimes.fr`

Abstract

In this article we propose a novel method for automatically extracting and classifying argument components from raw texts. We introduce a multi-task deep learning framework exploiting weight parameters trained on auxiliary simple tasks, such as Part-Of-Speech tagging or chunking, in order to solve more complex tasks that require a fine-grained understanding of natural language. Interestingly, our results show that the use of advanced deep learning techniques framed in a multi-task setting enables competing with state-of-the-art systems that depend on handcrafted features.

1 Introduction

Argumentation consists in a set of methods aiming at making an interlocutor adhere to an introduced point of view or conclusion -or at least to increase its adherence to the latter. In its simplest form, argumentation is a reasoning process selecting and structuring premises to attack or defend a given conclusion. Although the study of argumentation is well established in fields such as Logic, Philosophy, or Linguistics, automatic extraction and analysis of arguments from natural language, commonly referred as Argument Mining, is a relatively new research area. Advances in Argument Mining are of major importance for Natural Language Understanding and Processing, in particular due to their several direct applications and relationships with other tasks, e.g. fake news detection, knowledge base enrichment and population, source trustworthiness estimation. To date, most advanced argument mining systems aims at generating argument-based graphs identifying and structuring premises, claims and conclusion from raw texts (Cabrio and Villata, 2018). They can

usually be split into sequences of subtasks including argument detection and argument linking (Lippi and Torroni, 2016). This article focuses on analyzing argumentative micro-structure, i.e., how different argumentative components interact with each other within a single text.

Three types of argument components are often used in the annotation scheme considered in Argument mining: (i) major claims, reflecting the author's standpoint on the debated topic, (ii) claims, which are statements needing further justifications to be accepted, and (iii) premises, which are justifications used in order to make a claim stand (Stab and Gurevych, 2017). Those components are further structured into a directly acyclic graph in which nodes account for argumentative components and edges account for oriented links between them. Directed edges in the graph are labeled either as a *support* or *attack* relationship, and are only allowed a) from a premise to another premise, b) from a premise to a (major) claim, and c) from a claim to a (major) claim. Such an annotation schema is adopted by (Stab and Gurevych, 2017) in the Argument Annotated Essays corpus (version 2) composed of 402 manually annotated student essays taken from essayforum.com.

A pipeline of treatments is generally applied to automatically obtain the graph reflecting the underlying argumentative structure of an essay. The following intuitive decomposition involving four subtasks is moreover often considered in practice (Stab and Gurevych, 2017): (1) argument components identification, (2) argument components classification, (3) assessment of the existence of directed edges between argument components, and (4) tagging of the existing directed edges either as a support or as an attack relation-

"

ship. This article will focus on solving subtasks (1) and (2). It presents a novel multi-task approach to argument mining that does not require handcrafted features as input. We are in particular interested by evaluating if recent deep learning techniques, such as recurrent neural network mixed with multi-task learning, can compete with traditional approaches based on handcrafted features.

The paper is organized as follows. Section 2 introduces an overview of related work proposed on tasks similar to (1) and (2). Section 3 introduces our approach to solve those two tasks. Section 4 describes the training details of the proposed model. Section 5 describes our experiments and results. Section 6 provides directions and perspectives for future works.

2   Related work

Argument components detection consists in determining the boundaries separating the textual units carrying arguments from the rest of the text. This task is generally considered as a supervised text segmentation problem at word level. Models exploiting the sequential aspect of texts, inherent in the construction of a convincing argumentation, seem particularly adapted and are often used. (Madnani et al., 2012) used a CRF (Conditional Random Field) to identify non-argumentative segments within dissertations. (Levy et al., 2014) identified the boundaries of textual units detailing conclusions which were supporting or attacking topics discussed in threads from Wikipedia. (Ajjour et al., 2017) used LSTM (Long shortterm memory, recurrent neural network) to extract arguments from essays, editorials, and from user-generated comments. (Goudas et al., 2014) first identified sentences containing arguments and then detected their boundaries within social media using a CRF. (Sardianos et al., 2015) determined argument components boundaries in news articles using also using a CRF. Similarly, (Stab and Gurevych, 2017) used a CRF to extract argument components in essays. (Eger et al., 2017) leveraged deep learning techniques to extract arguments from raw texts.

Determining the type of argument components (premise, conclusion, etc.) has often been treated as a supervised text classification problem. (Eckle-Kohler et al., 2015) distinguished premises and conclusions in news articles using Naive Bayes, Random Forest and SVM (Support Vector Machine). (Park and Cardie, 2014) also used a SVM to determine the extent to which claims are justified in citizen's comments related to possible new legislation projects. (Stab and Gurevych, 2017) classified argumentative components into premises, claims and major claims in essays using a SVM. (Persing and Ng, 2016) used maximum entropy classification to determine the type of argument components. (Potash et al., 2016) used sequence-to-sequence recurrent neural networks to infer the type of argument components.

Multi-tasks models are able to handle several different problems by sharing a subset of shared parameters. They have been subject to recent interest within the Natural Language Processing community (Hashimoto et al., 2016; Søgaard and Goldberg, 2016; Eger et al., 2017; Yang et al., 2016). This type of models is bio-inspired: human beings are able to carry out a multitude of different tasks and can exploit, when necessary, knowledge related to different types of problems, making the learning of new tasks faster and easier. (Ruder, 2017) states the reasons why this type of model is effective from a machine learning point of view: the use of several different corpora induces an implicit increase in the number of examples available during the training phase. In addition, the model has to look for characteristics which may be useful for all the tasks to be processed, which limits the noise modeling and thus, leads to a better generalization.

(Søgaard and Goldberg, 2016) showed that inducing *a priori* knowledge in a multi-task model, by ordering the tasks to be learned, leads to better performance. (Yang et al., 2016) have shown that driving a multi-task and multi-language model can improve performance on problems where data is only partially annotated. (Hashimoto et al., 2016) obtained competitive results on several different tasks with a single model. However, we should note that there is no guarantee on the benefits of using multi-task models, and that their success depends on the data distribution related to the various problems treated (Mou et al., 2016; Alonso and Plank, 2016; Bingel and Søgaard, 2017). (Schulz et al., 2018) proposed a multi-task framework to perform end-to-end argument mining. The result they obtained are very promising. In this paper, we are interested in leveraging auxiliary informa-

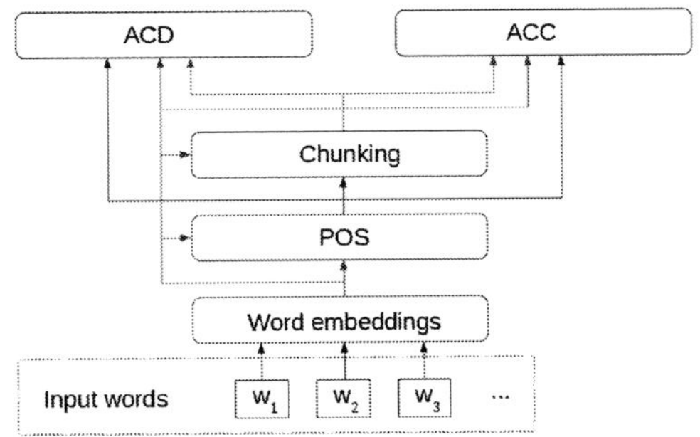

Figure 1: Overview of the model architecture (Layer-wise). POS, ACD and ACC are respectively acronyms for Part-Of-Speech, Argument Components Detection and Argument Components Classification.

tions such as Part-Of-Speech and Chunking tags in a multi-task learning setup, in order to perform argument component detection and classification.

3 Proposed approach

We propose a model which aims at 1) determining argument components boundaries within a set of essays and 2) determining the type of each argument component within the latter essays. We draw inspiration from the work of (Hashimoto et al., 2016) and opt for a multi-task model without the definition of handcrafted features. Specifically, we use deep learning techniques and develop a model that performs Part-Of-Speech (POS) tagging, chunking, argument components boundaries detection, and argument components classification. An overview of the model architecture is given in Figure 1. The different layers used in the architecture are described below.

3.1 Word embeddings

We first use a word embedding layer, assigning a vector representation e_t to each word w_t given in input to the system. We use GloVe (Pennington et al., 2014) to obtain a set of pre-trained embeddings in an unsupervised fashion[1]. Note that, word embeddings are continually optimized while training the model on the different tasks described below. Out-of-vocabulary words are mapped to a special $<UNK>$ token.

---

[1] We used pre-trained embeddings from https://nlp.stanford.edu/projects/glove/.

3.2 POS tagging

The second layer of the model corresponds to a POS tagging task, consisting in assigning a POS tag (noun, verb, adjective, etc.) to each word w_t given in input to the system. We use a bi-directional Gated Recurrent Unit (GRU) (Cho et al., 2014) to encode input word sequences.

GRU is a recurrent neural network using a gating mechanism and avoiding the use of a separate memory cell. At each time step t, GRU computes the hidden state h_t as follows:

$$h_t = (1 - z_t) * n_t + z_t * h_{(t-1)}$$

with

$$n_t = tanh(W_n x_t + b_n + r_t * (W_{hn} h_{(t-1)} + b_{hn}))$$

$$r_t = \sigma(W_r x_t + b_r + W_{hr} h_{(t-1)} + b_{hr})$$

$$z_t = \sigma(W_z x_t + b_z + W_{hz} h_{(t-1)} + b_{hz})$$

where x_t is the input at time step t, r_t, z_t and n_t are respectively the reset, update and new gates, σ is the sigmoid function, and W and b are matrice and vector parameters.

In order to exploit the past and future contexts of an element from a sequence of N inputs $[x_1, x_1, ..., x_N]$, we construct a bi-directional encoding by concatenating the hidden states obtained with a forward encoding (e.g, at time step $t = 1$, the input is x_1, at time step $t = 2$, the input is x_2, etc.) and a backward encoding (e.g, at time step $t = 1$, the input is x_N, at time step $t = 2$, the input is x_{N-1}, etc.):

$$\overrightarrow{h_t} = \overrightarrow{GRU}(x_t), t \in [1, N]$$

$$\overleftarrow{h_t} = \overleftarrow{GRU}(x_t), t \in [N, 1]$$

$$h_t = [\overrightarrow{h_t}; \overleftarrow{h_t}]$$

We use word embeddings as input of the POS tagging layer:

$$\overrightarrow{h_t^{(1)}} = \overrightarrow{GRU}(e_t)$$

$$\overleftarrow{h_t^{(1)}} = \overleftarrow{GRU}(e_t)$$

$$h_t^{(1)} = [\overrightarrow{h_t^{(1)}}; \overleftarrow{h_t^{(1)}}]$$

Then for each time step t we compute the probability of assigning the label k to the word w_t as follows:

$$p(y_t^{(1)} = k | h_t^{(1)}) =$$

$$\frac{exp(W_{sm_{(1)}} fc_t^{(1)} + b_{sm_{(1)}})}{\sum_{c_1} exp(W_{sm_{(1)}} fc_t^{(1)} + b_{sm_{(1)}})} \quad (1)$$

$$fc_t^{(1)} = relu(W_{fc_{(1)}} h_t^{(1)} + b_{fc_{(1)}}) \quad (2)$$

where W and b are parameter matrices and vectors, $ReLU$ is the Rectified Linear Unit function (Nair and Hinton, 2010), and c_1 is the set of possible POS tags.

3.3 Chunking

Chunking is a task aiming at assigning a chunk tag (noun phrase, verb phrase, etc.) to each word. We compute hidden chunking states by exploiting what the model has learned for the POS tagging task:

$$\overrightarrow{h_t^{(2)}} = \overrightarrow{GRU}([e_t; h_t^{(1)}; y_t^{(POS)}])$$

$$\overleftarrow{h_t^{(2)}} = \overleftarrow{GRU}([e_t; h_t^{(1)}; y_t^{(POS)}])$$

$$h_t^{(2)} = [\overrightarrow{h_t^{(2)}}; \overleftarrow{h_t^{(2)}}]$$

where $h_t^{(1)}$ is the hidden state obtained at time step t on the POS tagging task and $y_t^{(POS)}$ is the weighted POS label embedding. Following (Hashimoto et al., 2016), $y_t^{(POS)}$ is defined as follows:

$$y_t^{(POS)} = \sum_{j=1}^{card(c_1)} p(y_t^{(1)} = j | h_t^{(1)}) l(j) \quad (3)$$

where $l(j)$ is an embedding of the j-th POS tag. POS tag embeddings are pre-trained using GloVe.

The probability to assign a chunk tag to each word is then computed in a similar way to the one for POS tags (eq. (1) and (2)), but with a set of parameters specific to the chunking layer.

3.4 Argument Components Detection (ACD)

Argument components detection aims at delimiting the boundaries of each argument component within essays at the word level. We follow (Stab

and Gurevych, 2017) and treat this task as a supervised text segmentation problem, where labels follow an IOB-tagset (Ramshaw and Marcus, 1999): the first word of each argument component carries an "Arg-B" label, remaining words of said argument component bear an "Arg-I" tag, and the words not belonging to any argument component bear an "O" tag.

Each essay is considered as a single word sequence which we encode as follows:

$$\overrightarrow{h_t^{(3)}} = \overrightarrow{GRU}([e_t; h_t^{(1)}; y_t^{(POS)}; h_t^{(2)}; y_t^{(chunk)}])$$

$$\overleftarrow{h_t^{(3)}} = \overleftarrow{GRU}([e_t; h_t^{(1)}; y_t^{(POS)}; h_t^{(2)}; y_t^{(chunk)}])$$

$$h_t^{(3)} = [\overrightarrow{h_t^{(3)}}; \overleftarrow{h_t^{(3)}}]$$

where $y_t^{(chunk)}$ is the weighted chunk label embedding, computed in a similar way as the one for POS labels (eq. (3)).

The probability to assign a chunk tag to a word is then computed in a similar way as the one for POS labels, but with a set of parameters specific the ACD layer.

3.5 Argument Components Classification (ACC)

Argument components classification aims at determining the type of each argument component between premise, claim and major claim. We treat this task as a segment labeling problem. We consider that a segment can be the sequence of words belonging to a same argument component or can be the sequence of words belonging to a same portion of continuous text whose words do not belong to an argument component. The notion of segment is illustrated in Figure 2.

We encode each segment $s_i, i \in [1, L]$ as follows:

$$\overrightarrow{h_{it}} = \overrightarrow{GRU}([e_{it}; h_{it}^{(1)}; y_{it}^{(POS)}; h_{it}^{(2)}; y_{it}^{(chunk)}])$$

$$\overleftarrow{h_{it}} = \overleftarrow{GRU}([e_{it}; h_{it}^{(1)}; y_{it}^{(POS)}; h_{it}^{(2)}; y_{it}^{(chunk)}])$$

$$h_{it} = [\overrightarrow{h_{it}}; \overleftarrow{h_{it}}]$$

where it is the time step t for the segment s_i.

Figure 2: Excerpt from an essay of the corpus illustrat-
ing the notion of segments. Text regions underlined by
a solid line are premises, those underlined by a dashed
line are claims, and the bold regions are major claims.
Segment numbers [S$_\#$] were added as indications. The
first segment is the region from the beginning of the text
to the first premise. The second segment corresponds
to the first premise. The third segment is the not underlined region between the first premise and the first
claim, and so on.

In order to help the model focusing on the most
important markers (such as "I firmly believe that"
or "we can receive the same conclusion that")
we use an attention mechanism (Bahdanau et al.,
2014), which in addition allows us to synthesize
the information carried by segments hidden states
into fixed size vectors:

$$u_{it} = tanh(W_{att}h_{it} + b_{att})$$

$$\alpha_{it} = \frac{exp(u_{it}^{\intercal}u_{att})}{\sum_t exp(u_{it}^{\intercal}u_{att})}$$

$$sh_i = \sum_t \alpha_{it}h_{it}$$

where W_{att}, b_{att} and u_{att} are respectively parameter matrices, bias and vectors.

Then we encode each essay using the synthetic
segments hidden states sh_i:

$$\overrightarrow{h_j^{(4)}} = \overrightarrow{GRU}(sh_i), i \in [1, L]$$

$$\overleftarrow{h_j^{(4)}} = \overleftarrow{GRU}(sh_i), i \in [L, 1]$$

$$h_j^{(4)} = [\overrightarrow{h_j^{(4)}}; \overleftarrow{h_j^{(4)}}]$$

The probability of assigning a label to each segment is then computed similarly to that for POS
tags, but with a set of parameters specific to the
ACC layer.

4 Model Training

For each epoch of training, we optimized the
model's parameters for each layer. That is, at each
epoch we trained the layers in the following order: POS tagging, chunking, ACD and ACC. In
order to assess the relevance of implementing a
multi-task model, we trained two versions of the
model: a version where we trained every layer (referred as "w/ POS & chunking"), and a version for
which we voluntary omitted to train the POS tagging and chunking layers (referred as "w/o POS &
chunking"). The training details of each layer are
described below.

4.1 POS tagging layer

Following (Hashimoto et al., 2016), we denote
$\theta_{POS} = (W_{POS}, b_{POS}, \theta_e)$ the set of parameters
involved in the POS tagging layer. W_{POS} represents the set of parameter matrices for the POS
tagging layer, b_{POS} the set of biases of the POS
tagging layer, and θ_e the set of parameters of the
words embedding layer. The cost function is defined as:

$$J^{(1)} = -\sum_s \sum_t log\, p(y_t^{(1)} = k|h_t^{(1)})$$
$$+\lambda \|W_{POS}\|^2 + \delta \|\theta_e - \theta_e'\|^2$$

where $p(y_t^{(1)} = k|h_t^{(1)})$ is the probability of as-
signing the right label k to the word w_t of the word
sequence s, $\lambda \|W_{POS}\|^2$ is the L2 regularization
term and $\delta \|\theta_e - \theta_e'\|^2$ is a secondary regulariza-
tion term. λ and δ are hyperparameters.

The secondary regularization term aims at stabi-
lizing the training by preventing θ_e from being too
specifically optimized to fit the POS tagging task.
Indeed, since θ_e is shared across all layers of the
model, excessive modifications of its parameters
would prevent the model from learning efficiently.
θ_e' is the set of parameters involved in the word
embedding layer at last epoch.

4.2 Chunking layer

We denote $\theta_{chunk} = (W_{chunk}, b_{chunk}, E_{POS}, \theta_e)$
the set of parameters involved in the chunking

layer. W_{chunk} et b_{chunk} are respectively parameter matrices and bias of the chunking layer, including those of θ_{POS}. E_{POS} is the set of parameters characterizing the POS label embeddings. The cost function is defined as follows:

$$J^{(2)} = -\sum_{s}\sum_{t} log\, p(y_t^{(2)} = k|h_t^{(2)})$$
$$+\lambda \|W_{chunking}\|^2 + \delta \|\theta_{POS} - \theta'_{POS}\|^2$$

with $p(y_t^{(2)} = k|h_t^{(2)})$ the probability of assigning the right label k to the word w_t of the word sequence s. θ'_{POS} is the set of parameters of the POS tagging layer right before the training of the chunking layer for the current epoch.

4.3 ACD layer

We denote θ_{ACD} the set of parameters involved in the ACD layer, with $\theta_{ACD} = (W_{ACD}, b_{ACD}, E_{POS}, E_{chunk}, \theta_e)$. W_{ACD} and b_{ACD} are respectively parameter matrices and bias of the ACD layer, including those of the chunking and POS tagging layers. E_{chunk} is the set of parameters characterizing the chunk label embeddings. The cost is defined as follows:

$$J^{(3)} = -\sum_{d}\sum_{t} log\, p(y_t^{(3)} = k|h_t^{(3)})$$
$$+\lambda \|W_{ACD}\|^2 + \delta \|\theta_{chunk} - \theta'_{chunk}\|^2$$

with $p(y_t^{(3)} = k|h_t^{(3)})$ the probability of assigning the right label k to the word w_t of the essay d. θ'_{chunk} is the set of parameters of the chunking layer right before the training of the ACD layer for the current epoch.

4.4 ACC layer

We denote θ_{ACC} the set of parameters involved in the ACC layer, with $\theta_{ACC} = (W_{ACC}, b_{ACC}, E_{POS}, E_{chunk}, \theta_e)$. W_{ACC} and b_{ACC} are respectively parameter matrices and bias of the ACC layer, including those of the chunking and POS tagging layers. The cost function is defined as follows:

$$J^{(4)} = -\sum_{d}\sum_{i} log\, p(y_i^{(4)} = k|sh_i^{(4)})$$
$$+\lambda \|W_{ACC}\|^2 + \delta \|\theta_{chunk} - \theta'_{chunk}\|^2$$

with $p(y_i^{(4)} = k|sh_i^{(4)})$ is the probability of assigning the right label k to the segment s_i of the essay d.

5 Experiments and discussion

5.1 Hyperparameters and training corpora

5.1.1 Optimization

We trained the model alternating, for each epoch, the layers to be trained in the following order: POS tagging, chunking, ACD and ACC. We used Adam (Kingma and Ba, 2014) as learning algorithm, with $\beta_1 = 0.9$, $\beta_2 = 0.999$ and $\epsilon = 10^{-8}$. The learning rate was shared across all layers and was fixed to 10^{-3} at the beginning of the training, and then multiplied by 0.75 every 10 epochs. In order to limit the gradient exploding problem, we used a gradient clipping strategy (Pascanu et al., 2013). We followed (Hashimoto et al., 2016) and used a clipping value of $min(3.0, depth)$, where $depth$ stands for the number of bi-GRU involved in the trained layer.

5.1.2 Parameters initialization

In order to smooth the backpropagation of the gradient during the training phase, we used random orthogonal matrices as initial weights for parameter matrices of every GRU, as suggested by (Saxe et al., 2013). The remaining parameter matrices were initialized with values drawn from a gaussian $\mathcal{N}(0, \sqrt{\frac{2}{n_{in}}})$, with n_{in} being the number of input neurons in the layer, as proposed by (He et al., 2015). Bias vectors were initialized as zero vectors.

5.1.3 Vector dimensions used

We used 50 dimensional vectors for the words and labels embeddings. We used 100 dimensional vectors for the hidden states of every GRU in the model.

5.1.4 Regularization

Following (Hashimoto et al., 2016), we used $\lambda = 10^{-6}$ for the parameter matrices of every GRU and $\lambda = 10^{-5}$ for the remaining parameter matrices. The secondary regularization term rate δ was set to 10^{-2} for each layer. We also used Dropout (Srivastava et al., 2014) on every layer, with a probability to affect neurons set to 0.2.

5.1.5 POS tagging and chunking corpora

We used the corpora from the shared task CoNLL-2000 (Sang and Buchholz, 2000) and the associated labels to train the POS tagging and chunking layers.

5.1.6 ACD and ACC corpora

We used the Argument Annotated Essays (version 2) corpora released by (Stab and Gurevych, 2017) following the train/test split given to train the ACD and ACC layers.

5.1.7 Training termination criteria

For a mono-task model, a common practice is to stop the training right before overfitting. However, it is not clear to determine when to stop the training when dealing with multi-task models since it is possible that the model overfits only on a subset of the target tasks. Thus, we decided to stop the training when the model overfitted both on the ACD and the ACC tasks on a held-out validation set[2]. The reported results are the best we obtained for each task on the test set, before overfitting on the validation set. Note that hyperparameters can be chosen so that the model overfits roughly at the same time on the ACD and ACC tasks.

5.1.8 Simple ACC

We denote Simple ACC the ACC task with the following modification: every segment corresponding to an argument component was treated as a single special token $<EMPTY>$. We hypothesize that this transformation will prevent the model from focusing on words inside argument components, but rather on its context, thus allowing a better generalization process.

5.2 Results and discussion

We report the obtained results on the test data for the tasks ACC, ACD and Simple ACC in Table 1. The column "w/o POS & chunking" refers to the model version for which we omitted the training of the POS tagging and chunking layers, while the column "w/ POS & chunking" refers to the model version optimized for every tasks. As a baseline, we use the human performances[3] and the results reported by (Stab and Gurevych, 2017), shown in Table 2.

---

[2]We randomly sampled 10% essays from the training data to build the validation set.

[3]Human performance corresponds the average performances reached by human agents, as presented in (Stab and Gurevych, 2017).

Table 1: Macros f1-scores obtained on the ACC, ACD and Simple ACC tasks.

Task	w/o POS & chunking	w/ POS & chunking
ACD	0.5922	0.8870
ACC	0.6950	0.7257
Simple ACC	0.7670	0.7980

Table 2: F1-scores reported on the ACD and ACC tasks by Stab and Gurevych (Stab and Gurevych, 2017) and human agents.

Task	F1-score from (Stab and Gurevych, 2017)	Human f1-score
ACD	0.867	0.886
ACC	0.826	0.868

5.2.1 General performance discussion

We obtained a macro f1-score of 0.8870 on ACD with the "w/ POS & chunking" model version, reaching human performance. This result was obtained without using handcrafted features, and is comparable to the one reported in (Stab and Gurevych, 2017). Regarding the ACC task, we obtained a macro f1-score of 0.7980 with Simple ACC for the "w/ POS & chunking" version, representing 96.6 % of the performance obtained in (Stab and Gurevych, 2017) and 91.9% of the human performance.

5.2.2 Simple ACC assessment

We consider that the words composing argument components are not really relevant to determine if they are major claims, claims or premises. Hence, we hypothesize that focusing on those words will lead to model noise. Conversely, the context surrounding argument components should be a good indicator: sequences such as "we can receive the same conclusion that" seem to be strong indicators that the upcoming argument component is not a premise. This could explain the gap in performance obtained between ACC and Simple ACC, more particularly for the "w/ POS & chunking" version, with respective f1-scores of 0.7257 and 0.7980 (9.96% performance increase).

5.2.3 Multi-task framework assessment

Regarding the tasks ACD and Simple ACC, we obtained f1-scores of 0.5922 and 0.7670 for the "w/o POS & chunking" version and of 0.8870 and 0.7980 for the "w/ POS & chunking", representing respectively a 49.78% and a 4.1% performance gain. Those results show the benefits of using a multi-task framework and suggests that more sub-tasks could be added to the model.

6 Upcoming work and perspectives

The results we got are encouraging and could probably be improved, particularly by analyzing optimal hyperparameters in a deeper way. The performance difference between the "w/ POS & chunking" and "w/o POS & chunking" models tends to show that implementing more auxiliary tasks could be beneficial. One exploration way could be to insert a dependency parsing layer on top of the chunking layer, as done in (Hashimoto et al., 2016).

In order to implement a complete argument mining system, as introduced by (Stab and Gurevych, 2017), we plan to implement layers which enable to automatically generate argument graphs. Therefore, it is necessary to determine if a directed edge exists between each ordered pair of argument components, and also to label those edges either as support or as attack relationships.

7 Conclusion

This article introduced the use of a novel model based on a multi-task framework for automatically extracting and classifying argument components from raw texts. Interestingly, our results show that the use of advanced deep learning techniques enables competing with state-of-the-art systems that depend on handcrafted features. The variation of performance between the model exploiting auxiliary tasks (POS tagging and chunking) and a version skipping those tasks clearly promotes the added-value of a multi-task framework.

References

Yamen Ajjour, Wei-Fan Chen, Johannes Kiesel, Henning Wachsmuth, and Benno Stein. 2017. Unit segmentation of argumentative texts. In *Proceedings of the 4th Workshop on Argument Mining*, pages 118–128.

Héctor Martínez Alonso and Barbara Plank. 2016. When is multitask learning effective? semantic sequence prediction under varying data conditions. *arXiv preprint arXiv:1612.02251*.

Dzmitry Bahdanau, Kyunghyun Cho, and Yoshua Bengio. 2014. Neural machine translation by jointly learning to align and translate. *arXiv preprint arXiv:1409.0473*.

Joachim Bingel and Anders Søgaard. 2017. Identifying beneficial task relations for multi-task learning in deep neural networks. *arXiv preprint arXiv:1702.08303*.

Elena Cabrio and Serena Villata. 2018. Five years of argument mining: a data-driven analysis. In *IJCAI*, pages 5427–5433.

Kyunghyun Cho, Bart Van Merriënboer, Caglar Gulcehre, Dzmitry Bahdanau, Fethi Bougares, Holger Schwenk, and Yoshua Bengio. 2014. Learning phrase representations using rnn encoder-decoder for statistical machine translation. *arXiv preprint arXiv:1406.1078*.

Judith Eckle-Kohler, Roland Kluge, and Iryna Gurevych. 2015. On the role of discourse markers for discriminating claims and premises in argumentative discourse. In *Proceedings of the 2015 Conference on Empirical Methods in Natural Language Processing*, pages 2236–2242.

Steffen Eger, Johannes Daxenberger, and Iryna Gurevych. 2017. Neural end-to-end learning for computational argumentation mining. *arXiv preprint arXiv:1704.06104*.

Theodosis Goudas, Christos Louizos, Georgios Petasis, and Vangelis Karkaletsis. 2014. Argument extraction from news, blogs, and social media. In *Hellenic Conference on Artificial Intelligence*, pages 287–299. Springer.

Kazuma Hashimoto, Caiming Xiong, Yoshimasa Tsuruoka, and Richard Socher. 2016. A joint many-task model: Growing a neural network for multiple nlp tasks. *arXiv preprint arXiv:1611.01587*.

Kaiming He, Xiangyu Zhang, Shaoqing Ren, and Jian Sun. 2015. Delving deep into rectifiers: Surpassing human-level performance on imagenet classification. In *Proceedings of the IEEE international conference on computer vision*, pages 1026–1034.

Diederik P Kingma and Jimmy Ba. 2014. Adam: A method for stochastic optimization. *arXiv preprint arXiv:1412.6980*.

Ran Levy, Yonatan Bilu, Daniel Hershcovich, Ehud Aharoni, and Noam Slonim. 2014. Context dependent claim detection. In *Proceedings of COLING 2014, the 25th International Conference on Computational Linguistics: Technical Papers*, pages 1489–1500.

Marco Lippi and Paolo Torroni. 2016. Argumentation mining: State of the art and emerging trends. *ACM Transactions on Internet Technology (TOIT)*, 16(2):10.

Nitin Madnani, Michael Heilman, Joel Tetreault, and Martin Chodorow. 2012. Identifying high-level organizational elements in argumentative discourse. In *Proceedings of the 2012 Conference of the North American Chapter of the Association for Computational Linguistics: Human Language Technologies*, pages 20–28. Association for Computational Linguistics.

Lili Mou, Zhao Meng, Rui Yan, Ge Li, Yan Xu, Lu Zhang, and Zhi Jin. 2016. How transferable are neural networks in nlp applications? *arXiv preprint arXiv:1603.06111*.

Vinod Nair and Geoffrey E Hinton. 2010. Rectified linear units improve restricted boltzmann machines. In *Proceedings of the 27th international conference on machine learning (ICML-10)*, pages 807–814.

Joonsuk Park and Claire Cardie. 2014. Identifying appropriate support for propositions in online user comments. In *Proceedings of the first workshop on argumentation mining*, pages 29–38.

Razvan Pascanu, Tomas Mikolov, and Yoshua Bengio. 2013. On the difficulty of training recurrent neural networks. In *International conference on machine learning*, pages 1310–1318.

Jeffrey Pennington, Richard Socher, and Christopher Manning. 2014. Glove: Global vectors for word representation. In *Proceedings of the 2014 conference on empirical methods in natural language processing (EMNLP)*, pages 1532–1543.

Isaac Persing and Vincent Ng. 2016. End-to-end argumentation mining in student essays. In *Proceedings of the 2016 Conference of the North American Chapter of the Association for Computational Linguistics: Human Language Technologies*, pages 1384–1394.

Peter Potash, Alexey Romanov, and Anna Rumshisky. 2016. Here's my point: Joint pointer architecture for argument mining. *arXiv preprint arXiv:1612.08994*.

Lance A Ramshaw and Mitchell P Marcus. 1999. Text chunking using transformation-based learning. In *Natural language processing using very large corpora*, pages 157–176. Springer.

Sebastian Ruder. 2017. An overview of multi-task learning in deep neural networks. *arXiv preprint arXiv:1706.05098*.

Erik F Sang and Sabine Buchholz. 2000. Introduction to the conll-2000 shared task: Chunking. *arXiv preprint cs/0009008*.

Christos Sardianos, Ioannis Manousos Katakis, Georgios Petasis, and Vangelis Karkaletsis. 2015. Argument extraction from news. In *Proceedings of the 2nd Workshop on Argumentation Mining*, pages 56–66.

Andrew M Saxe, James L McClelland, and Surya Ganguli. 2013. Exact solutions to the nonlinear dynamics of learning in deep linear neural networks. *arXiv preprint arXiv:1312.6120*.

Claudia Schulz, Steffen Eger, Johannes Daxenberger, Tobias Kahse, and Iryna Gurevych. 2018. Multi-task learning for argumentation mining in low-resource settings. *arXiv preprint arXiv:1804.04083*.

Anders Søgaard and Yoav Goldberg. 2016. Deep multi-task learning with low level tasks supervised at lower layers. In *Proceedings of the 54th Annual Meeting of the Association for Computational Linguistics (Volume 2: Short Papers)*, pages 231–235.

Nitish Srivastava, Geoffrey Hinton, Alex Krizhevsky, Ilya Sutskever, and Ruslan Salakhutdinov. 2014. Dropout: a simple way to prevent neural networks from overfitting. *The journal of machine learning research*, 15(1):1929–1958.

Christian Stab and Iryna Gurevych. 2017. Parsing argumentation structures in persuasive essays. *Computational Linguistics*, 43(3):619–659.

Zhilin Yang, Ruslan Salakhutdinov, and William Cohen. 2016. Multi-task cross-lingual sequence tagging from scratch. *arXiv preprint arXiv:1603.06270*.

Multi Sense Embeddings from Topic Models

Shobhit Jain
Amazon Web Services
jainshob@amazon.com

Sravan Babu Bodapati
Amazon Web Services
sravanb@amazon.com

Ramesh Nallapati
Amazon Web Services
rnallapa@amazon.com

Abstract

Distributed word embeddings have yielded state-of-the-art performance in many NLP tasks, mainly due to their success in capturing useful semantic information. These representations assign only a single vector to each word whereas a large number of words are polysemous (i.e., have multiple meanings). In this work, we approach this critical problem in lexical semantics, namely that of representing various senses of polysemous words in vector spaces. We propose a topic modeling based skip-gram approach for learning multi-prototype word embeddings. We also introduce a method to prune the embeddings determined by the probabilistic representation of the word in each topic. We use our embeddings to show that they can capture the context and word similarity strongly and outperform various state-of-the-art implementations.

1 Introduction

Representing words as dense, low dimensional embeddings (Mikolov et al., 2013a,b; Pennington et al., 2014) allow the representations to capture useful syntactic & semantic information making them useful in downstream Natural Language Processing tasks. However, these embedding models ignore the lexical ambiguity among different meanings of the same word. They assign only a single vector representative of all the different meanings of a word. In this work, we attempt to address this problem by capturing the multiple senses of a word using the global semantics of the document in which the word appears. Li and Jurafsky (2015) indicated that such sense specific vectors improve the performance of applications related to semantic understanding, such as Named Entity Recognition, Part-Of-Speech tagging.

In this work, we first train a topic model on our corpus to extract the topic distribution for each document. We treat these extracted topics as a heuristic to model word senses. We hypothesize that these word senses correlate quite well with the human notion of word senses, and validate it through our rigorous experiments as we demonstrate in our results section. We then use this topic distribution to train sense-specific word embeddings for each sense. We train these embeddings by weighing the learning procedure in proportion to the corresponding topic representation for each document. However, a word need not strongly correlate with each of these extracted senses. To address it, we propose a variant of this model which restricts the learning to only those embeddings where the word has a strong correlation with the topic extracted, i.e., high $p(word|topic)$.

The major contributions of our work are (i) training multi-sense word embeddings based on structured skip gram using topic models as a precursor (ii) non-parametric approach which prunes the embeddings to capture variability in the number of word senses.

2 Prior Work

Recently, learning multi-sense word embedding models has been an active area of research and has gained a lot of interest. TF-IDF (Reisinger and Mooney, 2010), SaSA (Wu and Giles, 2015), MSSG (Neelakantan et al., 2015), Huang et al. (2012) used cluster-based techniques to cluster the context of a word and comprehend word senses from the cluster centroids. Tian et al. (2014) proposed to use EM-based probabilistic clustering to assign word senses. Li and Jurafsky (2015) used Chinese Restaurant Process to model the word senses. All these techniques are just local context based and thus ignore the essential correlations amongst words and phrases in a broader document-level context. In contrast, our method enriches the embeddings with the document level information, capturing word interactions in a broader document-level context.

AutoExtend (Rothe and Schütze, 2015), Sensembed (Iacobacci et al., 2015), Nasari (Camacho-Collados et al., 2016), Deconf (Pilehvar and Collier, 2016), Chen et al. (2014); Jauhar et al. (2015); Pelevina et al. (2017) have used multi-step approach to learn sense & word embeddings but require an external lexical database like WordNet to achieve it. SW2V(Mancini et al., 2016) train the embeddings in a single joint training phase. Nonetheless, all these methods assign same weight to every sense of a word, ignoring the extent to which each sense is associated with it's context.

MSWE (Nguyen et al., 2017) trained sense and word embeddings separately, with sense specific word embeddings computed as a weighted sum of the two, where the weights are calculated using topic modeling. Similarly, Liu et al. (2015a,b); Cheng et al. (2015); Zhang and Zhong (2016) used skip-gram based approach to obtain separate word & topic embeddings. Lau et al. (2013) also used topic models to distinguish between different senses of a word. All these techniques express the sense-specific word representation as a function of word & sense embeddings which essentially belongs to two different domains. Our work trains more robust compositional word embeddings formulated as a weighted sum of sense specific word embeddings, thus, taking into consideration all the different word senses while operating in the same vector space.

More recent techniques like ELMo (Peters et al., 2018), BERT (Devlin et al., 2018) compute the contextual representations of a word based on the sentence in which the word appears, whereas, our method yields precomputed embeddings for each sense of a word within the same vector space.

3 Multi Sense Embeddings Model

3.1 Topic Modeling

Mixed membership models like topic models allow us to discover topics that occur in a collection of documents. A *topic* is defined as a distribution over words and consists of cluster of words that occur frequently. This formulation benefits us in inferring the probability distribution over different contexts(topics) the word can occur in. Latent Dirichlet Allocation(LDA) (Blei et al., 2003) is a topic modeling technique that assigns multiple topics in different proportions to each document along with the

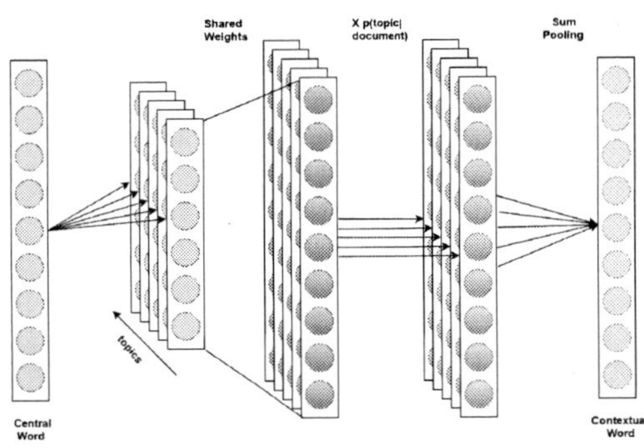

Figure 1: We feed our model a central word as input and predict the context word from it. First we learn separate word embeddings corresponding to each topic, E_{w_t, z_i}. Each of these embeddings are then multiplied with global word embeddings, $v_g(w)$, weighed in proportion to the topic distribution of the document from which the words have been chosen, and summed up to predict the neighboring context word.

probability distribution over words for each of the topics. Topic models based on Gibbs Sampling (Geman and Geman, 1987) achieve this by computing the posterior for a word based on the topic proportion at document level coupled with how often the word appears together with other words in the topic. We use Gibbs Sampling based approach to compute the topic distribution for each document. We use the LDA implementation from MALLET *topic modeling* toolkit (McCallum, 2002) for our experiments.

3.2 Embeddings from Topic Models (ETMo)

In this section we present our baseline approach for training sense-specific word embeddings. We formulate our approach as follows. Let $E_w \in R^{k \times n}$ represent the embedding matrix for word w, where k is the number of topics(treated as number of word senses) and n is the dimensionality of embeddings. We represent the embedding of word w corresponding to topic z_i as E_{w,z_i}. Let $v_g(w)$ be the *output* vector representation for word w, which is shared across senses, and enforces the embeddings of different senses to be within the same vector space.

We introduce a latent variable z, representing the topic dimension, to model separate embedding for each topic. Inline with the skip-gram(Mikolov et al., 2013a) approach, we maximize the probability of predicting the context word w_{t+j}, given a central word w_t for a document d as:

$$p(w_{t+j}|w_t, d) =$$
$$\sum_{i=1}^{k} p(w_{t+j}|w_t, z_i, d) * p(z_i|d) \quad (1)$$

$p(z_i|d)$ represents the topic distribution of the document d, obtained from the trained topic model. In the above equation, we reasonably make the assumption, $p(z_i|w_t, d) = p(z_i|d)$, owing to the fact that the topic distribution is computed at the document level. Using Negative Sampling (Mikolov et al., 2013b), we reduce the first term in the above equation as:

$$p(w_{t+j}|w_t, z_i) =$$
$$\sigma(E_{w_t, z_i} * v_g(w_{t+j})) + \sum_{w \in S} \sigma(-E_{w_t, z_i} * v_g(w)) \quad (2)$$

Formally, given a large corpus of documents, with size D, having a words sequence $w_1, w_2, ..., w_{N_d-1}, w_{N_d}$, where N_d is the number of words in document d, skip-window size c, number of topics k, the objective is to maximize the following log likelihood:

$$L = \sum_{d=1}^{D} \sum_{t=1}^{N_d} \sum_{j=-c}^{c} log\, p(w_{t+j}|w_t, d) =$$
$$\sum_{d=1}^{D} \sum_{t=1}^{N_d} \sum_{j=-c}^{c} log \sum_{i=1}^{k} p(w_{t+j}|w_t, z_i, d) * p(z_i|d) \quad (3)$$

As shown in Figure 1, we use a neural network architecture to compute the log likelihood. We feed the central word, in its BoW representation, as input to the model and compute the probability of the context word. Refer to the figure for detailed explanation.

During inference, we first compute the topic distribution for the given document, $p(z_i|d)$, using our pre-trained topic model. Finally, for a document d and for each word w, we infer the word embedding as:

$$v_{w,d} = \sum_{i=1}^{k} p(z_i|d) * E_{w, z_i} \quad (4)$$

Model	$avgSim$	$globalSim$
GloVe	-	63.2
(Pennington et al., 2014)		
Huang et al. (2012)	64.2	71.3
csmRNN	-	64.58
(Luong et al., 2013)		
GC-SINGLE	62.3	-
(Jauhar et al., 2015)		
NP-MSSG	69.1	68.6
(Neelakantan et al., 2015)		
MSWE-I	-	**72.40**
(Nguyen et al., 2017)		
Gensense	54.0	-
(Lee et al., 2018)		
ETMo (Ours)	68.5	68.2
ETMo + NP (Ours)	**69.3**	69.1

Table 1: Spearman's correlation $\rho \times 100$ on WS-353

3.3 ETMo + Non-parametric

In this section, we substantiate the flaws in our baseline approach and present our non-parametric method to learn the embeddings.

Our previous approach assigns an embedding to every word corresponding to each topic. As one can see, this method would undesirably accumulate a fair amount of noisy updates to those word embeddings that have minimal representation in a topic. Hence, we extend our model by exploiting the information from topic models to learn only those embeddings where the word has a strong correlation with the topic.

In particular, we train only those embedding E_{w_t, z_i} such that $p(w_t|z_i) > p_{thres}$, where p_{thres} is chosen empirically, which we will explain later. For the words where none of the senses satisfy the above condition (might be the case for some monosemous words), we chose the embedding $E_{w_t, x}$ to be trained, such that $x = \text{argmax}_{z_i}\, p(w_t|z_i)$.

4   Experimental Setup

We use the English Wikipedia corpus dump (Shaoul and Westbury, 2010) for training both, topic models and embedding models. Though many previous research works have used a larger training corpus, but for a fair comparison, we only compare our results with those works which have used the same corpus. We could also improve obtained results by using a larger training corpus, but this is not central point of our paper. The main aim of our work is to compute sense specific embed-

Model	$avgSim$	$avgSimC$
TF-IDF	60.4	-
Huang et al. (2012)	62.8	65.7
Tian et al. (2014)	-	65.4
Chen et al. (2014)	66.2	68.9
Cheng et al. (2015)	-	65.9
GC-MULTI	-	65.9
(Jauhar et al., 2015)		
SENSEMBED	62.4	-
(Iacobacci et al., 2015)		
SaSA	-	66.4
(Wu and Giles, 2015)		
TWE-I (Liu et al., 2015b)	-	68.1
NP-MSSG	67.2	**69.3**
(Neelakantan et al., 2015)		
SG+Greedy	-	69.1
(Li and Jurafsky, 2015)		
MSWE	66.7	66.6
(Nguyen et al., 2017)		
ETMo (Ours)	65.4	65.8
ETMo + NP (Ours)	**67.5**	69.1

Table 2: Spearman's correlation $\rho \times 100$ on SCWS

Model	Accuracy(%)
Word2Vec	67
Huang et al. (2012)	12
Neelakantan et al. (2015)	64
ETMo (Ours)	**67**
ETMo + NP (Ours)	66

Table 3: Results on Word Analogy task

dings for a word using topic models and demonstrate the strength of our model empirically.

The raw dataset consists of nearly 3.2 million documents and 1 billion tokens. Training topic models on such a large and diverse corpus helps in obtaining clearly demarcated senses for each topic.

To tune the hyper parameters of our neural network model, we sample 20% of our corpus as validation data and chose those parameters that give the lowest validation loss. Later, we use these parameter values for training on the entire corpus. For all our experiments, we use a skip-window of size 2, 8 negative samples, embeddings of dimensionality 200, and fix the number of topics to 10. A detailed analysis on how we chose the number of topics, using perplexity score, can be found later in the analysis section. We initialize the embeddings using pre-trained GloVe embeddings to ensure all our target embeddings are in the same vector space. We choose the value for p_{thres} as 1e-4 and give an analysis on how we chose the parameter value in the results section.

5 Results

We evaluate our model on two tasks, namely, word similarity and word analogy. For word similarity evaluation, we evaluate our embeddings on standard word similarity benchmark datasets including WS-353 (Finkelstein et al., 2001) & SCWS-2003 (Huang et al., 2012). WS-353 includes 353 pairs

of words and a human judgment score of the similarity measure between the two words. Similarly, SCWS-2003 consists of 2003 pairs of words, but, given with a context.

We note that our embeddings can capture only those senses that are represented by the extracted topics, and due to the restricted number of topics extracted, they might not be able to capture all the senses for a word. However, at a specific number of topics, our model is effective in capturing various senses of words in standard word similarity datasets. We demonstrate this effect qualitatively and quantitatively in this section.

For each of the datasets, we report the Spearman correlation between the human judgment score and model's similarity score computed between two words w and w'. We follow Reisinger and Mooney (2010) to compute the following similarity measures. For a pair of words w and w' and given their respective contexts c and c', we represent the cosine distance between the embeddings $E_{w,i}$ and $E_{w',j}$ as $d(E_{w,i}, E_{w',j})$.

$$globalSim = d(v_g(w),)$$

$$avgSim = \frac{1}{N_1 * N_2} \sum_{i=1}^{N_1} \sum_{j=1}^{N_2} d(E_{w,i}, E_{w',j})$$

$$avgSimC = \sum_{i=1}^{N_1} \sum_{j=1}^{N_2} p(z_i|c) * p(z_j|c') * \\ d(E_{w,i}, E_{w',j})$$

(5)

N_1 and N_2 are chosen such that they satisfy $p(w_t|z_i) > p_{thres}$. $v_g(w)$ represents the *output* vector for word w, as mentioned in section 3.2. We infer the probabilities, $p(z_i|c)$ & $p(z_j|c')$ using our pre-trained topic model.

In contrast to our model, methods such as ELMo, BERT requires a document context to compute an embedding, which makes it unfair to compare on avgSim metric since it doesn't take any context into account. Additionally, ELMo gives a set of 3 different embeddings making it unclear to compare on the avgSimC metric as well.

5.1 Quantitative Results

We present the results of our approach in Tables 1 and 2. A higher Spearman's correlation translates to a better model.

As can be seen in Table 1, our non-parametric approach clearly outperforms other multi-sense embeddings models using the *avgSim* metric on WS-353. Further, though our method focusses on sense specific embeddings and not on the global word embeddings, for the purpose of completeness, we also report our results on the *globalSim* metric. Using *globalSim*, expectedly we obtain slightly lower results since *globalSim* is more suited for global word embeddings.

In Table 2, we compare our models on the SCWS dataset. Using *avgSim* metric, our model obtain state-of-the-art results, outperforming other embeddings model. Using the *avgSimC* metric, we produce competitive results and perform better than most of the models, including Nguyen et al. (2017) which also uses topic models.

These superior results indicate the usefulness of our method to accurately capture word representations that can take into account different word senses. Additionally, our non-parametric approach consistently outperforms our baseline ETMo approach, validating our hypothesis to threshold the topics.

We also evaluate our model on the word analogy task (Mikolov et al., 2013a). [1] Our answer is correct if this word matches the correct word given in the dataset. As can be seen in Table 3, our ETMo approach obtains similar results as the baseline word2vec model, and we beat other implementations.

5.2 Qualitative Comparison

We show a qualitative comparison of some polysemous words in Table 4, with the nearest neighbors of words in the table, for Glove embeddings and the embeddings trained from our model. For each of the words in Table 4, we can clearly see that the different senses of words are being effectively captured by our model whereas Glove embeddings could only capture most frequently used meaning

---

[1] The word analogy task aims to answer the question of the form: *a is to b as c is to ?*. To answer the question, we compute the word vector nearest to '$v_g(b) - v_g(a) + v_g(c)$', where $v_g(w)$ represents the *output* vector for word w, as mentioned in section 3.2.

for the word. Moreover, each of these senses can be easily correlated with the topic that these embeddings correspond to which can be seen from Table 5. Consider the word *Play*. The first sense for *play* corresponds to *Music* (topic 2). The second embedding corresponds to *Sports* (topic 7).

An interesting qualitative result is shown for the word *Network*. The nearest neighbors to Glove embeddings show that they are only able to capture one meaning which is in the subject of *Television Network*. However, our model is able to capture 3 different meanings for the word quite powerfully. The first one, which corresponds to topic 2, occurs in the context of *Television Network* which is the sense Glove was able to capture. The second sense, which corresponds to topic 5, occurs in the context of *Computer Networks*. The third sense, which corresponds to topic 6, remarkably relates to the context *Geography*.

5.3 Number of Topics Analysis

In this section, we perform a study on choosing the right number of topics(k) in Table 6. Here, topic uniqueness refers to the proportion of unique words in a topic, computed over the top words in the vocabulary. Higher the topic uniqueness score, more distinct are the obtained topics. We compute the Spearman correlation on the *avgSim* metric using the word pairs from RG-65 (Rubenstein and Goodenough, 1965). With k = 10, we obtained a topic uniqueness of 32.23, which dropped to 27.12 for k=20 topics. Thus increasing the number of topics increases overlap which harms our model as the topic weight gets divided while training the embeddings. This effect can be clearly seen in the correlation coefficient which drops from 68.5 to 66.9 for 10 & 20 topics respectively. Using k=5 improved the topic uniqueness score to 34.05, but the perplexity score (Blei et al., 2003) reduced, indicating that the topic model requires more degrees of freedom to fit the corpus. We also observed not very distinct topics at k=5 (i.e. a topic could be mixture of sports and history), resulting in reduced correlation coefficient of 67.1.

5.4 Threshold Parameter Analysis

In this section, we study the effect of p_{thres} on the model performance. We tune its value by comparing the Spearman correlation on the *avgSim* metric using the word pairs from RG-65 (Rubenstein and Goodenough, 1965). However, we hypothesize that the threshold parameter depends only on the output

Word	Topic #	Nearest Neighbors
play	Glove	playing, played, plays, game, players, player, match, matches, games
	2	played. performance, musical, performed, plays, stage, release, song, work, time
	7	season, players, played, one, game, first, football, teams, last, year, clubs
rock	Glove	band, punk, pop, bands, album, rocks, music, indie, singer, albums, songs, rockers
	2	metal, pop, punk, members, jazz, alternative, indie, folk, band, hard, recorded, blues
	6	island, point, valley, hill, large, creek, granite, railroad, river, lake
bank	Glove	banks, banking, central, credit, bankers, financial, investment, lending, citibank
	6	river, tributary, flows, valley, side, banks, mississippi, south, north, mouth, branch
	8	company, established, central, first, group, one, investment, organisation, development
plant	Glove	plants, factory, facility, flowering, produce, reactor, factories, production
	1	plants, bird, genus, frog, rodent, flowering, fish, species, tree, endemic, asteraceae
	5	design, plants, modern, power, process, technology, standard, substance, production
war	Glove	wars, conflict, battle, civil, military, invasion, forces, fought, fighting, wartime
	4	combat, first, world, army, served, american, battle, civil, outbreak, forces
	7	series, championship, cup, fifa, champion, chess, records, wrestling, championships
network	Glove	cable, channel, television, broadcast, internet, stations, programming, radio
	2	series, program, shows, bbc, broadcast, station, channel, aired, nbc, radio, episode
	5	data, information, computer, system, applications, technology, control, standard, design
	6	light, station, car, stations, railway, commuter, lines, rail, trains, commute

Table 4: Nearest neighbours of some polysemous words for Glove, and for each sense identified by our algorithm, based on the cosine similarility. We take only those senses corresponding to topics where $p(w_t|j) > p_{thres}$.

TOPIC #	TOPIC KEYS	TOPIC NAME
1	species south india island north found small indian region family district water large east long spanish central village west area	Agriculture
2	film music album released band series show song time television single songs live rock records video release appeared episode films	Music/Television
3	party government state states united president law member general court house election served political elected national born council	Politics
4	war air army force british battle service aircraft japanese forces world military time ship fire navy command attack september car	Military
5	system formula number time called form data systems process high energy type common set space based power similar standard	Technology
6	city age county area population town located years north river south west station park line road district village income living	Geography
7	team season game league played club football games world year career player born time final cup play championship national	Sports
8	school university college company students education, public program business national research development services million service	Education
9	church book work life published century time english works art people world books language great written god early death called	Religion
10	french german france war king germany century russian part italian son chinese empire soviet republic born died emperor paris	History

Table 5: The top words for each topics according to topic modeling

# of topics	uniqueness	perplexity	$\rho \times 100$
5	34.05	9.88	67.1
10	32.23	9.78	68.5
15	29.57	9.70	67.8
20	27.12	9.65	66.9

Table 6: effect of number of topics on Spearman correlation on 50 word pairs from WordSim-353

p_{thres}	$\rho \times 100$	senses captured for *network*
1e-3	68.3	television, IT
1e-4	69.1	television, IT, transportation
1e-5	68.4	mixed senses

Table 7: Spearman's correlation $\rho \times 100$ on 50 word pairs from WS-353 and the word senses captured for *network*. The word senses are adjudged qualitatively.

of topic modeling, particularly $p(word|topic)$, and thus is independent of the this chosen subset, as can be seen in the results on other datasets. In Table 7, we can see that the optimal value for p_{thres} is 1e-4 for the non-parametric model at which it can strongly differentiate between the different senses for *network*. A higher threshold value of 1e-3 captures a fewer number of senses. A lower threshold value of 1e-5 allows training of more than the actual number of true senses leading to noisy updates, thus becoming ineffective in capturing any sense. The corresponding lower correlation coefficients in Table 7 confirm these effects quantitatively.

6 Conclusion & Future Work

In this work, we presented our approach to learn word embeddings to capture the different senses of a word. Unlike previous sense-based models, our model exploits knowledge from topic modeling to induce mixture weights in structured skip-gram approach, for learning sense specific representations. We extend this model further by pruning the embeddings conditioned on the number of word senses. Finally, we showed our model achieves state-of-the-art results on word similarity tasks, and demonstrated the strength of our model in capturing multiple word senses qualitatively. Future work should aim towards using these embeddings for downstream tasks.

References

David M Blei, Andrew Y Ng, and Michael I Jordan. 2003. Latent dirichlet allocation. *Journal of machine Learning research*, 3(Jan):993–1022.

José Camacho-Collados, Mohammad Taher Pilehvar, and Roberto Navigli. 2016. Nasari: Integrating explicit knowledge and corpus statistics for a multilingual representation of concepts and entities. *Artificial Intelligence*, 240:36–64.

Xinxiong Chen, Zhiyuan Liu, and Maosong Sun. 2014. A unified model for word sense representation and disambiguation. In *Proceedings of the 2014 Conference on Empirical Methods in Natural Language Processing (EMNLP)*, pages 1025–1035.

Jianpeng Cheng, Zhongyuan Wang, Ji-Rong Wen, Jun Yan, and Zheng Chen. 2015. Contextual text understanding in distributional semantic space. In *Proceedings of the 24th ACM International on Conference on Information and Knowledge Management*, pages 133–142. ACM.

Jacob Devlin, Ming-Wei Chang, Kenton Lee, and Kristina Toutanova. 2018. Bert: Pre-training of deep bidirectional transformers for language understanding. *arXiv preprint arXiv:1810.04805*.

Lev Finkelstein, Evgeniy Gabrilovich, Yossi Matias, Ehud Rivlin, Zach Solan, Gadi Wolfman, and Eytan Ruppin. 2001. Placing search in context: The concept revisited. In *Proceedings of the 10th international conference on World Wide Web*, pages 406–414. ACM.

Stuart Geman and Donald Geman. 1987. Stochastic relaxation, gibbs distributions, and the bayesian restoration of images. In *Readings in computer vision*, pages 564–584. Elsevier.

Eric H Huang, Richard Socher, Christopher D Manning, and Andrew Y Ng. 2012. Improving word representations via global context and multiple word prototypes. In *Proceedings of the 50th Annual Meeting of the Association for Computational Linguistics: Long Papers-Volume 1*, pages 873–882. Association for Computational Linguistics.

Ignacio Iacobacci, Mohammad Taher Pilehvar, and Roberto Navigli. 2015. Sensembed: Learning sense embeddings for word and relational similarity. In *Proceedings of the 53rd Annual Meeting of the Association for Computational Linguistics and the 7th International Joint Conference on Natural Language Processing (Volume 1: Long Papers)*, volume 1, pages 95–105.

Sujay Kumar Jauhar, Chris Dyer, and Eduard Hovy. 2015. Ontologically grounded multi-sense representation learning for semantic vector space models. In *Proceedings of the 2015 Conference of the North American Chapter of the Association for Computational Linguistics: Human Language Technologies*, pages 683–693.

Jey Han Lau, Paul Cook, and Timothy Baldwin. 2013. unimelb: Topic modelling-based word sense induction for web snippet clustering. In *Second Joint Conference on Lexical and Computational Semantics (* SEM), Volume 2: Proceedings of the Seventh International Workshop on Semantic Evaluation (SemEval 2013)*, volume 2, pages 217–221.

Yang-Yin Lee, Ting-Yu Yen, Hen-Hsen Huang, Yow-Ting Shiue, and Hsin-Hsi Chen. 2018. Gensense: A generalized sense retrofitting model. In *Proceedings of the 27th International Conference on Computational Linguistics*, pages 1662–1671.

Jiwei Li and Dan Jurafsky. 2015. Do multi-sense embeddings improve natural language understanding? *arXiv preprint arXiv:1506.01070*.

Pengfei Liu, Xipeng Qiu, and Xuanjing Huang. 2015a. Learning context-sensitive word embeddings with neural tensor skip-gram model. In *Twenty-Fourth International Joint Conference on Artificial Intelligence*.

Yang Liu, Zhiyuan Liu, Tat-Seng Chua, and Maosong Sun. 2015b. Topical word embeddings. In *AAAI*, pages 2418–2424.

Thang Luong, Richard Socher, and Christopher Manning. 2013. Better word representations with recursive neural networks for morphology. In *Proceedings of the Seventeenth Conference on Computational Natural Language Learning*, pages 104–113.

Massimiliano Mancini, Jose Camacho-Collados, Ignacio Iacobacci, and Roberto Navigli. 2016. Embedding words and senses together via joint knowledge-enhanced training. *arXiv preprint arXiv:1612.02703*.

Andrew Kachites McCallum. 2002. Mallet: A machine learning for language toolkit. Http://mallet.cs.umass.edu.

Tomas Mikolov, Kai Chen, Greg Corrado, and Jeffrey Dean. 2013a. Efficient estimation of word representations in vector space. *CoRR*, abs/1301.3781.

Tomas Mikolov, Ilya Sutskever, Kai Chen, Greg S Corrado, and Jeff Dean. 2013b. Distributed representations of words and phrases and their compositionality. In *Advances in neural information processing systems*, pages 3111–3119.

Arvind Neelakantan, Jeevan Shankar, Alexandre Passos, and Andrew McCallum. 2015. Efficient non-parametric estimation of multiple embeddings per word in vector space. *arXiv preprint arXiv:1504.06654*.

Dai Quoc Nguyen, Dat Quoc Nguyen, Ashutosh Modi, Stefan Thater, and Manfred Pinkal. 2017. A mixture model for learning multi-sense word embeddings. *arXiv preprint arXiv:1706.05111*.

Maria Pelevina, Nikolay Arefyev, Chris Biemann, and Alexander Panchenko. 2017. Making sense of word embeddings. *arXiv preprint arXiv:1708.03390*.

Jeffrey Pennington, Richard Socher, and Christopher Manning. 2014. Glove: Global vectors for word representation. In *Proceedings of the 2014 conference on empirical methods in natural language processing (EMNLP)*, pages 1532–1543.

Matthew E Peters, Mark Neumann, Mohit Iyyer, Matt Gardner, Christopher Clark, Kenton Lee, and Luke Zettlemoyer. 2018. Deep contextualized word representations. *arXiv preprint arXiv:1802.05365*.

Mohammad Taher Pilehvar and Nigel Collier. 2016. De-conflated semantic representations. *arXiv preprint arXiv:1608.01961*.

Joseph Reisinger and Raymond J Mooney. 2010. Multi-prototype vector-space models of word meaning. In *Human Language Technologies: The 2010 Annual Conference of the North American Chapter of the Association for Computational Linguistics*, pages 109–117. Association for Computational Linguistics.

Sascha Rothe and Hinrich Schütze. 2015. Autoextend: Extending word embeddings to embeddings for synsets and lexemes. *arXiv preprint arXiv:1507.01127*.

Herbert Rubenstein and John B Goodenough. 1965. Contextual correlates of synonymy. *Communications of the ACM*, 8(10):627–633.

C. Shaoul and Edmonton AB: University of Alberta Westbury, C. (2010) The Westbury Lab Wikipedia Corpus. 2010. The westbury lab wikipedia dataset. Data downloaded from http://www.psych.ualberta.ca/ westbury-lab/downloads/westburylab.wikicorp.download.html.

Fei Tian, Hanjun Dai, Jiang Bian, Bin Gao, Rui Zhang, Enhong Chen, and Tie-Yan Liu. 2014. A probabilistic model for learning multi-prototype word embeddings. In *Proceedings of COLING 2014, the 25th International Conference on Computational Linguistics: Technical Papers*, pages 151–160.

Zhaohui Wu and C Lee Giles. 2015. Sense-aaware semantic analysis: A multi-prototype word representation model using wikipedia. In *Twenty-Ninth AAAI Conference on Artificial Intelligence*.

Heng Zhang and Guoqiang Zhong. 2016. Improving short text classification by learning vector representations of both words and hidden topics. *Knowledge-Based Systems*, 102:76–86.

Automatic Arabic Text Summarization Based on Fuzzy Logic

Lamees M. Al Qassem
The Emirates ICT Innovation Center
Electrical and Computer Engineering Department,
Khalifa University,
Abu Dhabi, UAE
`lamees.alqassem@ku.ac.ae`

Di Wanga
The Emirates ICT Innovation Center
Khalifa University,
Abu Dhabi, UAE.
`di.wang@ku.ac.ae`

Hassan Barada
Electrical and Computer
Engineering Department,
Khalifa University,
Abu Dhabi, UAE
`hassan.barada@ku.ac.ae`

Ahmad Al Rubaiea, Nawaf Al Moosaa
The Emirates ICT Innovation Center
Khalifa University,
Abu Dhabi, UAE.
`{ahmad.al-rubaie,nawaf.almoosa}@ku.ac.ae`

Abstract

The unprecedented growth in the amount of online information available in many languages to users and businesses, including news articles and social media, has made it difficult and time consuming for users to identify and consume sought after content. Hence, automatic text summarization for various languages to generate accurate and relevant summaries from the huge amount of information available is essential nowadays. Techniques and methodologies for automatic Arabic text summarization are still immature due to the inherent complexity of the Arabic language in terms of both structure and morphology. This work attempts to improve the performance of Arabic text summarization. We propose a new Arabic text summarization approach based on a new noun extraction method and fuzzy logic. The proposed summarizer is evaluated using EASC corpus and benchmarked against popular state of the art Arabic text summarization systems. The results indicate that our proposed Fuzzy logic approach with noun extraction outperforms existing systems.

1 Introduction

In the recent two decades, the exponential growth in the amount of information like email, online news articles, reports, social media content and memos, introduced new challenges and made it harder for users to sift through and extract the key information they need. Hence, a smart system that can automatically identify important information from vast amount of data and generate concise summaries from these identified data is highly demanded nowadays. Automatic accurate text summarization is the key to addressing this challenge. Text summarization is the process of conveying important information from the original text source(s). The summary is typically no longer than half of the original text(s) and usually significantly less than that (Das and Martins, 2007). Techniques for automatic text summarization for widely-used and relatively simple-grammar languages such as English are mature. However, little work has been done for Arabic summarization (Al Qassem et al., 2017) due to the complexity of the language in terms of both structure and morphology. Nevertheless, Arabic summarization systems are highly needed nowadays. There are more than 300 million Arabic speakers in the world, and Arabic is an official language in the United Nations (Nenkova et al., 2011) and 22 other countries (Al-Shalabi et al., 2009). Therefore, researchers are working on improving Arabic text summarization methods and developing real world systems. A smart system is needed to automatically generate summaries from Arabic texts and deliver these summaries to the user, either directly or on-demand. The generated summaries need to be coherent, readable, grammatically correct, and comprise the key information of the original texts. This requires an in-depth study to achieve better preprocessing for Arabic text and a better methodology to extract the main information and generate a more accurate summary.

In this work, we propose and develop a smart

Arabic summarization system with better accuracy than the current state of the art. The system has been applied to generate summaries from online news in real time and delivers the summary instantly to the right users who just need it. The paper is organized as follows. The state of art for text summarization (mainly English and Arabic summarization systems) is discussed in Section 2. Our proposed summarization system is described in Section 3. The evaluation and comparison results are explained in Section 4. Our conclusion is given in Section 5.

2 Related Work

The first automatic summarization system was proposed by (Luhn, 1958). Luhn came up with the assumption that says the more frequent the word appears in the text the more important it is; excluding the very common words (called stop words). Ten years later, (Edmundson, 1969) expanded Luhns work by adding more features, such as resemblance to the title feature (the vocabulary overlap between the title and the sentence) and the position feature (the relevant position of the sentence within the text). The results showed that the word frequency is set to be the least important feature. It is important to note that the author assigned weights to the features subjectively; thus, these assigned weights could be imprecise and uncertain. In 1995, (Kupiec et al., 1995) developed a trainable document summarizer to automatically train the weights of the features using a corpus instead of defining the weights subjectively. The evaluation results agreed with Edmundsons results (Edmundson, 1969). As a conclusion, both work claimed that the best combination of features is made of the position feature, key word feature, and the title feature.

Although a lot of work has been done for text summarization for English, the work for Arabic summarization is very recent and limited. Lakhas (Douzidia and Lapalme, 2004) considered one of the first known Arabic text summarization system that was evaluated and compared to English systems. The system produces a summary of size of 10 words only and translates it to English. The authors claimed that the translation process is the reason for the bad evaluation scores. Using TF-IDF (term frequency-inverse document frequency) as the main feature to score sentences is a common method in Arabic summarization systems.

TF-IDF is the ratio of the frequency of a term in a document over its frequency in a corpus. TF-IDF is a good indicator of the importance of a word in a document and a topic, and hence highlights the importance of the corresponding sentence. (Haboush et al., 2012) used TF-IDF on clustered word roots and obtained competitive accuracy. (Al-Radaideh and Afif, 2009) developed a system that focuses on the inner product between TF in a sentence and the document frequency DF for each extracted noun. ACBTSS and AQBTSS (El-Haj et al., 2009) are two most recent systems that used TF-IDF with Vector Space Model (VSM). Semantic connectedness among sentences and documents is another important factor when generating summaries with minimum redundancy. LCEAS system (Sarmini, 2015) used lexical cohesion to identify important topics and text entailment to remove redundancy. Their system outperformed (Haboush et al., 2012), (Al-Radaideh and Afif, 2009), Sakhr, AQBTSS (El-Haj et al., 2009), Gen-Summ (El-Haj et al., 2010) and LSA-Summ (El-Haj et al., 2010), by containing more significant sentences and less redundancy. In recent work, more features/indicators are researched to represent the importance of sentences. Therefore, deciding which features to use and the weights for these features become a hard task and more research is needed. Some researchers followed the machine learning approach and modeled the summarization process as a classification problem (i.e. the sentences are classified as summary and non-summary sentences). The work in (Boudabous et al., 2010) and (Belkebir and Guessoum, 2015) includes examples of systems that followed the machine learning approach. In (Boudabous et al., 2010), SVM (Support Vector Machine) was used to classify the sentences using 15 features. In (Belkebir and Guessoum, 2015) an Arabic summarizer was proposed using AdaBoost. Machine learning approaches give researchers the ability to efficiently utilize a large number of features in the scoring process, which is desirable. Using fuzzy logic in text summarization is a very recent approach in English text summarization (Yadav and Meena, 2016). (Suanmali et al., 2009) used the fuzzy logic approach to select the sentences based on eight features. The system was compared to a baseline summarizer that generates summaries by selecting the first 200 words in the input document and MS word 2007 summa-

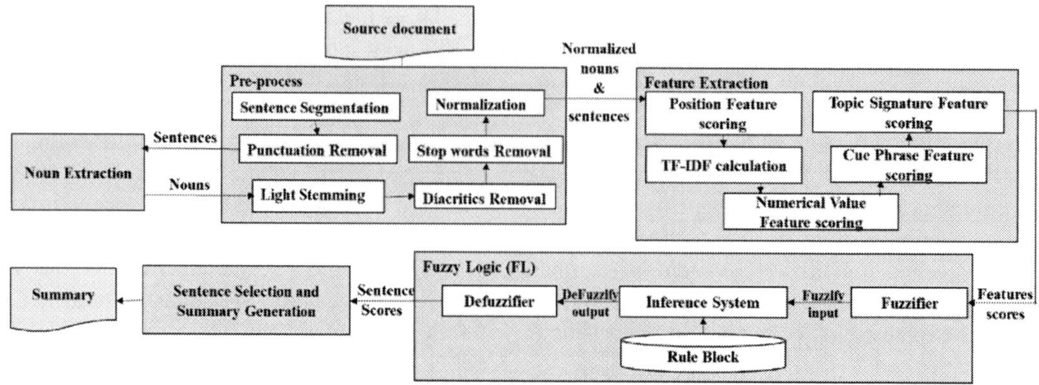

Figure 1: System Architecture.

rizer. The results showed that their proposed approach outperformed the baseline summarizer and MS word 2007 summarizer. (Yadav and Meena, 2016) used fuzzy logic along with WordNet synonyms and bushy path, a graph-based method, to improve the performance of extractive text summarization system. The WordNet synonyms is used for the semantic similarity of the text; bushy path is used for the relationship between different parts of the text; finally, fuzzy logic is used to solve the issue of uncertainty and vagueness related to the weights for different features of the sentences. The system generated three summaries from the three approaches and then selected the sentences that appeared in all summaries to form the final summary. The three approaches were evaluated and compared against the proposed approach using ROUGE-1 and ROUGE-2. The results showed that the proposed approach outperformed the other three approaches. In addition, the evaluation results showed that the fuzzy logic approach outperformed the bushy path and the WordNet synonyms methods. (Sarmini, 2015) proposed an Arabic text summarizer based on fuzzy logic and genetic algorithm. The genetic algorithm was used to select the optimal member functions of the selected features. The fuzzy system is used to score the sentences. To sum up, all reviewed systems claimed that using fuzzy logic improved the performance of the summarization systems and the quality of the summaries. Fuzzy logic approaches handled the issues related to the uncertainty, imprecision and vagueness of determining the importance of different features using machine learning approaches, leading to better summaries.

3 Proposed Fuzzy Logic Arabic Summarizer

Condensing all the discussions and comparisons in the literature review, we propose an Arabic summarization system with five main components (pre-processing, noun extraction, features extraction, fuzzy logic, sentence selection) to generate the final summary. Figure 1 shows the five components in the proposed system. The first two steps in the proposed system are Pre-processing and Noun extraction. Pre-processing prepares the text before sentences are further treated and summarized. Noun extraction extracts the nouns from the text output of the pre-processor. From the state of art noun words are considered to carry important information than other words (Al Qassem et al., 2017; Al-Radaideh and Afif, 2009). A noun is any word representing an idea, a thing or a person. To have a good summary, we need to make sure all sentences representing the main ideas are selected. To assure this, all nouns in the text should be processed and evaluated. The importance of a sentence will then be scored by the extracted nouns only. Furthermore, using nouns only will reduce noise and increase efficiency by avoiding unnecessary processing. In our previous work, we proposed a linguistic-rule-based noun extraction system (Al Qassem et al., 2018) that extracts nouns according to Arabic grammar rules. The system is evaluated against the widely used Stanford Arabic Part of Speech (POS) tagger (Stanford Log-linear Part-Of-Speech Tagger, n.d.). The results show that the proposed method is more efficient when achieving comparable benchmark accuracies. The details of our proposed Arabic noun extraction method has been explained in our previous paper (Al Qassem et al., 2018) and will not be repeated here due to the size limit of the paper. After that the feature extraction module extracts key features (sentence position, TF-IDF, cue phrase, topic signature and numerical data) representing the importance of the sentences. Finally, the extracted features/scores are input into the fuzzy logic module to generate the final scores of the sentences. The sentence' score indicates how important a sentence is within the whole article. The sentences with the highest scores are selected to form the final summary. In our system we used five features based on the discussion and experimental results from the state of art (Ferreira et al., 2013; Fattah and Ren, 2009); they are: (1) Sentence position: this is just the position of the sentence within the full text; (2) TF-IDF: it is calculated for the extracted nouns only as a feature that indicates the importance accumulation of the extracted nouns in a sentence; (3) Cue phrases: they are phrases that give a good indication about the content of this sentence such as in conclusion, the most important ... etc., and defined as positive cue phrases (Ferreira et al., 2013). (Haboush et al., 2012) claimed that the existence of these cue phrases increases the probability for a sentence to be selected. On the contrary, there are list of phrases that give a detailed explanation or indicates redundant information like in other words and for example. These phrases are called negative cue phrases (Fattah and Ren, 2009). In our system, we use both types of cue phrases to either increase or decrease the importance score of the sentences. The two other features are: (4) Topic Signature: each topic has a list of topic signature words used across all documents within this topic but not frequently used across other topics(the score of the sentence that contains topic signature words is supposed to increase); and finally (5) Numerical Data: sentences that contain numbers are more likely to be added to the summary because numbers refer to important information like money transaction, dates, address ... etc. (Ferreira et al., 2013; Fattah and Ren, 2009). The final score of the sentences is calculated by combining all the features. The linear combination of all features (feature-weight equation) is usually used for the final score. The main challenge in this step is assigning a weight for each feature. As discussed previously, not all features are equally important and different features should be given different weights representing their importance and contribution to generate a high quality summary. Therefore, we use fuzzy logic. At this stage the features extracted from the sentence are inputs to the fuzzy logic system, and the sentence final score is the output. According to (Hüllermeier, 2011), fuzzy logic can contribute in solving issues related to uncertainty, vagueness, ambiguity, and imprecision that result from incomplete and imprecise information. Fuzzy logic provides the ability to map rules using concept (e.g. long vs short, big vs small) rather than numbers (numerical data). Furthermore, representing gradual concepts is a key feature of fuzzy logic compared with machine learning that failed to do so (Hüllermeier, 2011). Fuzzy logic is transparent, data-driven and makes use of available expert knowledge (for model initialization) to generate a robust model. It is considered an approximate reasoning solution that can be initialized from expert knowledge and optimized from data with very strong reasoning capabilities (Megala et al., 2014). Finally, the sentences with highest scores from the fuzzy logic system are selected to form the summary. The sentences in the summary are ordered by their original position in the article. The proposed Arabic summarization system can generate different sizes of the summaries based on user choice. Our observations and evaluation of the generated model are aligned with our hypothesis, in that the first few sentences represent the main ideas. This is expected in news articles that tend to be relatively short; important words repeat more frequently within the text and cue phrases are used to attract the attention of the reader.

4   System Evaluation

Evaluating an Arabic text summarizer is a challenging task due to the lack of gold standard corpora and the different measures used in assessing summarization systems. We have therefore, decided to choose the corpus and evaluation metrics that are used by most benchmark systems in the literature, to provide as objective comparison as possible. Based on this approach, we found that ROUGE-N (N=1and 2) with EASC corpus (El-Haj et al., 2010) are used by many recent systems. ROUGE correlates well with human judgement for single-document summarization tasks. In addition, the correlation increases by using multiple references. This gives an advantage for EASC

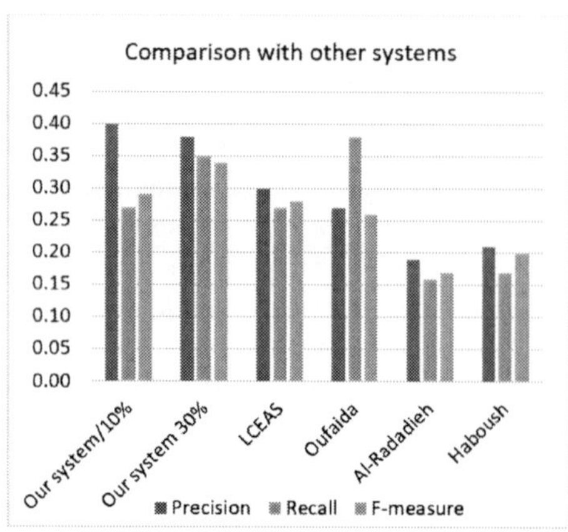

Figure 2: Performance comparison with other systems in the literature.

System	Average Recall		Average Precision		Average F-measure	
	ROUGE-		ROUGE-		ROUGE-	
	1	2	1	2	1	2
Oufaida (2014)	0.41	0.38	0.37	0.27	0.36	0.26
Our Sys 10%	0.34	0.27	0.51	0.40	0.37	0.29
Our Sys 30%	0.45	0.35	0.48	0.38	0.44	0.34

Table 1: ROUGE evaluation results for our system and Oufaida system.

corpus as each document has five reference summaries.

We compared our system with the state of art systems (LCEAS 2015 (Al-Khawaldeh and Samawi, 2015), (Al-Radaideh and Afif, 2009), (Haboush et al., 2012) and (Oufaida et al., 2014)). Figure 2 below illustrates the comparison of ROUGE-2 results for our summarizer and the other systems. The 30% summary size represents the reference summaries that are neither too long nor too short, the 10% summary size represents the shortest summary. As shown in the Figure, the ROUGE-2 scores for LCEAS (Al-Khawaldeh and Samawi, 2015), (Al-Radaideh and Afif, 2009) and (Haboush et al., 2012) are less than 0.3 for recall and less than 0.2 for precision, where the best scores were obtained by LCEAS. The F-measure for LCEAS system is approximately 0.22. To compare our system against these three systems, we use the ROUGE results when the summary size is 10% from the proposed Arabic summarization system (the smallest possible size). The average ROUGE-2 recall, precision and F-measure scores for our system are 0.27, 0.40 and 0.29, respectively. Our system outperformed the three systems in F-measure scores despite the fact that these systems were compared against our worst-case results.

Furthermore, LCEAS was compared against Sakhr, AQBTSS (El-Haj et al., 2009), Gen-Summ and LSA-Summ (El-Haj et al., 2010). The authors claimed that LCEAS outperformed all these three systems. Since our fuzzy logic summarizer outperformed LCEAS, it is our logical assumption that our system will outperform these three systems too.

For (Oufaida et al., 2014), the system was evaluated using ROUGE-N (N=1 and 2) and EASC corpus.

The generated summary size of a document is equal to its reference summary. The EASC has five summaries per article. Consequently, the system generated five summaries per document and computed their average ROUGE-N scores. The system ROUGE-1 and ROUGE-2 scores are shown in Table 1. We compared our system against Oufaida using the ROUGE-results obtained for the summary sizes 30% and 10%, which are the percentages used in the state of art methods for our fair comparison. In the real world application, this percentage can be changed and adjusted by users based on the requirements. The less the percentage is, the more concise the summary is but some information might be missed. On the contrary, summary with higher percentage of length provides more information (sentences) but the summary takes more human beings time to read (hence not a very efficient summary). According to both summary sizes 10% and 30% and ROUGE-N (N=1,2) results, our system outperformed Oufaidas.

5 Conclusion

Due to the increase in the amount of information available online, consuming a broad range of relevant, concise but important information has become a laborious task. Automatic text summarization methods are put forward to address this problem. Text summarization for English is advanced and many approaches have been studied and evaluated. However, this field is still in its early stages for the Arabic language. In this paper, we discussed different text summarization approaches and methodologies and proposed our approach by using fuzzy logic for a more accurate and efficient Arabic summarization system. Fuzzy logic is still very recent in English summarization and showed improvement in the quality of the generated summaries. We compared our summarizer against five state of the art Arabic text summarizers that reported good results. The results showed that fuzzy logic improved the performance of the summarization system. The system is able to create very short summaries containing the most important ideas, and performed better than five state of art Arabic summarization systems. The future work might be looking into better Arabic preprocessing, (e.g. http://arabicnlp.pro/alp/) for more accurate Arabic summarizer.

References

F Al-Khawaldeh and V Samawi. 2015. Lexical cohesion and entailment based segmentation for arabic text summarization (lceas). *The World of Computer Science and Information Technology Journal (WSCIT)*, 5(3):51–60.

Lamees Al Qassem, Di Wang, and Hassan Barada. 2018. Noun extraction tool for anlp applications. In *2018 IEEE 12th International Conference on Semantic Computing (ICSC)*, pages 308–309. IEEE.

Lamees Mahmoud Al Qassem, Di Wang, Zaid Al Mahmoud, Hassan Barada, Ahmad Al-Rubaie, and Nawaf I Almoosa. 2017. Automatic arabic summarization: a survey of methodologies and systems. *Procedia Computer Science*, 117:10–18.

Q Al-Radaideh and Mohammad Afif. 2009. Arabic text summarization using aggregate similarity. In *International Arab conference on information technology (ACIT2009), Yemen*.

Riyad Al-Shalabi, Ghassan Kanaan, Bashar Al-Sarayreh, Khalid Khanfar, Ali Al-Ghonmein, Hamed Talhouni, Salem Al-Azazmeh, et al. 2009. Proper noun extracting algorithm for arabic language. In *International conference on IT, Thailand*.

Riadh Belkebir and Ahmed Guessoum. 2015. A supervised approach to arabic text summarization using adaboost. In *New Contributions in Information Systems and Technologies*, pages 227–236. Springer.

Mohamed Mahdi Boudabous, Mohamed Hédi Maaloul, and Lamia Hadrich Belguith. 2010. Digital learning for summarizing arabic documents. In *International Conference on Natural Language Processing*, pages 79–84. Springer.

Dipanjan Das and André FT Martins. 2007. A survey on automatic text summarization. *Literature Survey for the Language and Statistics II course at CMU*, 4(192-195):57.

Fouad Soufiane Douzidia and Guy Lapalme. 2004. Lakhas, an arabic summarization system. *Proceedings of DUC2004*.

Harold P Edmundson. 1969. New methods in automatic extracting. *Journal of the ACM (JACM)*, 16(2):264–285.

Mahmoud El-Haj, Udo Kruschwitz, and Chris Fox. 2009. Experimenting with automatic text summarisation for arabic. In *Language and Technology Conference*, pages 490–499. Springer.

Mahmoud El-Haj, Udo Kruschwitz, and Chris Fox. 2010. Using mechanical turk to create a corpus of arabic summaries.

Mohamed Abdel Fattah and Fuji Ren. 2009. Ga, mr, ffnn, pnn and gmm based models for automatic text summarization. *Computer Speech & Language*, 23(1):126–144.

Rafael Ferreira, Luciano de Souza Cabral, Rafael Dueire Lins, Gabriel Pereira e Silva, Fred Freitas, George DC Cavalcanti, Rinaldo Lima, Steven J Simske, and Luciano Favaro. 2013. Assessing sentence scoring techniques for extractive text summarization. *Expert systems with applications*, 40(14):5755–5764.

Ahmad Haboush, Maryam Al-Zoubi, Ahmad Momani, and Motassem Tarazi. 2012. Arabic text summarization model using clustering techniques. *World of Computer Science and Information Technology Journal (WCSIT) ISSN*, pages 2221–0741.

Eyke Hüllermeier. 2011. Fuzzy sets in machine learning and data mining. *Applied Soft Computing*, 11(2):1493–1505.

J Kupiec, J Pedersen, and F Chen. 1995. A trainable document summarizer. dans les actes de acm special interest group on information retrieval (sigir), 68–73.

Hans Peter Luhn. 1958. The automatic creation of literature abstracts. *IBM Journal of research and development*, 2(2):159–165.

S Santhana Megala, A Kavitha, and A Marimuthu. 2014. Enriching text summarization using fuzzy logic. *International Journal of Computer Science and Information Technologies*, 5(1):863–867.

Ani Nenkova, Kathleen McKeown, et al. 2011. Automatic summarization. *Foundations and Trends® in Information Retrieval*, 5(2–3):103–233.

Houda Oufaida, Omar Nouali, and Philippe Blache. 2014. Minimum redundancy and maximum relevance for single and multi-document arabic text summarization. *Journal of King Saud University-Computer and Information Sciences*, 26(4):450–461.

Mohamad Sarmini. 2015. Design and implementation
of hybrid syntactic-fuzzy genetic system for extractive arabic text summarization. *International Journal of Computer Science and Engineering in Arabic*,
6:69–98.

Ladda Suanmali, Naomie Salim, and Mohammed Salem Binwahlan. 2009. Feature-based
sentence extraction using fuzzy inference rules. In
*2009 International Conference on Signal Processing
Systems*, pages 511–515. IEEE.

Jyoti Yadav and Yogesh Kumar Meena. 2016. Use of
fuzzy logic and wordnet for improving performance
of extractive automatic text summarization. In *2016
International Conference on Advances in Computing, Communications and Informatics (ICACCI)*,
pages 2071–2077. IEEE.

An Arabic Multi-Domain Spoken Language Understanding System

Mohamed Lichouri, Mourad Abbas
Computational Linguistics Dept.,CRSTDLA
Algeria
`m.lichouri@crstdla.dz`
`m.abbas@crstdla.dz`

Rachida Djeradi, Amar Djeradi
USTHB University
Algeria
`rdjeradi@usthb.dz`
`adjeradi@usthb.dz`

Abstract

In this paper, we suggest the generalization of an Arabic Spoken Language Understanding (SLU) system in a multi-domain human-machine dialog. We are interested particularly in domain portability of SLU system related to both structured (DBMS) and unstructured data (Information Extraction), related to four domains. In this work, we used the thematic approach for four domains which are School Management, Medical Diagnostics, Consultation domain and Question-Answering domain (DAWQAS). We should note that two kinds of classifiers are used in our experiments: statistical and neural, namely: Gaussian Naive Bayes, Bernoulli Naive Bayes, Logistic Regression, SGD, Passive Aggressive Classifier, Perceptron, Linear Support Vector and Convolutional Neural Network.

1 Introduction

With the increasing spread of internet content, there is a mutually growing number of web applications pushing human being in a race against time to exploit and to master all of these applications. In such a situation, a human-machine dialogue system is needed to assist humans for acquiring information efficiently and accurately. However, the existing dialogue systems cannot cover all application domains. That is why, we tackle in this paper the multi-domain task. We should note that a little initial work with regard to the multi-domain problem has been presented in (Minker, 1998; Liu and Lane, 2016), which remains an open issue. We have witnessed recently a renewed interest in the extension of application domain, where some systems use Latent Semantic Mapping (LSM) for the identification of any abrupt change towards another application (Nakano et al., 2011). In other works, a Markovian decision-making process was considered for

the selection of an application among several ones (Wang et al.) or the extension to a new application in the Web (Komatani et al., 2008). While in (Jung et al., 2009), a study related to comparable applications (within the same domain) has been conducted. In the case of more than two applications, we can mention task-based applications (where the dialogue is finalized and specific to a given domain) as presented in (Lee et al., 2009) or managing specific applications of the Web (Jiang et al., 2014). In (Jaech et al., 2016; Chelba and Acero, 2006; Daumé-III, 2007; Daumé-III and Marcu, 2006), the principle of adaptation from application to another has been applied, where the system is trained in the first application and tested in the second one (Daumé-III and Jagarlamudi, 2011; Kim and Sarikaya, 2015). The majority of researches done on multi-domain are dealing with domains structured within DBMS(Lefevre et al., 2012) such as (Information on the schedules of trains, planes, tourism, car navigation, weather information, Guide of TV program, chat, etc). We aim to provide a portable system, with minimal intervention from experts, across four domains. Three domains are based on information extraction, which are *Medical Diagnostic*, *Diverse Consultation* and *Question-Answering (DAWQAS)*[1] domains (Ismail and Homsi, 2018), in addition to the *University Schooling Management* domain which is based on database information retrieval. In this paper, we first present, in section 2, an SLU system based on thematic approach, followed by a description of the feature selection process as well as the dataset we prepared. In section 3, we present experiments and the corresponding results, and we conclude in section 4.

---

[1] A Dataset for Arabic Why Question Answeing System

DBMS Information Retrieval	University Schooling Management Domain	على كم تحصلت في مادة المجال الكهرومغناطيسي
		How much I got in the electromagnetic field module
Information Extraction	Medical Diagnostic Domain	لقد أغمي علي وانا أشعر بالتوتر لأن نبضات قلبي سريعة
		I'm fainting and I feel nervous because my heartbeat is fast
	Consultation Domain	هل يمر الإنسان بدورات نفسية متعاقبة ليس لها علاقة بالظروف ؟
		Does the person undergo successive psychological courses that have nothing to do with the circumstances?
	Question-Answering Domain (DAWQAS)	لماذا التحدث عن نقاط ضعفك خلال مقابلة العمل أمر رائع بالنسبة لك
		Why talking about your weaknesses during a job interview is great for you

Table 1: Samples of requests related to the four domains.

2 Spoken Language Understanding

The SLU system is based on some of the cognitive properties of humans which is tendency to understand an utterance in two different ways: Slot Filling and Intent Identification. Note that Slot Filling consists in identifying significant terms of this utterance followed by the identification of relationships between these terms, which leads him to understand the meaning of the utterance. While Intent Identification aims to identify the subject of the utterance without understanding the words one by one. In this work, we adopt Intent Identification to implement the SLU system, using text categorization (Lichouri et al., 2015, 2018b). The techniques used include statistical and neural methods: Multinomial Naive Bayes(MNB), Bernoulli Naive Bayes(BNB), Logistic Regression, Stochastic Gradient Descent(SGD), Passive Aggressive Classifier, Perceptron, Linear Support Vector Classification(LSVC) and Convolutional Neural Networks(CNN).

2.1 Feature Selection

We first processed the requests by removing all the punctuation. Then we conducted experiments, with and without stop words, in order to show the impact of Arabic stop words on intent identification which yields the request (sentence) intent. Second we used both word and character analyzers (Lichouri et al., 2018a) as an input to the vectorization process either by using TF-IDF for statistical classification or One hot encoder for CNN. We should note that we applied n-grams as features in the case of word analyzer.

2.2 Data acquisition and description

In this section, we will present a description of the corpus related to the four domains. For *University Schooling Management* which is a DBMS Information Retrieval Domain, We collected from around 300 students which formulated their requests to access their information from the education office. After discarding the repeated requests, we obtained a corpus made of 127 different requests expressed in French. The collected corpus, which was initially in French, was translated manually by experts to Arabic (?). Some examples of these queries are given in the table 1. These queries express what do students request from the office of education such as Marks, Certificates and Diplomas. The second domain which is *Medical Diagnostic*, We collected a corpus from a medical care forum known as Doctissimo (Alexandre, 2000). Some examples of these queries are also given in the table 1. These queries express the symptoms and feelings of ill people describing their health states to a doctor on the forum so that he could administer their treatment or the advice to give. We choose seven diseases, namely: Allergy, Anemia, Bronchitis, Diarrhea, Fatigue, Flu and Stress. For the *Consultation* domain, We collected the dataset from Islamtoday website (Today, 2000). It contains four main tasks which are: Educational, Psychological, Social and Religion Consulting. An example of this corpus is presented in table 1. We have shared the first two corpora (University Schooling Management and Medical Diagnostic) in a github repository[2]

---

[2]https://github.com/licvol/Arabic-Spoken-Language-Understanding

for research purpose, where às the third will be shared in our future works. The fourth corpus related to Question-Answering domain, we used the DAWQAS[3] corpus which contains a set of QA couples including 13 tasks, which are: Animal, Art and Celebrities, Community, Food, Health, Nature, Philosophy, Politics, Religion, Science and Technology, Space, Sports, and Women. More details of the datasets related to the four domains are summarized in table 2.

Corpus	School	Medical	Consultation	DAWQAS
#Sentence	126	152	3541	2525
#word	700	866	400.972	19.836
#class	3	7	4	13

Table 2: Description of the four used corpora.

3 Experiments and results

We conducted experiments on SLU portability between two kinds of domains: DBMS Information Retrieval and Information Extraction. The request is considered to be well understood if it is assigned a correct category. We achieved a comparison between statistical methods (Pedregosa et al., 2011) and neural method[4]. The training has been achieved on 70% of the shuffled datasets and the testing on the rest of dataset. For the CNN, we considered two tests with 10 and 100 iteration, respectively. We compared the performance of the classifiers by combining the different sets of features. Figures 1 and 2 represent the different values of F1-score obtained using the different classifiers, where SW_r, CA, WA_u, WA_b, WA_t and SW stand for, respectively, stop words removal, using character analyzer, word analyzer on unigram, bigram, trigram and using stop words. We should note that each combination of the aforementioned features is attributed a number (from 1 to 8) where: 1=SW+WA_u, 2=SW+WA_b, 3=SW+WA_t, 4=SW+CA, 5=SW_r+WA_u, 6=SW_r+WA_b, 7=SW_r+WA_t and 8=SW_r+CA.

We can see that the average of F1 measure is around 63%, 25%,39% and 32% for the School, Medical, Consultations and DAWQAS domains, respectively. Whereas the maximum values of F1 scored for the four domains are: 100%, 54%, 74%

[3]https://github.com/masun/DAWQAS
[4]https://github.com/tensorflow/workshops/blob/master/extras/keras-bag-of-words/keras-bow-model.ipynb

	Best results(%)			Feaures		
	Prec	Recall	F1	Stop Words	Analyzer	n-gram
MNB	86	84	84	Yes	Word	1
BNB	90	89	89	Yes/No	Char	-
LSVC	98	97	97	Yes/No	Word	1
LogReg	81	71	67	Yes	Word	1
SGD	98	97	97	Yes/No	Word	1
PassAgg	98	97	97	Yes/No	Word	1
Perceptron	100	100	100	Yes/No	Word	1
CNN	95	95	95	No	Word	1

Table 3: Best performance for the School domain

and 63%. In addition, it is noticeable through results shown in tables 3, 4, 5 and 6 that it is unclear which features combination yields the best performance. For instance, the absence of stop words gives the best performance for SGD while it doesn't for other classifiers.

As shown in table 3, in the case of School application, the best performance was achieved by the Perceptron classifier, with a perfect result by using a word analyzer with or without Arabic stop words. Whereas in table 4, for the medical application, the best result was performed by the SGD classifier, with an F1-score of 54% by also using the word analyzer and without removing the Arabic stop words.

	Best results(%)			Features		
	Prec	Recall	F1	Stop Words	Analyzer	n-gram
MNB	64	46	42	Yes	Word	1
BNB	21	26	23	Yes/No	Char	-
LSVC	66	52	49	No	Word	1
LogReg	60	43	39	Yes	Word	1
SGD	66	57	54	No	Word	1
PassAgg	61	52	52	Yes	Word	1
Perceptron	53	46	46	No	Word	1
CNN	74	39	47	No	Word	1

Table 4: Best performance for the Medical domain

Table 5 shows results for the Consultations domain. Note that both SGD and Logistic Regression classifiers achieved the best F1-score of 74% by using word analyzer. The SGD has performed equally by using either a unigram or bigram as input for the word analyzer, where the Logistic Regression has performed better with the trigram as an input.

For the last application related to DAWQAS corpus, the best results have been achieved with both LSVC and Passive Aggressive classifiers with F1-score of 63%. The first one has achieved equally by either filtering or not the Arabic stop words in plus to applying the word analyzer with a unigram as input. For the latter classifier, the same analyzer was used but without filtering the

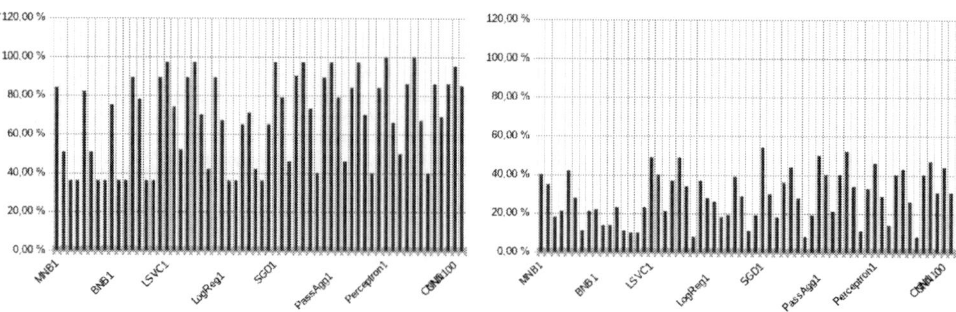

Figure 1: F1-score of the two domains: School (above), Medical (below).

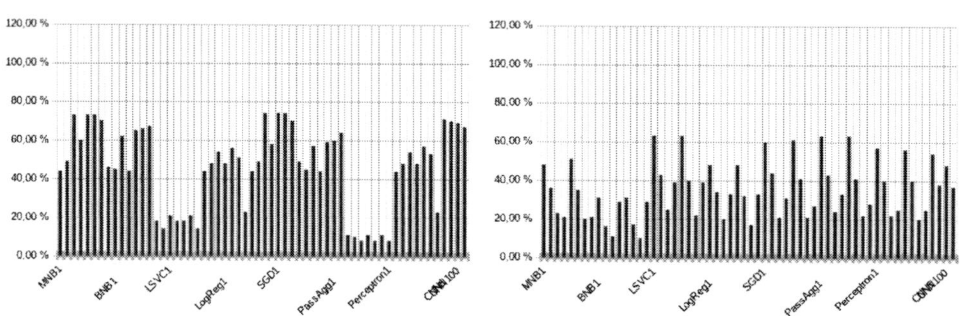

Figure 2: F1-score of the two domains: Consultations (above), DAWQAS (below).

	Best results(%)			Features		
	Prec	Recall	F1	Stop Words	Analyzer	n-gram
MNB	73	75	73	No	Word	2;3
BNB	69	67	67	Yes	Word	2
LSVC	55	62	54	Yes	Char	-
LogReg	74	75	74	Yes	Word	3
SGD	74	75	74	No	Word	1;2
PassAgg	65	65	64	No	Word	2
Perceptron	55	60	57	Yes	Word	2
CNN	73	69	71	No	Word	1

Table 5: Best performance for the Consult domain

Arabic Stop words.

	Best results(%)			Features		
	Prec	Recall	F1	Stop Words	Analyzer	n-gram
MNB	60	57	51	Yes	Word	1
BNB	40	42	31	No	Word	1
LSVC	64	64	63	Yes/No	Word	1
LogReg	57	54	48	No	Word	1
SGD	62	62	61	Yes	Word	1
PassAgg	64	64	63	No	Word	1
Perceptron	58	58	57	No	Word	1
CNN	57	53	54	No	Word	1

Table 6: Best performance for the DAWQAS domain

By comparing the performance of the different classifiers for the four domains, we can conclude that (i) the Arabic Stop words change the meaning or intent of utterance according the task and the domain. (ii) There is no perfect classifier to perform an acceptable SLU portability across domains, especially for the Arabic language, which is known for its richness at the lexical level.(iii) There is not a perfect size for a corpus to be considered when porting to a new domain. Indeed, performance for Consult domain is better than DAWQAS though the Consult corpus is smaller.

4 Conclusion and Perspective

This paper is a modest contribution to the ongoing research about the generalization of a Spoken Language Understanding System in a multi-domain Human-Machine Dialog. To our knowledge, this is the first study to investigate the possibility of a portable SLU system across domains, especially for the Arabic Language. The findings were quite interesting since the F1 scores obtained from experiments to adapt the Schooling Management domain to Medical, Consultations and DAWQAS were 54%, 74% and 63%, respectively.

References

Drs Claude Malhuret Laurent Alexandre. 2000. Sant et bien ltre avec doctissimo. `http://www.doctissimo.fr/`. [Online; accessed 07/08/2018].

C. Chelba and A. Acero. 2006. Adaptation of maximum entropy capitalizer: Little data can help a lot. *Computer Speech & Language*, 20(4):382–399.

H. Daumé-III. 2007. Frustratingly Easy Domain Adaptation. In *Proc. of the Annual Meeting of the Association for Computational Linguistics (ACL)*, Columbus, Ohio, USA.

Hal Daumé-III and Jagadeesh Jagarlamudi. 2011. Domain adaptation for machine translation by mining unseen words. In *Proceedings of the 49th Annual Meeting of the Association for Computational Linguistics: Human Language Technologies: Short Papers - Volume 2*, pages 407–412.

Hal Daumé-III and Daniel Marcu. 2006. Domain adaptation for statistical classifiers. *Journal of Artificial Intelligence Research*, 26.

Walaa Saber Ismail and Masun Nabhan Homsi. 2018. Dawqas: A dataset for arabic why question answering system. *Procedia computer science*, 142:123–131.

A Jaech, L Heck, and M Ostendorf. 2016. Domain adaptation of recurrent neural networks for natural language understanding. In *http://arxiv.org/abs/1604.00117*.

Ridong Jiang, Rafael E Banchs, Seokhwan Kim, Kheng Hui Yeo, Arthur Niswar, and Haizhou Li. 2014. Web-based multimodal multi-domain spoken dialogue system. In *Proceedings of 5th International Workshop on Spoken Dialog Systems*.

Sangkeun Jung, Cheongjae Lee, Kyungduk Kim, Minwoo Jeong, and Gary Geunbae Lee. 2009. Data-driven user simulation for automated evaluation of spoken dialog systems. *Computer Speech & Language*, 23(4):479–509.

Y Kim and R Sarikaya. 2015. New Transfer Learning Techniques For Disparate Label Sets. In *Proceedings of the Annual Meeting of the Association for Computational Linguistics (ACL)*, Beijing, China.

Kazunori Komatani, Satoshi Ikeda, Tetsuya Ogata, and Hiroshi G Okuno. 2008. Managing out-of-grammar utterances by topic estimation with domain extensibility in multi-domain spoken dialogue systems. *Speech Communication*, 50(10):863–870.

Cheongjae Lee, Sangkeun Jung, Seokhwan Kim, and Gary Geunbae Lee. 2009. Example-based dialog modeling for practical multi-domain dialog system. *Speech Communication*, 51(5):466–484.

Fabrice Lefevre, Djamel Mostefa, Laurent Besacier, Yannick Esteve, Matthieu Quignard, Nathalie Camelin, Benoit Favre, Bassam Jabaian, and Lina Maria Rojas Barahona. 2012. Leveraging study of robustness and portability of spoken language understanding systems across languages and domains: the portmedia corpora. In *The International Conference on Language Resources and Evaluation*.

Mohamed Lichouri, Mourad Abbas, Abed Alhakim Freihat, and Dhiya El Hak Megtouf. 2018a. Word-level vs sentence-level language identification: Application to algerian and arabic dialects. *Procedia Computer Science*, 142:246–253.

Mohamed Lichouri, Amar Djeradi, and Rachida Djeradi. 2015. A new automatic approach for understanding the spontaneous utterance in human-machine dialogue based on automatic text categorization. In *Proceedings of the International Conference on Intelligent Information Processing, Security and Advanced Communication*, page 50. ACM.

Mohamed Lichouri, Rachida Djeradi, and Amar Djeradi. 2018b. Combining topic-based model and text categorisation approach for utterance understanding in human-machine dialogue. *International Journal of Computational Science and Engineering*, 17(1):109–117.

Bing Liu and Ian Lane. 2016. Joint online spoken language understanding and language modeling with recurrent neural networks. *arXiv preprint arXiv:1609.01462*.

Wolfgang Minker. 1998. *Speech Understanding for Spoken Language Systems: Portability Across Domains and Languages*. Hänsel-Hohenhausen.

Mikio Nakano, Shun Sato, Kazunori Komatani, Kyoko Matsuyama, Kotaro Funakoshi, and Hiroshi G Okuno. 2011. A two-stage domain selection framework for extensible multi-domain spoken dialogue systems. In *Proceedings of the SIGDIAL 2011 Conference*, pages 18–29. Association for Computational Linguistics.

Fabian Pedregosa, Gaël Varoquaux, Alexandre Gramfort, Vincent Michel, Bertrand Thirion, Olivier Grisel, Mathieu Blondel, Peter Prettenhofer, Ron Weiss, Vincent Dubourg, et al. 2011. Scikit-learn: Machine learning in python. *Journal of machine learning research*, 12(Oct):2825–2830.

Islam Today. 2000. Alistisharat. `http://www.islamtoday.net/istesharat/index.htm`. [Online; accessed 21/11/2018].

Zhuoran Wang, Hongliang Chen, Guanchun Wang, Hao Tian, Hua Wu, and Haifeng Wang. Policy learning for domain selection in an extensible multi-domain spoken dialogue system.

Building a Speech Corpus based on Arabic Podcasts for Language and Dialect Identification

Khaled Lounnas
USTHB University, Algeria
klounnas@usthb.dz

Mourad Abbas and Mohamed Lichouri
Computational Linguistics Dept., CRSTDLA, Algeria
{m.abbas, m.lichouri}@crstdla.dz

Abstract

In this paper, we present ArPod, a new Arabic speech corpus made of Arabic audio podcasts. We built this dataset, mainly for both speech-based multi-lingual and multi-dialectal identification tasks. It includes two languages: Modern Standard Arabic (MSA) and English, and four Arabic dialects: Saudi, Egyptian, Lebanese and Syrian. A set of supervised classifiers have been used: Support Vector Machines (SVM), Multi Layer Perceptron (MLP), K-Nearest Neighbors (KNN), Extratrees and Convolutional Neural Networks (CNN), using acoustic and spectral features. For both tasks, SVM yielded encouraging results and outperformed the other classifiers. Language Identification, Dialect Identification, CNN, Acoustic features, spectral features, SVM, Arabic Podcast

1 Introduction

The most popular researches on spoken audio language/dialects identification has been conducted based on acoustic information, Phonotactic and prosodic approaches and other techniques. Acoustic information is the lowest and nevertheless simplest level of features that can denote a speech waveform. Indeed, in (Koolagudi et al., 2012), MFCC features have been extracted to study the impact of MFCC's coefficients on Indian language recognition . Phonotactic and prosodic information have been used in(Biadsy et al., 2009) and (Biadsy and Hirschberg, 2009). The authors applied a phonotactic approach to automatically detect Arabic dialects by using phone recognizer followed by dialect modeling using trigram models. They also examined the role of prosodic features (intonation and rhythm) for identification of dialects from four Arabic regions: Gulf, Iraq, Levantine and Egypt. In other researches like in (Alshutayri and Albarhamtoshy, 2011), authors trained HMM to characterize part of speech, to implement a dialect identification system.

In order to establish robust systems for Language/dialect identification, spoken corpora have been developed by research community for several languages, but many other languages still lack such resources such as Arabic. That is why we developed a new speech corpus, Arpod-1.0, which is a Multilingual Arabic spoken dataset extracted from the web podcast. This dataset is composed of more than 8 hours, devoted for Arabic and some of its dialects: Saudi, Lebanese, Egyptian and Syrian, in addition to English. The dataset has been separated to two categories: Languages and dialects without code switching, and dialects with code switching. We trained SVM, Extratrees and kNN using acoustic and spectral features, and CNN using spectorgram. In addition, we conducted experiments to find the impact of duration on speech utterances language identification. Indeed, three duration values have been considered: 6 sec, 30 sec and 1 min.

This paper is organized as follows, we present an overview of the works on speech based language identification in section 2. In section 3 we give a description of the the collected dataset. In section 4 and 5, we present the models used as well the experimental setup and results, respectively and we conclude in section 6.

2 Speech based Language Identification: an Overview

For Spoken Language Identification, we cite the work done in (Ali et al., 2015) where authors investigated different approaches for dialect identification in Arabic broadcast speech, based on phonetic and lexical features obtained from a speech recognition system, and bottleneck features using the i-vector framework. By using a binary classifier to discriminate between MSA and dialectal Arabic, they obtained an accuracy of 100% . While, they obtained an accuracy of 59.2% to discriminate five Arabic dialects, namely: Egyptian, Gulf, Levantine, North African, and MSA. In (Moftah et al., 2018), the authors have introduced a new technique for extracting the characteristics of different Arabic dialects from speech by discovering the repeated sequences (motifs) that characterize each dialect. They adopted an extremely fast parameter-free Self-Join motif discovery algorithm called Scalable Time series Ordered search Matrix Profile (STOMP) and extracted 12 Mel Frequency Cepstral Coefficients (MFCC) from each motif, which were used to train the Gaussian Mixture Model-Universal Background Model (GMM-UBM) classifier. This approach was applied on three different motif lengths 500 ms, 1000 ms, and 1500 ms on a data set that was downloaded from Qatar Computing Research Institute domain and carried out some experiments on Egyptian (EGY) and Levantine (LEV). Whereas in (Bougrine and Abdelali, 2018), a system based on prosodic speech information, for intra-country dialects has been proposed. DNN and SVM have been used to evaluate KALAM'DZ, a Web-based corpus dedicated to Algerian Arabic Dialectal varieties. The authors have obtained results that show the close-performance between the DNNs and SVM. In (Lounnas et al., 2019), the problem of identifying languages as Persian, German, English, Arabic and Kabyl [1], has been addressed using Voxforge speech corpus [2].

3 Dataset

We downloaded more than 8 hours of speech data from "Arab podcast" website[3]. This dataset covers MSA and some of its dialects from the following regions: Saudi Arabia (KSA), Syria (SYR), Egypt (EGY), Lebanon (LEB) in addition to English (ENG). The language/dialects are of duration ranging from 50 min to 1 h 30 min. Note that LEB, EGY and KSA-E dialectal corpora include some English expressions along with the conversations. Accordingly this may cause performance degradation compared to the remaining corpora. For training requirements and system design it was necessary to split the downloaded speech files into a smaller segments of around five minutes each, using MKVToolNix GUI v31.0.0 [4]. The whole corpus is sampled at 44.1 khz and encoded on 16 bits. Each language/dialect involves conversations spoken by two speakers or more (male and female). Table 1 summarizes the overall statistics of Arpod-1.0 corpus, describing the duration per language/dialect.

Language/Dialect	Duration (hours)
KSA	00:50:05
MSA	00:50:05
SYR	00:50:05
ENG	00:50:05
EGY	01:30:00
KSA-E	01:30:00
LEB	01:30:00
Total	**08:10:00**

Table 1: ArPod dataset used for language/dialect identification

The targeted applications that will be trained using Arpod-1.0 are several and not only for the two aforementioned tasks. Since it might be of great help for researchers, we will make it available next[5].

---

4 General System

The system includes two types of data representation: acoustic and spectral ones. We used many acoustic features as MFCC, Entropy of Energy, Zero Crossing Rate, Spectral centroid and many others. We used two schemes according to the work mentioned in (Giannakopoulos, 2015). The second type of speech data representation is by using spectogram. We give more details in the following subsections. In our experiments, We used a set of classifiers, namely: kNN, SVM, MLP and Extratrees.

4.1 Acoustic Features based Classification

Scheme 1

In this scheme, 34 features are selected.

1. MFCC coefficients (13)

2. energy(1) & energy of entropy(1)

3. Zero Crossing Rate(1) & Spectral Centroid(1)

4. Spectral Spread (1) & Spectral Entropy(1)

5. Spectral Rolloff(1) & Chroma Vector(12)

6. Spectral Flux(1) & Chroma Deviation(1)

Scheme 2

We have used a framework[6] on the basis of Librosa (McFee et al., 2015), which includes spectral features and rhythm characteristics. We present in the following the features used in this framework, with a total of 193 components:

1. MFCC coefficients (40)

2. Mel spectrogram (128) & Chroma Vector (12)

3. Spectral contrast (7) & Tonnetz(6)

4.2 Spectogram based Classification

In this approach, We opted for an image recognition process to solve the problem of spoken language identification. The idea is to extract the spectogram for our speech dataset which is under .wav format. Then, we applied a CNN classifier to identify languages and dialects based on their respective spectograms.

5 Experiments and Results

In this study, we divided Arpod-1.0 dataset into two parts according to their content: the first one includes 3 hours and 40 minutes of speech, covering two languages: MSA and English (ENG) and two dialects: Saudi (KSA) and Syrian (SYR). The second part -4 hours 30 minutes- is composed of three dialects characterized by language alternation or code switching: Egyptian (EGY), Lebanese (LEB) and Saudi (KSA-E). Note that, in this second part of dataset, speakers alternate between their dialects and English. Experiments have been achieved on speech segments with different durations: 6, 30 and 60 sec.

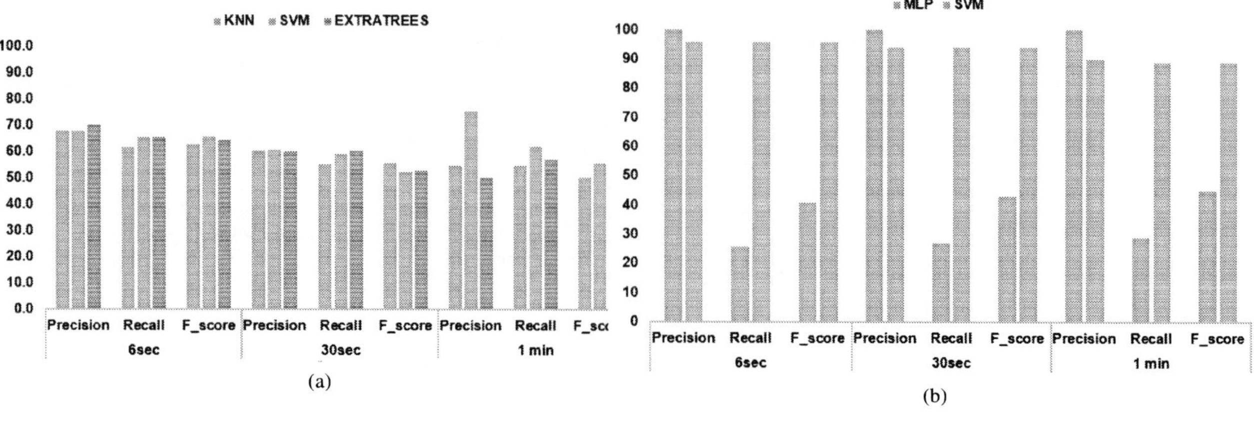

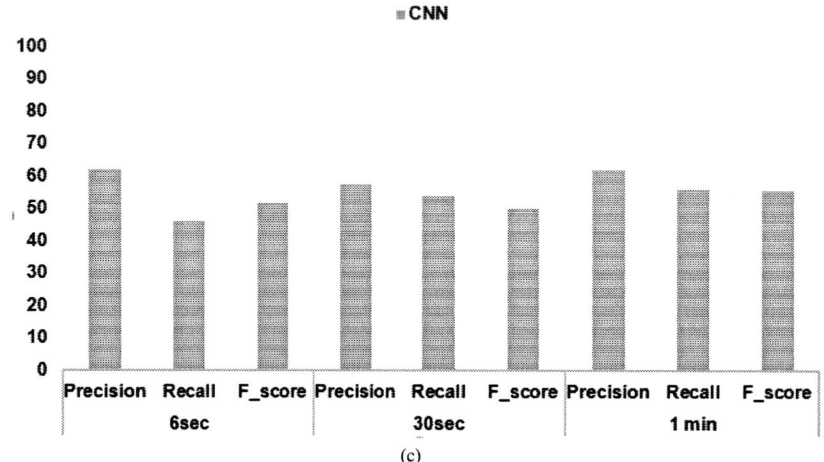

Figure 1: Languages and dialects without code switching, (a) System's performance with scheme 1, (b) System's performance with scheme 2, (c) System's performance using spectrogram based approach.

5.1 Languages and Dialects without Code Switching

As aforementioned, the first experiment has been devoted to identifying languages and dialects that do not contain any kind of code switching. It is about MSA, English, Syrian and Saudi dialects. We should note that all the experiments have been conducted by taking into account the different durations of utterances which are: 6, 30 and 60 seconds.

Based on the results reported in figures 1, we conclude that SVM based on scheme 2 outperforms scheme 1 and spectrogram based approaches, with F1 measure equal to 96%, through short utterances (6 sec). The spectogram based approach yielded an F1 score of 56 % for utterances with 1 min of duration. We should emphasize that performance based on schemes 1 and 2 is inversely proportional to duration, and it is better when dealing with shorter utterances. This is true for kNN, SVM and Extratrees classifiers, except for MLP performance which increases slightly whith duration.

5.2 Dialects with Code Switching

In this experiment, we study whether the system is robust to the code switching phenomenon or not. The speech corpora selected to be used are in Egyptian, Saudi and Lebanese dialects where speakers alternate between English and these dialects. Figure2, shows that the best result was achieved by SVM using the second scheme with an F1 of 98%, for the shortest utterances (6 seconds).

However, unlike experiments dealing with languages and dialects without code switching, performance obtained using the two schemes and the spectrogram based approach is not influenced by the duration of the test utterances.

6   Conclusion

In this paper, we presented the dataset Arpod-1.0 that we collected from Arabic podcasts and prepared to be used for Arabic dialect identification. we conducted a set of experiments to find the model giving the best performance for our language identification system. We have taken into consideration different circumstances like duration of speech utterances and the presence of code switching phenomenon. The findings showed, in the absence of code switching, that shorter utterances are well identified and performance decrease when utterances are longer. Surprisingly, utterances taken from datasets including code

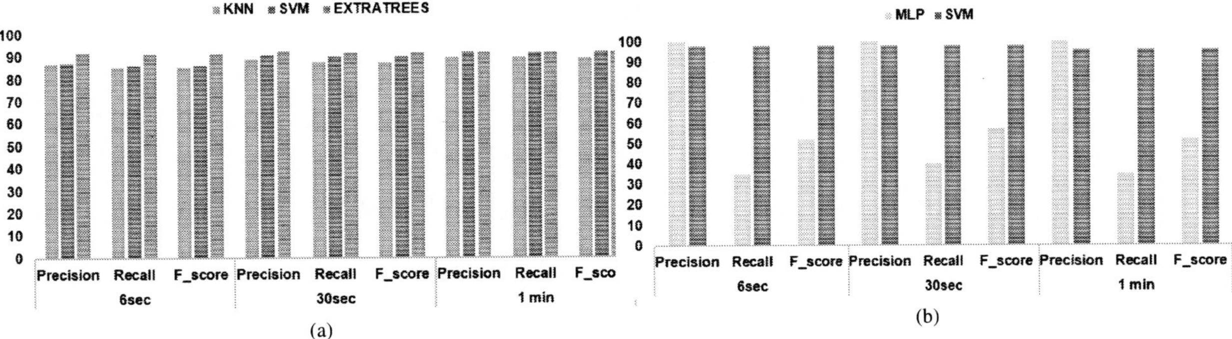

(a)   (b)

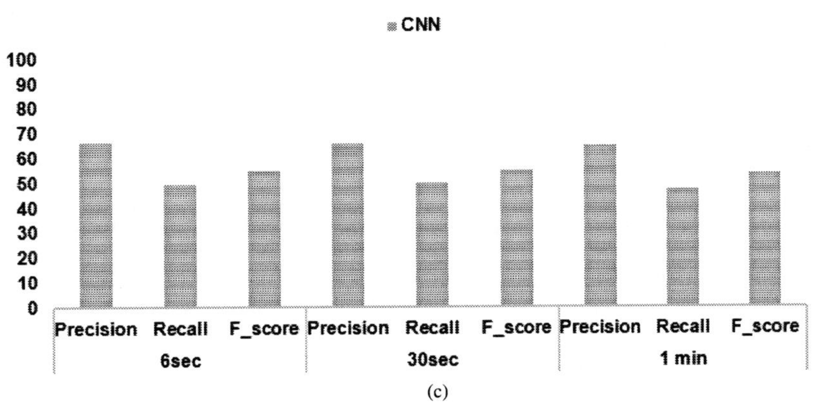

(c)

Figure 2: Dialects with code switching, (a) System's performance with scheme 1, (b) System's performance with scheme 2, (c) System's performance using spectrogram based approach.

switched dialects, are well identified using SVM and Extratrees -schemes 1 and 2 - and seem that these models are robust to code switching and duration variation.

In future work, we aim to build a robust model based on other features, like the Shifted delta coefficients (SDCs) which have proven to be efficient in language identification (Lee et al., 2016; Jiang et al., 2014; Ferrer et al., 2015).

Acknowledgment

We thank the reviewers for their valuable comments.

References

Ahmed Ali, Najim Dehak, Patrick Cardinal, Sameer Khurana, Sree Harsha Yella, James Glass, Peter Bell, and Steve Renals. 2015. Automatic dialect detection in arabic broadcast speech. *arXiv preprint arXiv:1509.06928*.

Areej Alshutayri and Hassanin Albarhamtoshy. 2011. Arabic spoken language identification system (aslis): A proposed system to identifying modern standard arabic (msa) and egyptian dialect. In *International Conference on Informatics Engineering and Information Science*, pages 375–385. Springer.

Fadi Biadsy and Julia Hirschberg. 2009. Using prosody and phonotactics in arabic dialect identification. In *Tenth Annual Conference of the International Speech Communication Association*.

Fadi Biadsy, Julia Hirschberg, and Nizar Habash. 2009. Spoken arabic dialect identification using phonotactic modeling. In *Proceedings of the eacl 2009 workshop on computational approaches to semitic languages*, pages 53–61. Association for Computational Linguistics.

Hadda Cherroun Soumia Bougrine and Ahmed Abdelali. 2018. Spoken arabic algerian dialect identification. In *2018 2nd International Conference on Natural Language and Speech Processing (ICNLSP)*, pages 1–6. IEEE.

Luciana Ferrer, Yun Lei, Mitchell McLaren, and Nicolas Scheffer. 2015. Study of senone-based deep neural network approaches for spoken language recognition. *IEEE/ACM Transactions on Audio, Speech, and Language Processing*, 24(1):105–116.

Theodoros Giannakopoulos. 2015. pyaudioanalysis: An open-source python library for audio signal analysis. *PloS one*, 10(12):e0144610.

Bing Jiang, Yan Song, Si Wei, Jun-Hua Liu, Ian Vince McLoughlin, and Li-Rong Dai. 2014. Deep bottleneck features for spoken language identification. *PloS one*, 9(7):e100795.

Shashidhar G Koolagudi, Deepika Rastogi, and K Sreenivasa Rao. 2012. Identification of language using mel-frequency cepstral coefficients (mfcc). *Procedia Engineering*, 38:3391–3398.

Kong Aik Lee, Haizhou Li, Li Deng, Ville Hautamäki, Wei Rao, Xiong Xiao, Anthony Larcher, Hanwu Sun, Trung Hieu Nguyen, Guangsen Wang, et al. 2016. The 2015 nist language recognition evaluation: the shared view of i2r, fantastic4 and singams.

Khaled Lounnas, Mourad Abbas, Hocine Teffahi, and Mohamed Lichouri. 2019. A language identification system based on voxforge speech corpus. In *International Conference on Advanced Machine Learning Technologies and Applications*, pages 529–534. Springer.

Brian McFee, Colin Raffel, Dawen Liang, Daniel PW Ellis, Matt McVicar, Eric Battenberg, and Oriol Nieto. 2015. librosa: Audio and music signal analysis in python. In *Proceedings of the 14th python in science conference*, volume 8.

Mohsen Moftah, Mohammed Waleed Fakhr, and Salwa El Ramly. 2018. Arabic dialect identification based on motif discovery using gmm-ubm with different motif lengths. In *2018 2nd International Conference on Natural Language and Speech Processing (ICNLSP)*, pages 1–6. IEEE.

Automatic Text Tagging of Arabic News Articles Using Ensemble Deep Learning Models

Ashraf Elnagar, Omar Einea and **Ridhwan Al-Debsi**
Machine Learning and Arabic Language Processing Research Group
Dept. Computer Science
University of Sharjah
Sharjah, UAE
`{ashraf,oeinea,raldebsi}@sharjah.ac.ae`

Abstract

Automatic document categorization gains more importance in view of the plethora of textual documents added constantly on the web. Text categorization or classification is the process of automatically tagging a textual document with most relevant label. Text categorization for Arabic language become more challenging in the absence of large and free datasets. We propose new, rich and unbiased dataset for the single-label (SANAD) text classification, which is made freely available to the research community on Arabic computational linguistics. In contrast to the majority of the available categorization systems of Arabic text, we offer several deep learning classifiers. With deep learning, we eliminate the heavy pre-processing phase usually used to on the data. Our experimental results showed solid performance on SANAD corpus with a minimum accuracy of 93.43%, achieved by CGRU, and top performance of 95.81%, achieved by HANGRU. In pursuit of superior performance, we implemented an ensemble model to combine best deep learning models together in a majority-voting paradigm.

1 Introduction

As a result of the rise of the Internet and Web 2.0, unimaginable amount of data is constantly on the rise, which is produced by several sources including social media users. The presence of such unstructured data makes a great resource for data processing and management in order to extract useful information. One important task is text classification and clustering, which is a field of research that gained much momentum in the last few years. The recent advances in machine learning paved the road for proposing successful text categorization systems.

The terms text categorization and text classification are used interchangeably to indicate the process of predicting predefined categories or domains to a given document. The automated categorization process may report the most relevant single category or multiple close ones (Figure 1). For the huge amount of available documents (or text) on the internet, manual classification by domain experts becomes ineffective and unfeasible. Therefore, automated classifiers had become not only an alternative but a necessity utilizing machine learning algorithms. However, the unstructured nature of the textual documents necessitates the need of machine learning algorithms to represent the data in a compatible format such as using numeric vectors. Text categorization is a key prerequisite to several evolving applications in different areas such as language (and dialects) identification (Lulu and Elnagar, 2018), sentiment analysis (Elnagar and Einea, 2016; Elnagar et al., 2018b,a), genre classification (Onan, 2018), and spam filtering (Li et al., 2018) to list few.

Text categorization is well studied in several languages and in particular the English language. Despite of the importance of Arabic language being the fourth used language on the Internet and 6th official language reported by United Nations ((Eldos, 2003)), few research attempts are reported on the Arabic language text classification as detailed in the next section. According to Wikipedia, as of 2018, there are 25 independent nations where Arabic is an official language and the number of Arabic speakers reach 380 million. With the rise of Arabic data on the internet, the need for an effective and robust automated classification system becomes a must. The research attempts at addressing this problem for Arabic text are limited to using shallow deep learning classifiers and were conducted on small and mostly unavailable datasets. As a result, we report the construction of a dataset for Arabic categorization tasks collected from news sources. The dataset is made free to use for the research community. In addition and unlike previous research works, we utilize deep learning models for investigating both single-label Arabic text categorization and provide comparative results of the different models.

We constructed a new corpus for the Arabic classification tasks, namely, SANAD (Single-label Arabic News Articles Dataset), (Einea et al., 2019). This corpus consists of more than one dataset. It is made available on Mendely[1]. It is our objective to make the dataset accessible for the research community.

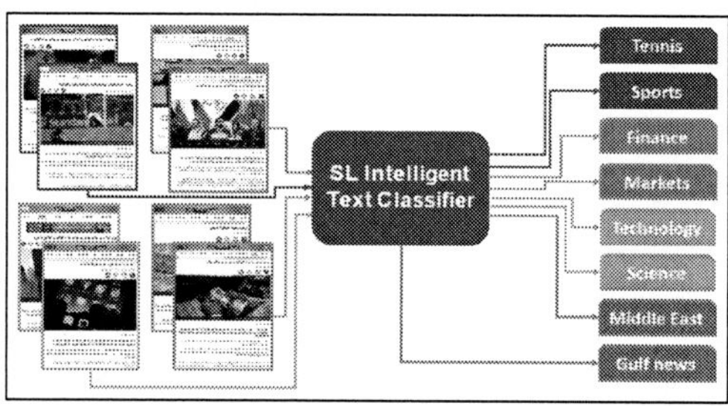

Figure 1: Single-label text classifier.

Several reported works proposed robust text classifiers but mostly designed for English text. As for Arabic, reported works are conducted on small datasets. Besides, the reported accuracies of such solutions have a big room for improvement. We implement nine robust deep neural network based classifiers that are tested on large datasets and yield high accuracy on single-label categorization tasks.

The remainder of this paper is organized as follows. In Section 2, we describe previous research work on Arabic text categorization. Next, we describe the datasets in detail in Section 3. In Section 4, we list the deep learning models implemented for the Arabic categorization task. In Section 5, we demonstrate the performance and improvement of our models over existing systems on SANAD as well as a recently reported benchmark dataset. Finally, we conclude our research in Section 6.

------

[1]http://dx.doi.org/10.17632/57zpx667y9.1

2 Literature Review

Numerous papers addressed the problem of automatic text categorization proposing different techniques and solutions. This is mainly true for the English language. Comprehensive surveys already exist and provide a thorough coverage of text categorization classifiers (Sebastiani, 2002; Aggarwal and Zhai, 2012; Korde and Mahender, 2012; Joachims, 2002). A relatively recent good survey on Arabic text categorization is available in (Hmeidi et al., 2014).

As our emphasis, in this work, is Arabic language, we pay more attention to research work on Arabic text categorization. The early work of Saad, (Saad, 2010), used several shallow learning supervised classifiers including Decision Tree, KNN, SVM, and Naïve Bayes. He studied the impact of pre-processing on text categorization results. For this purpose, he used the widely spread, but relatively small, BBC and CNN Arabic news datasets. Similarly, the effect of pre-processing of Arabic text in order to reduce the feature spaces are reported in (Duwairi et al., 2009; Al-Kabi et al., 2011; Yaseen and Hmeidi, 2014) in which the authors investigated the impact of stemming, light stemming, and synonyms-clustering on the features space reduction and accuracy. For the same purpose, Feature Subset Selection (FSS) metrics, (Mesleh, 2011), were used with SVM classifier to categorize text. Although the training time is reduced, accuracy deteriorates as well.

Furthermore, Maximum Entropy (ME) is used to classify news articles, (Sawaf et al., 2001). The work concluded that the Dice measures with N-gram produce better results than the Manhattan distance. Combining both ME and pre-processing is reported in (A, 2007). The author showed that the use of normalization and stop-words removal has enhanced F1-measure.

The use of Neural Networks (NN) for Arabic text categorization was first reported in (Umer and Khiyal, 2007) using Learning Vector Quantization (LVQ) classifier and self-organization Maps (SOM). Good accuracy results were reported while using a relatively small dataset. Similarly, the authors of (Harrag et al., 2011) showed that NN outperforms SVM after reducing the features space.

The majority of reported research on Arabic text classification used classical supervised machine learning classifiers such as NB (El Kourdi et al., 2004; Mesleh, 2007; Hadi et al., 2008; Joachims, 1998; Alsaleem, 2011; Khorsheed and Al-thubaity, 2013), SVM (Mesleh, 2007; Joachims, 1998; Alsaleem, 2011; Khorsheed and Al-thubaity, 2013), Rocchio (Joachims, 1998), KNN (Mesleh, 2007; Hadi et al., 2008; Joachims, 1998), and decision trees (Joachims, 1998; Khorsheed and Al-thubaity, 2013; Harrag et al., 2009). The results mostly conclude that SVM is reported as the top classifier for categorizing Arabic texts followed by NB and decision trees.

Different from the previous research works, El-Mahdaouy et al (El Mahdaouy et al., 2017) performed Arabic document classification using Word and document Embedding rather than relying on text pre-processing and word counting representation. It was shown that document Embedding outperformed text pre-processing techniques either by learning them using Doc2Vec or averaging word vectors. The results are in line with the conclusions reported by Baroni et al. (Baroni et al., 2014) which evaluated the use of word embedding against classical approaches that rely on pre-processing or word counting on an array of applications such as concept categorization on the English language. Besides, it has been shown that neural network based models are more robust when it comes for sensitivity to parameters settings.

In our work, we introduce new benchmark datasets for both single-label and multi-label Arabic text categorization. However, the datasets may serve the research community on Arabic computational linguistics working on other supervised learning tasks. Therefore, the datasets are publicly available. Moreover, we investigate the use of nine deep learning models to solve the single-label as well as the multi-label Arabic text categorization problem.

3 Dataset

We use three different datasets that we collected using web scraping (Python Selenium, Requests

Source	Categories	Train	Test
Alarabiya.net	5	22203	4075
Khaleej.ae	7	42000	3500
Akhbarona.com	7	42000	4900

Table 1: Number of articles in SANAD.

and BeautifulSoup or PowerShell), from three popular news websites (alarabiya.net, alkhaleej.ae and akhbarona.com). All datasets have the categories [Finance, Medical, Politics, Sports, Tech, Culture and Religion] except alarabiya.net; it does not have the last 2 categories. As these datasets were collected from news portals, the articles are expressed in modern standard Arabic, so there are no dialects involved. Since all datasets are tagged with single labels, we grouped them in one corpus called SANAD. We partitioned the datasets into training and testing sets, Table 1 details the number of articles and categories in each one of them.

The scraped articles are cleaned by removing Latin alphabet and punctuation marks. In the sequel, we describe each one of the 3 datasets that make SANAD:

3.0.1 alarabiya.net

All scraped articles were initially grouped into 7 categories. However, 2 of the categories did not have much data (i.e., 'Culture' and 'Iran News') when compared with the rest of the categories. We merged 'Iran News' with the 'Politics' category and dropped the 'Culture' set. The articles collected are until early 2018. Figure 2 shows the distribution of the five resulting categories of this dataset.

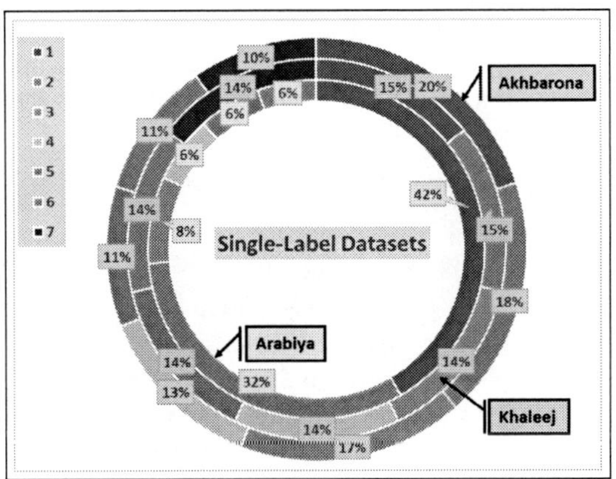

Figure 2: Distribution of categories in the proposed single-label datasets.

3.0.2 alkhaleej.ae

We collected around 1.2M (4GB) articles since 2008 until 2018. However, the tagging in the news portal was incomplete and vague. Therefore, we had to manually tag a reasonable amount of articles in each one of the aforementioned seven categories. This is a balanced dataset in which each category has 6.5k articles. the total size of the dataset is 45.5k articles. Figure 2 shows the balanced distribution of the 7 categories.

3.0.3 akhbarona.com

We scraped a large number of articles in the 7 categories. However, the 'Religion' category had half as much as other categories did. In order to increase the number, we scraped the remaining half of this category from a similar newspaper portal, which is `Alanba.com`. Figure 2 shows the resulting distribution of the seven categories of this dataset (Table 1).

4 Deep Leaning Models

- CNN The hierarchy of our CNN model consists of a dropout layer, followed by 3 CNN layers with kernel size of 5, and 128 filters, followed by global max-pooling with default values, and another dropout layer.

- RNN We used both GRU and LSTM models. The GRU model consists of 2 GRU layers. While our LSTM model consists of 1 LSTM layer. This selection has been determined by trying out different methods until we obtained the best accuracy. Both RNN layers are an improvement on the basic RNN layer to involve memory capabilities, where GRU has a memory, but LSTM was introduced to solve the Vanishing Gradient Problem (Hochreiter et al., 2001).

- BiRNN Both RNN models mentioned above were also wrapped around with a Bidirectional wrapper, giving us 2 more models; Bi-GRU and BiLSTM. Both models are composed of 1 BiRNN layer. The reason for implementing the bidirectional strategy is because of the nature of text, where each word is defined by the preceding and the proceeding words. Bidirectional wrappers allow the layers to go over the data in both directions, resulting in a vector that is 2 times as big as a uni-directional layer.

- Attention The attention mechanism was added only to the RNN models, as it was noted in (Raffel and Ellis, 2015) that it will solve the long term memory issues, hence it was applied to GRU and LSTM only. The attention models simply have an attention layer after the RNN model producing more models.

- CNN+RNN For our final 2 models, we used a combination of CNN and RNN layers to produce CRNNs (Convolution Recurrent Neural Networks). The hierarchy of the network consists of a dropout layer, followed by one CNN layer, one RNN layer, global max pooling, and another dropout layer.

5 Experimental Results and Discussion

5.1 Setup and Pre-processing

Our objective is to explore the success of using DNN models to classify Arabic news categories. We conducted several experiments involving categorization of Arabic text on different datasets. Our experiments involve single-label classification on our own three constructed datasets (`Arabiya`, `Khaleej`, and `Akhbarona`.

We split all datasets into 80% for training, 10% for cross-validation, and 10% for testing. We report the accuracy on testing datasets for each of the nine implemented deep learning models. It should be noted that embeddings are initialized at random for the input layer in all experiments. We chose Tensorflow and Keras frameworks for the implementation of all DNN models.

Simple text pre-processing is used to clean the dataset by filtering out non-Arabic content. This is particularly important when dealing with data collected from the web. Although Arabic character set is somehow unique, it is easy to eliminate non-Arabic characters. We further eliminate all diacritics, elongation (i.e., "جــمــيــل" is reduced to "جميل", punctuation marks, extra spaces, etc. Another widely adopted practice is to apply normalization on some Arabic characters. This involves replacing the letters "إ" , "أ" , and "آ" with letter "ا" , letter "ة" with "ه" , and letter "ي" with "ى" . In contrast with the majority of research works on Arabic computational linguistics, we argue that the normalization step is not required; we believe it can affect the contextual meaning for some words such as "فَأر" and "فَار" or "كرة" and "كره" . This is clear when producing word embedding models. As a result, we did not normalize the Arabic text.

5.2 Single-label Text Classification

We implemented 9 DNN models. Namely, 4 RNN models (GRU, BiGRU, LSTM, BiLSTM), 2 attention models (HANGRU, HANLSTM), and 3 CNN based models (CNN, CGRU, CLSTM). We trained the 9 models on each of the 3 training datasets of SANAD. Then, we tested the resulting trained model on each of the 3 datasets. For example, we trained the BIGRU model on Arabiya training dataset and tested it on Arabiya testing dataset, Khaleej testing dataset, and Akhbarona testing dataset. The resulting accuracy scores of this comprehensive testing is depicted in Figures 4 and 3 for each of the 9 DNN models.

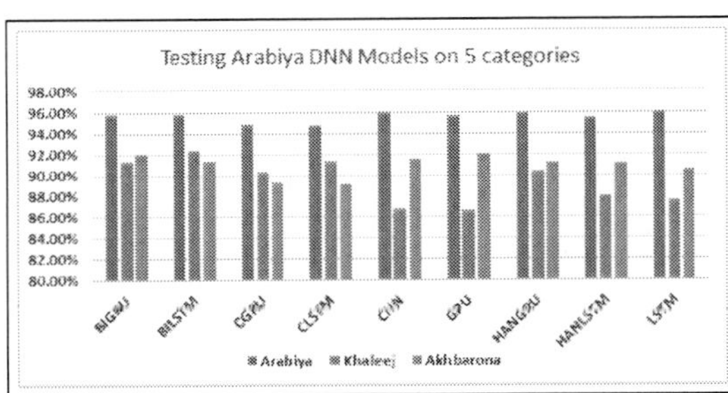

Figure 3: Performance evaluation of the 9 models on the 'Arabiya' datasets.

Figure 3 summarizes the accuracy results on our three constructed datasets. In the first experiment, we trained the nine DNN models on Arabiya dataset and then tested the models on Arabiya, Khaleej, and Akhbarona datasets on five categories. When testing on Arabiya dataset, six models out of the nine produced close results between 95.63% and 96.05% (CNN), one model (HANLSTM) reported 95.63, which is around average, and two models, CLSTM and CGRU, performed below average with accuracy scores of 94.67% and 94.87%, respectively. We further tested the Arabiya-trained model on totally different testing data from Khaleej and Akhbarona datasets. On Khaleej testing dataset, the best and worst results are reported by BiLSTM model with accuracy of 92.40% and GRU model with accuracy of 86.64%. As for Akhbarona test dataset, the best and worst results are reported by GRU model with accuracy of 92.00% and CLSTM model with accuracy of 89.05%. In the second experiment (Figure 4), we trained the nine DNN models on Khaleej dataset and then tested the models on Arabiya, Khaleej, and Akhbarona datasets on seven categories. The

Table 2: Performance of the 9 DNN models on the datasets (AR-5, KH-7, and AB-7. Best and worst performing DL model is shown in Bold font for each dataset.

	AR-5	KH-7	AB-7
BIGRU	95.78%	95.00%	92.94%
BILSTM	95.75%	93.91%	93.53%
CGRU	94.87%	94.23%	**91.18%**
CLSTM	**94.67%**	94.57%	92.55%
CNN	**96.05%**	95.89%	93.94%
GRU	95.63%	**93.86%**	93.37%
HANGRU	95.85%	**96.94%**	**94.63%**
HANLSTM	95.36%	95.49%	94.08%
LSTM	95.95%	95.23%	93.26%

results on Khaleej test dataset ranged between 93.85% and 96.94%. Whereas the results on the other two test datasets ranged between 75.04% and 87.12% for Arabiya and 66.38% and 76.40% for Akhbarona. In the third experiment (Figure 4), we trained the nine DNN models on Akhbarona dataset and tested against the three datasets. The results ranged between 78.43% and 89.79% for Arabiya; and 70.14% and 80.46% for Khaleej; and 91.18% and 94.63% for Akhbarona. The results of these experiments show that Arabiya-training model is the best one to use for single-label classification of Arabic news articles.

The performance of the DNN models vary in the above set of experiments. While some DNN models produce above average results, few others are trailing behind. Figure 5 reflects the level of performance of each model in the experiments. For example, BiLSTM model yielded accuracy above average in eight of the nine experiments. Similarly, both HANGRU and BiGRU models were successfully producing solid results around or above average. However, GRU performed poorly compared to the rest.

Table 2 depicts the results on SANAD datasets. namely, Arabiya with 5 categories (AR), Khaleej with 7 categories (KH-7), and Akhbarona with 7 categories (AB-7).

5.3 Ensemble Models

To further enhance the accuracy results of the deep learning models, we employed the ensemble concept to produce better classifiers. Ensemble modeling is the process of combining more than one model together while producing a single accuracy

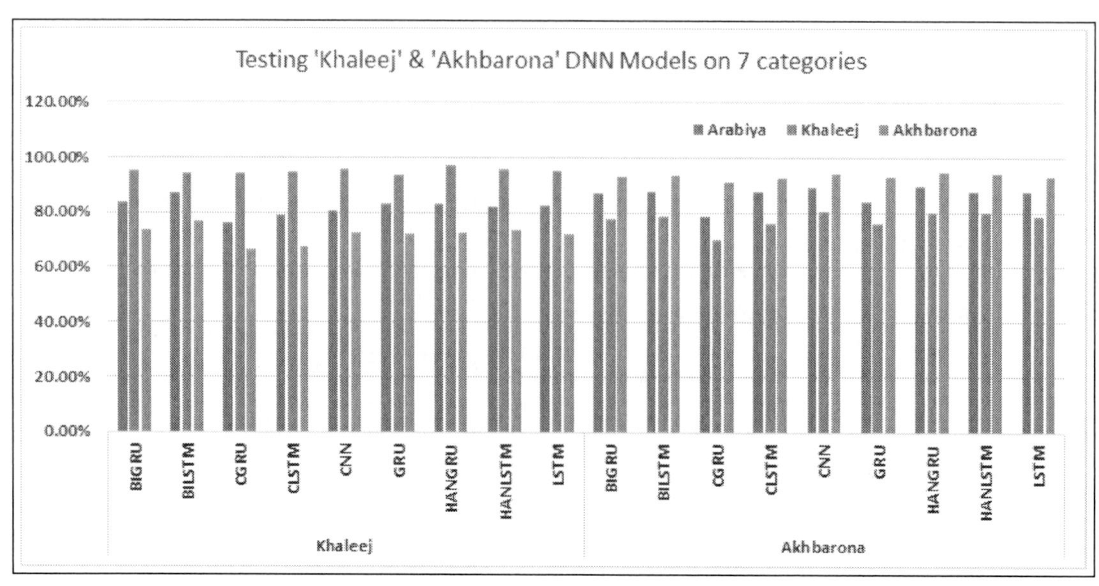

Figure 4: Performance evaluation of the 9 models on the datasets: Khaleej and Akhbarona.

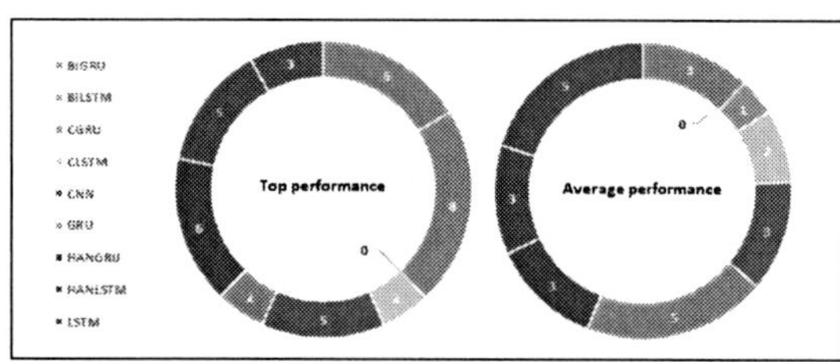

Figure 5: Top and average performing deep learning models in all experiments.

score. We use the majority voting principle to compute such score. By combining different models, we anticipate eliminating drawbacks of some models such as biases and high variability of data.

We performed a greedy ensemble on all combinations of DNN models. We solicited models that produce higher accuracy than the best single model reported above. As expected, a combination of two or more models outperformed the top individual model's accuracy. Although the number of generated ensemble models reached 459 models in some cases, the improvement in accuracy scores did not exceed 2.1%. This is was achieved when testing Khaleej models against Akhbarona dataset. On the other hand, no single ensemble model beat the top single model of testing Khaleej models on Khaleej dataset. It is worth noting that the impact is little because the reported accuracy scores of individual models are already high. Figure 6 compares top ensemble models

with top individual model for all nine tests.

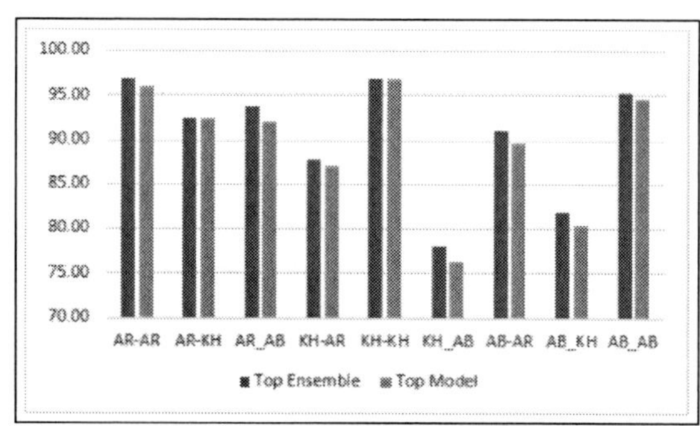

Figure 6: Top ensemble model vs. top individual model.

We observed that some of the DNN models had more contribution in the successful selected ensemble models than others. The model that had the most contribution is HANGRU, which appeared in 7 experiments out of the 9 ones; major contributor to the top ensemble models. CNN appeared 6 times. However, the BiGRU model is the least contributor (only once). Figure 7 shows the contribution percentages of each model in the top ensemble models.

6 Conclusion

In this work, we described a new large corpus for single-label Arabic text categorization tasks as a contribution to the research community on Arabic computational linguistics. SANAD is collected

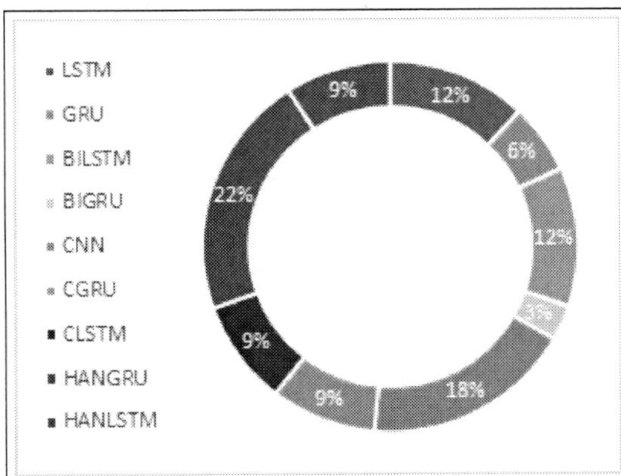

Figure 7: Contributions of DNN models to the top ensemble models.

from annotated Arabic news articles, and consists of 3 datasets; 2 (Arabiya and Akhbarona) are imbalanced while Khaleej dataset is a balanced one. The total number of Arabic articles amount to 200k, which makes it the largest freely available benchmark. The articles are classified into a maximum of seven categories.

We further implemented a variety of deep learning Arabic text classifiers and tested them thoroughly on SANAD corpus. Our treatment is different from existing Arabic single-label text systems that adopt standard machine learning classifiers with heavy pre-processing phase to prepare the data. Besides, we eliminated the heavy pre-processing requirements. Our experimental results showed that DNN models performed very well on SANAD corpus with a minimum accuracy of 93.43%, achieved by CGRU, and top performance of 95.81%, achieved by HANGRU. Furthermore, we introduced ensemble modeling to boost the performance, which resulted in enhancing the results in 8 experiments out of the 9 ones.

References

El-Halees A. 2007. Arabic text classification using maximum entropy. *The Islamic University Journal (Series of Natural Studies and Engineering)*, 15:167–167.

Charu C. Aggarwal and Cheng Xiang Zhai. 2012. *Mining Text Data*. Springer Publishing Company, Incorporated.

Mohammed N. Al-Kabi, Qasem A. Al-Radaideh, and Khalid W. Akkawi. 2011. Benchmarking and assessing the performance of arabic stemmers. *Journal of Information Science*, 37(2):111–119.

Saleh Alsaleem. 2011. Automated arabic text categorization using svm and nb. *International Arab Journal of eTechnology*.

Marco Baroni, Georgiana Dinu, and Germán Kruszewski. 2014. Don't count, predict! a systematic comparison of context-counting vs. context-predicting semantic vectors. In *Proceedings of the 52nd Annual Meeting of the Association for Computational Linguistics (Volume 1: Long Papers)*, pages 238–247. Association for Computational Linguistics.

Rehab Duwairi, Mohammad Nayef Al-Refai, and Natheer Khasawneh. 2009. Feature reduction techniques for arabic text categorization. *Journal of the American Society for Information Science and Technology*, 60(11):2347–2352.

Omar Einea, Ashraf Elnagar, and Ridhwan Al Debsi. 2019. Sanad: Single-label arabic news articles dataset for automatic text categorization. *Data in Brief*, page 104076.

Mohamed El Kourdi, Amine Bensaid, and Tajje-eddine Rachidi. 2004. Automatic arabic document categorization based on the naïve bayes algorithm. In *Proceedings of the Workshop on Computational Approaches to Arabic Script-based Languages*, Semitic '04, pages 51–58, Stroudsburg, PA, USA. Association for Computational Linguistics.

Abdelkader El Mahdaouy, Eric Gaussier, and Saïd Ouatik El Alaoui. 2017. Arabic text classification based on word and document embeddings. In *Proceedings of the International Conference on Advanced Intelligent Systems and Informatics 2016*, pages 32–41, Cham. Springer International Publishing.

T.M. Eldos. 2003. Arabic text data mining: a root-based hierarchical indexing model. *International Journal of Modelling and Simulation*, 23(3):158–166.

A. Elnagar and O. Einea. 2016. Brad 1.0: Book reviews in arabic dataset. In *2016 IEEE/ACS 13th International Conference of Computer Systems and Applications (AICCSA)*, pages 1–8.

Ashraf Elnagar, Yasmin S. Khalifa, and Anas Einea. 2018a. *Hotel Arabic-Reviews Dataset Construction for Sentiment Analysis Applications*, pages 35–52. Springer International Publishing.

Ashraf Elnagar, Leena Lulu, and Omar Einea. 2018b. An annotated huge dataset for standard and colloquial arabic reviews for subjective sentiment analysis. *Procedia Computer Science*, 142:182 – 189. Arabic Computational Linguistics.

Wael Hadi, S Al Hawari, Fadi Thabtah, and Jafar Ababneh. 2008. Naive bayesian and k-nearest neighbour to categorize arabic text data. In *The 22nd annual European Simulation and Modelling Conference (ESM'2008)*, pages 196–200.

F. Harrag, E. El-Qawasmeh, and P. Pichappan. 2009. Improving arabic text categorization using decision trees. In *2009 First International Conference on Networked Digital Technologies*, pages 110–115.

Fouzi Harrag, Eyas El-Qawasmah, and Abdul Malik S. Al-Salman. 2011. Stemming as a feature reduction technique for arabic text categorization. *2011 10th International Symposium on Programming and Systems*, pages 128–133.

Ismail Hmeidi, Mahmoud Al-Ayyoub, Nawaf Abdulla, Abdalrahman Almodawar, Raddad Abooraig, and Nizar A. Ahmed. 2014. Automatic arabic text categorization: A comprehensive comparative study. *Journal of Information Science*, 41:114–124.

Sepp Hochreiter, Yoshua Bengio, Paolo Frasconi, Jürgen Schmidhuber, et al. 2001. Gradient flow in recurrent nets: the difficulty of learning long-term dependencies.

Thorsten Joachims. 1998. Text categorization with support vector machines: Learning with many relevant features. In *Machine Learning: ECML-98*, pages 137–142, Berlin, Heidelberg. Springer Berlin Heidelberg.

Thorsten Joachims. 2002. *Learning to Classify Text Using Support Vector Machines: Methods, Theory and Algorithms*. Kluwer Academic Publishers, Norwell, MA, USA.

Mohammad Khorsheed and Abdulmohsen Al-thubaity. 2013. Comparative evaluation of text classification techniques using a large diverse arabic dataset. *Language Resources and Evaluation*, 47:513–538.

SVandana Korde and C. Namrata Mahender. 2012. Text classification and classifiers: A survey. *IJAIA Journal*, 3(2):85–99.

Yuancheng Li, Xiangqian Nie, and Rong Huang. 2018. Web spam classification method based on deep belief networks. *Expert Systems with Applications*, 96:261 – 270.

Leena Lulu and Ashraf Elnagar. 2018. Automatic arabic dialect classification using deep learning models. *Procedia Computer Science*, 142:262 – 269. Arabic Computational Linguistics.

Abdelwadood Moh'd Mesleh. 2011. Feature sub-set selection metrics for arabic text classification. *Pattern Recogn. Lett.*, 32(14):1922–1929.

Abdelwadood Moh'd A Mesleh. 2007. Chi square feature extraction based svms arabic language text categorization system. *Journal of Computer Science*, 3(6):430–435. Exported from https://app.dimensions.ai on 2019/02/03.

Aytuğ Onan. 2018. An ensemble scheme based on language function analysis and feature engineering for text genre classification. *Journal of Information Science*, 44(1):28–47.

Colin Raffel and Daniel PW Ellis. 2015. Feedforward networks with attention can solve some long-term memory problems. *arXiv preprint arXiv:1512.08756*.

Motaz Saad. 2010. The Impact of Text Preprocessing and Term Weighting on Arabic Text Classification. Master's thesis, Computer Engineering Dept., Islamic University of Gaza, Palestine.

Hassan Sawaf, Jörg Zaplo, and Hermann Ney. 2001. Statistical classification methods for arabic news articles. In *Arabic Natural Language Processing in ACL2001*, pages 1–6.

Fabrizio Sebastiani. 2002. Machine learning in automated text categorization. *ACM Comput. Surv.*, 34(1):1–47.

Muhammad Fahad Umer and M. Sikander Hayat Khiyal. 2007. Classification of textual documents using learning vector quantization. *Information Technology Journal*, 6:154–159.

Qussai Yaseen and Ismail Hmeidi. 2014. Extracting the roots of arabic words without removing affixes. *Journal of Information Science*, 40(3):376–385.

A Probabilistic Approach for Confidence Scoring in Speech Recognition

Punnoose A K
Flare Speech Systems
Bangalore, India
punnoose@flarespeech.com

Abstract

This paper discusses a method to derive a meaningful confidence score for a speech segment at the phoneme level, using a frame classifier. Multiple functions, which capture various aspects of the frame classifier output, are first introduced. The ability of these functions to discriminate between different phonemes is shown. A probabilistic approach is formulated to combine the functions to get a meaningful confidence score, which reflects the precision of the predicted phoneme chunk. Relevant real-world datasets are used to demonstrate the effectiveness of the proposed confidence scoring mechanism.

1 Introduction

In speech recognition, it is desirable to have a confidence score which has a strong correlation with the correctness of recognition. A low confidence score should imply wrong recognition, and a high score should signal correct recognition. For this, the confidence score should be derived out of features which are not directly used or overlooked, in the speech recognition. Modern automatic speech recognition is done in a multi-level manner. The bottom level corresponds to frame recognition. Next levels are phoneme, word and sentence recognition respectively. In the sentence level, language model plays a key role in the overall word error. The relationship between the frame level accuracy and the word level accuracy follows more of an S-curve. Word accuracy increases gradually as the frame accuracy increases, then it shoots up exponentially, and then gradually slows down. An error in frame level classification can be forgiving than an error in phoneme detection, especially in the case of large vocabulary speech recognition task. Ideally, the confidence scoring should be using low level features which are raw compared to higher level features.

Confidence scoring in speech recognition has a rich literature. A general survey for confidence scoring can be found in (Schaaf and Kemp, 1997; Jiang, 2005; Rose et al., 1995). Confidence scoring was treated as a classification problem with features derived from trained acoustic and language models along with derived word level features (Huang et al., 2013; Weintraub et al., 1997; Wessel et al., 1999; J. Hazen et al., 2002). Another approach is using backward language models (Duchateau et al., 2002). A trained generic confidence scoring mechanism can be recalibrated to output a more meaningful confidence score, by taking into account the end application specific scenarios (Yu et al., 2011). Another approach used for confidence scoring is by using word lattices (Kemp and Schaaf, 1997) and N-best lists (Rueber, 1997).

Multilayer perceptrons(mlp) based posteriors (Lee et al., 2004; Wang et al., 2009; Ketabdar, 2010; Bernardis and Bourlard, 1998) has been extensively used for confidence scoring. mlp posterior based score has the benefit of being at the frame level, rather than at the phoneme level. We propose a confidence scoring mechanism at the phoneme level, using a set of new features derived from an mlp based frame classifier.

The rest of the paper is organized as follows. First, the frame classifier details and datasets used are explained. Certain measures computed from the frame classifier output is explored. Then a set of phoneme level features are derived for confidence scoring. A probabilistic confidence scoring mechanism is formulated using the features derived. And finally, the approach is benchmarked using a test dataset. This is a meta-learning approach, as the confidence scoring stage depends on the output from a trained frame classifier.

Datasets & Definitions: Voxforge data is used for all the experiments. The foremost reason for using Voxforge data is that it is recorded in an uncontrolled environment by people with different accents, mother tongue, etc. This will give the necessary variability in the data and any confidence scoring mechanism derived out of this data will be applicable to a real-world speech based information access.

The whole Voxforge dataset is divided into 3 subsets, d_1, d_2 and d_3. d_1 is used to train the frame classifier. d_2 is fed to the frame classifier to get the output dubbed as d_m, which is eventually used for making distributions and functions needed for confidence scoring. d_3 is used for benchmarking the proposed confidence scoring approach.

1.1 Frame Classifier Details

An mlp is trained to predict phonemes from speech features. Perceptual Linear Prediction Coefficients(plp) along with delta and double delta features are used. Standard English phoneme set is used as the labels. Mini-batch gradient descent is used as the training mechanism. Cross-entropy error is used as the objective for backpropagation training. 3 hidden layers are used and weights of the mlp are initialized randomly between -1 and +1. Given an input, the softmax layer outputs a probability vector, where components of the probability vector correspond to phonemes.

Given a wave file, the frame classifier outputs a sequence of probability vectors, each corresponding to a frame size of 25ms. Each component in the probability vector corresponds to a phoneme and the phoneme with the highest probability is treated as the classified phoneme. The classified phoneme is labeled as the top phoneme for that frame. Define a phoneme chunk as multiple continuous frames, classified as the same phoneme. Chunk duration of a phoneme is the number of frames in that chunk. /p/ denotes the phoneme p.

The subset d_2 is passed through the frame classifier to get a set of classified phonemes and the associated probability vectors. This act as the dataset d_m, which is used to derive a set of features for the confidence scoring. First, we discuss these features by completely disregarding the associated ground truth phoneme label. Next, we use phoneme labels to fit distributions for true positives and false positives for all the features, phoneme wise. Finally, a confidence scoring mechanism with a focus on precision is derived.

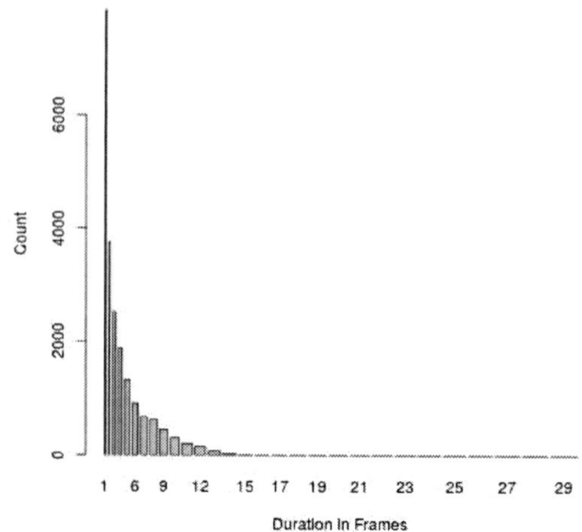

Figure 1: Phoneme /b/: Duration in frames

2 New Features

To derive new features for confidence scoring, three measures are first introduced. These are the duration of phoneme chunks, distribution of softmax probability, and the softmax probability of phoneme chunk. These measures are computed from the frame classifier output d_m, which has a sufficiently large amount of data, that allows us to treat this as a population feature. The measures are analyzed based on the top phoneme detected, framewise, by completely ignoring the ground truth phoneme labels. These measures are finally converted into phoneme chunk level features.

Duration of Phoneme Chunks: Fig 1 and 2 plots the duration of the detected phoneme chunks of /b/ and /ay/ respectively. Note that /b/ tends to have almost zero long phoneme chunks, while /ay/ has relatively plenty long chunks detected by the frame classifier. This difference in the detected duration of different phoneme chunks is significant enough to treat the phoneme chunk duration as a valid variable for confidence score prediction. Converting the counts to a simple discrete distribution,

$$g(k; p) = \frac{C(k)}{\sum_k C(k)} \tag{1}$$

where $c(k)$ is the number of chunks of size k of phoneme p.

Distribution of Softmax Probability: To understand how the highest softmax probability is

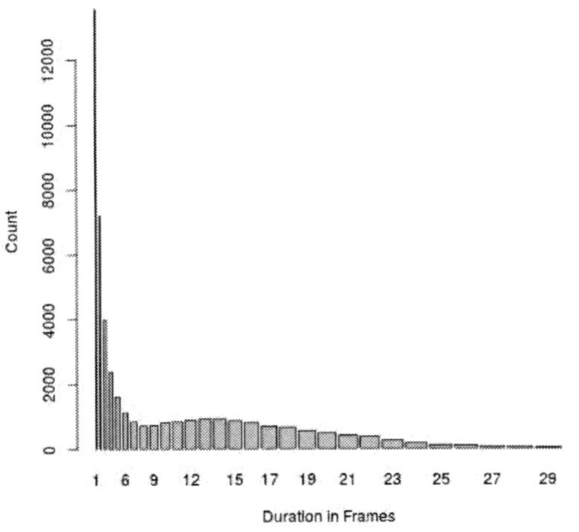

Figure 2: Phoneme /ay/: Duration in frames

distributed generally for different top phonemes, the histogram of probabilities for 2 different top phonemes are plotted for speech data.

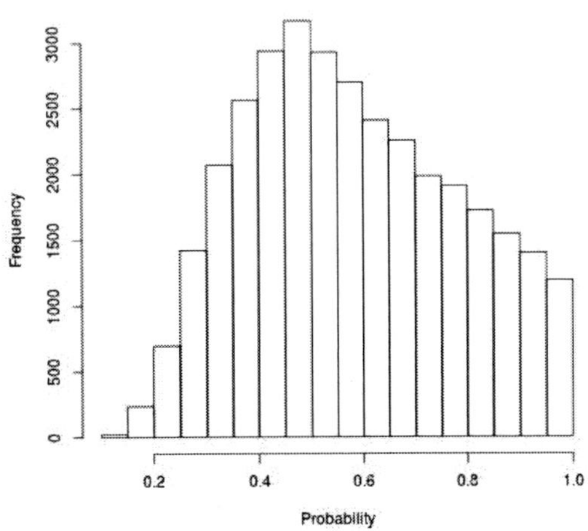

Figure 3: Softmax probability histogram for top phoneme /aa/

Fig 3 plots the histogram of the highest probabilities for top phoneme /aa/, which is a very common phoneme. It is clear from the histogram that the highest count peaks at 0.5 and as it moves up to 1, the count decreases. What it implies is that the number of instances a /aa/ phoneme is predicted with probability [0.9-1] are less than the number instances in which it is predicted with probability [0.4-0.5]. It could be due to the presence of similar sounding phonemes like /ae/, /ah/, etc so that probability gets divided. The issue with probabilities getting divided closely is that it is difficult to assign a meaningful confidence score.

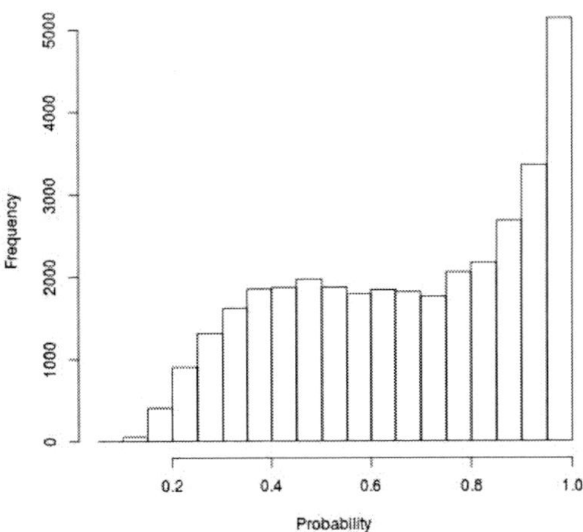

Figure 4: Softmax probability histogram for top phoneme /f/

Fig 4 plots the highest probabilities for the top phoneme /f/. It is apparent that /f/ is predicted with high probability, for most of the instances, rather than getting confused with other phonemes. From the 2 plots, it is clear that the softmax probability of the top phoneme is distributed differently for different phonemes, and could be useful in deriving a robust confidence score.

Softmax Probability of Phoneme Chunks: A related question is whether the softmax probability of a top phoneme is dependant on the neighboring same top phonemes. Fig 5 plots the mean of average softmax probability of phoneme chunks for different phoneme chunks sizes, for /f/. It is clear from the plot that as the phoneme chunk size increases, the average softmax probability also increases.

A strong correlation between the detected phoneme chunk size and mean of average softmax probabilities indicates that any confidence scoring mechanism should take into account the phoneme chunk size. As the above mentioned features are plotted from unlabelled data, it doesn't indicate whether the detected phoneme chunk is indeed correct or not. To assign a confidence score for a phoneme chunk predicted with a softmax proba-

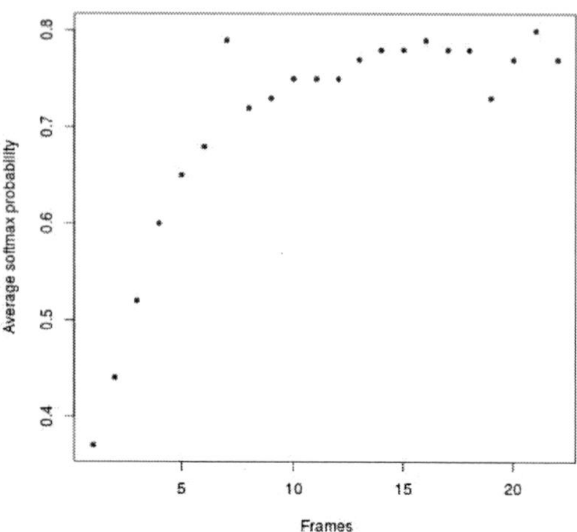

Figure 5: Average softmax probability against chunk size in frames for phoneme /f/

bility, ground truth labels of the phoneme chunks has to be taken into account.

2.1 New Features Using Label Information

Ground truth of the detected phoneme chunk provides the necessary discriminatory information needed to differentiate true positives from false positives. Ground truth label of a detected phoneme chunk is the sequence of true label phonemes. Due to the unpredictability of frame classifier, we consider a predicted phoneme chunk to be correct if at least one of the frames in the predicted phoneme chunk and the ground truth phoneme sequence, have the same phoneme. This is because as the ground truth phoneme sequence is from the output of a forced aligner, there could be the misalignment of phoneme boundaries. For eg, let a phoneme chunk predicted be $[p_1\ p_2\ p_3\ p_4\ p_5]$ and let the ground truth be $[q_1\ q_2\ q_3\ q_4\ p_5]$, the phoneme chunk predicted is assumed to be correct, because of the 1 common phoneme at the end of the chunks.

With an objective to maximize the precision of the final scoring system, probabilistic models are fit on the features derived from d_m, to capture multiple aspects of speech. For modeling a specific phoneme, on a particular feature, positive and negative data is first captured. Positive data for a phoneme is the feature values derived from d_m, which eventually is classified as the phoneme correctly. Negative data for a phoneme is the false

positive feature values derived from d_m, which incorrectly got classified as the phoneme. In the context of this paper, correctly detected refers to true positives and wrongly detected refers to false positives. Finally, probabilistic models are learned using the positive and negative data, for the particular feature, for the specific phoneme. The features are chunk size, chunk softmax average, chunk average softmax distribution, distinct phoneme count adjacent to the phoneme chunk.

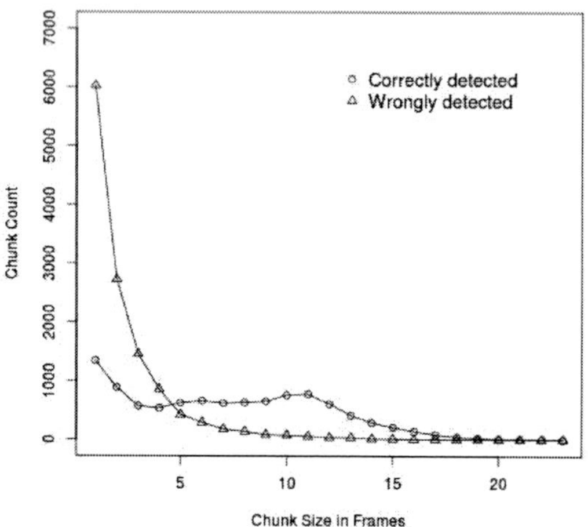

Figure 6: Count of correctly detected and wrongly detected phoneme chunks for /f/

Chunk Size: Phoneme chunk size is a crucial variable that indicates whether the detected phoneme chunk is indeed correct or not. In Fig 6, the true positives and false positives are plotted for phoneme /f/. As the phoneme chunk size increases, the detected phoneme chunk count also increases. Note that the for phoneme chunk size up to 4, the misrecognition rate is very high, which shows that small chunks are more likely to be misrecognized. From these type of plots, distributions on chunk size for true positives and false positives for specific phonemes can be fit.

The fact that even detected chunk size has an effect on the precision is very crucial. This information modeled using a distribution can be used in a full blown large vocabulary recognition engine to rescore the language model probabilities. But the downside is that it assigns a disproportionately low score for very short words.

Chunk Softmax Average: The average of softmax probabilities could be another differentiating variable, between correctly detected and falsely detected phoneme chunks.

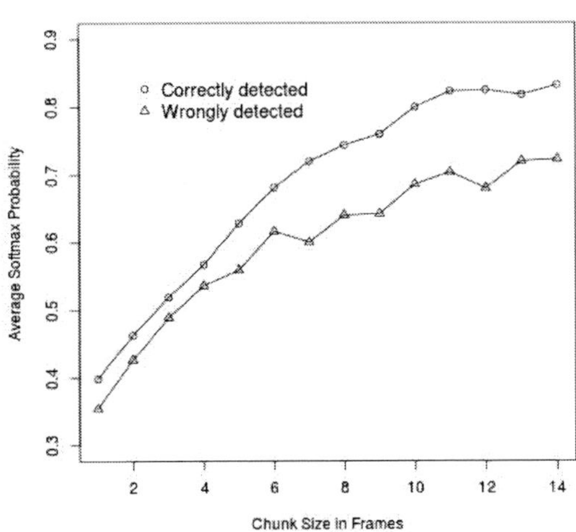

Figure 7: Mean of softmax probability across chunk size

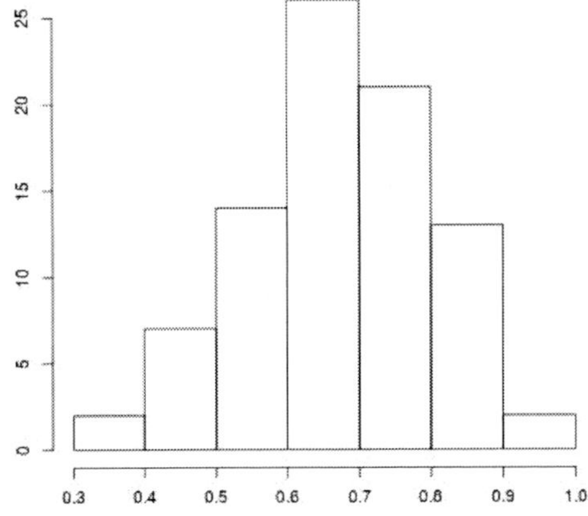

Figure 8: Wrongly detected phoneme chunk softmax probability histogram for /f/

Fig 7 plots the mean of average softmax probabilities of the phoneme chunks for the top phoneme /f/, averaged chunk size wise, for true positives and false positives. As the chunk size increases, the average softmax probability of the chunk increases. The average softmax probability of the phoneme chunk, for the correctly predicted and incorrectly predicted case, is very close to each other and does not provide much discriminatory information, when taken in isolation.

Chunk Average Softmax Distribution: Fig 8 and 9 plots the distribution of average softmax probability of top phoneme /f/, for wrongly detected and correctly detected phoneme chunks respectively. The chunk size used is 9 frames. It is apparent that both histograms are left skewed, but varies in the degree of skewness. The difference in skewness serves as another discriminatory feature.

As the histogram appears to be normally distributed and skewed, a skew normal distribution (Azzalini, 2013) can be used to model the data. A skew normal distribution models data which are normally distributed and skewed either left or right. A random variable Y is said to have a location-scale skew-normal distribution, with location λ, scale δ, and shape parameter α, and denote $Y \sim SN(\lambda, \delta^2, \alpha)$, if its probability density

function is given by

$$f(y; \lambda, \delta^2, \alpha) = \tfrac{2}{\delta}\phi(\tfrac{y-\lambda}{\delta})\Phi(\alpha\tfrac{y-\lambda}{\delta}) \qquad (2)$$

where $y, \alpha, \lambda \in R$ and $\delta \in R^+$. ϕ and Φ denote the probability density function and cumulative distribution function of the standard Normal distribution. If the shape parameter $\alpha = 0$, then the skew normal distribution equals a normal distribution. i.e.,

$$f(y; \lambda, \delta^2, \alpha) = \mathcal{N}(y; \lambda, \delta) \text{ when } \alpha = 0$$

Given a dataset, the maximum likelihood estimate(MLE) of parameters λ, δ, α does not have a closed loop solution and are calculated using numerical methods.

Distinct Phoneme Count Adjacent to the Phoneme Chunk: The number of distinct phonemes, in a small window to the phoneme chunk detected, can serve as a source of information on whether the phoneme chunk detected is correct or not.

Fig 10 and 11, plot the number of distinct phonemes in a 5 frame window preceding to the phoneme chunk /p/, where the /p/ is correctly detected and wrongly detected respectively. For the correctly detected case, as seen in Fig 10, the presence of a single phoneme or 2 phonemes are more, in the adjacent left window. This means the detection rate is high if it is a smooth transition between phonemes. Converting this information into a distribution,

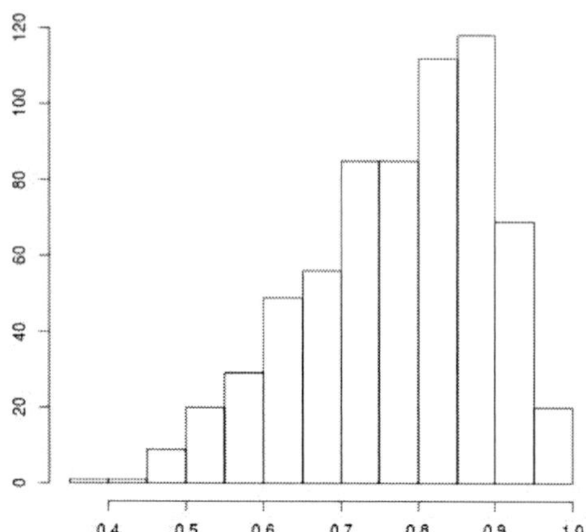

Figure 9: Correctly detected phoneme chunk softmax probability histogram for /f/

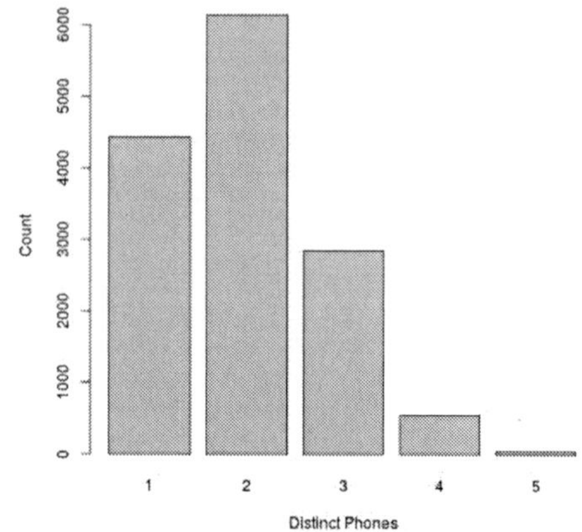

Figure 10: Distinct phoneme count preceding the correctly detected phoneme chunk /p/

$$h(n;p) = \frac{C(n)}{\sum_n C(n)} \tag{3}$$

where $C(n)$ is the count of n distinct phonemes in the left window, of a detected phone p, in the dataset d_m.

3 Confidence Prediction

We seek a confidence score that reflects the precision of the prediction of a phoneme chunk. Assume a phoneme chunk of phoneme p with chunk size k, predicted by the frame classifier, with an average softmax probability s and with n distinct phonemes in the adjoining left window of the phoneme chunk. The confidence score is given by the posterior odds ratio,

$$\frac{P(p|s,k,n)}{P(\neg p|s,k,n)} = \frac{\frac{P(p,s,k,n)}{P(s,k,n)}}{\frac{P(\neg p,s,k,n)}{P(s,k,n)}}$$

$$= \frac{P(s|k,n,p)P(k|n,p)P(n|p)P(p)}{P(s|k,n,\neg p)P(k|n,\neg p)P(n|\neg p)P(\neg p)}$$

With the following conditional independence assumptions,

$$P(k|n,p) = P(k|p)$$
$$P(s|k,n,p) = P(s|k,p)$$

The posterior odds ratio can be written as

$$\frac{P(p|s,k,n)}{P(\neg p|s,k,n)} = \frac{P(s|k,p)P(k|p)P(n|p)P(p)}{P(s|k,\neg p)P(k|\neg p)P(n|\neg p)P(\neg p)}$$

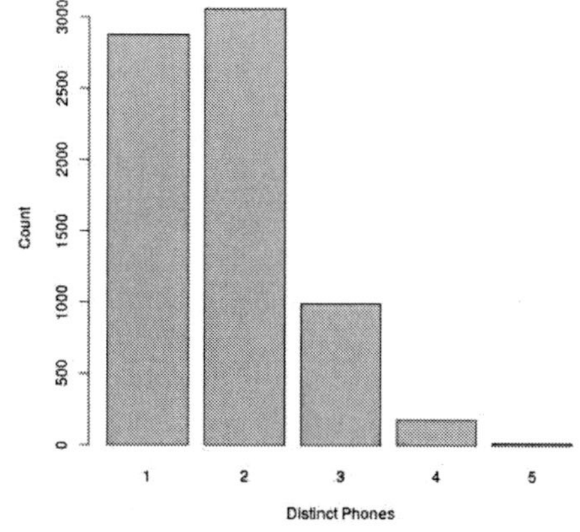

Figure 11: Distinct phoneme count preceding the wrongly detected phoneme chunk /p/

where the distributions are defined as,

$$
\begin{aligned}
P(k|p) &= g(k;p) \\
P(k|\neg p) &= g(k;\neg p) \\
P(n|p) &= h(n;p) \\
P(n|\neg p) &= h(n;\neg p) \\
P(s|k,p) &= f(s;\lambda_{pk},\delta^2_{pk},\alpha_{pk}) \\
P(s|k,\neg p) &= f(s;\lambda_{\neg pk},\delta^2_{\neg pk},\alpha_{\neg pk})
\end{aligned}
$$

where $\neg p$ represents the false positives of phoneme p, that is the cases where phoneme chunks are wrongly detected as p. $P(p)$ and $P(\neg p)$ represents the prior probabilities of true positive and false positive cases respectively. A high posterior ratio means high precision as the posterior ratio is directly proportional to the precision of the prediction.

Assuming equal prior probabilities for true positives and false positives, i.e., $P(p) = P(\neg p)$, and in the absence of any other information, the posterior odds ratio reduces to,

$$\frac{P(p|s,k,n)}{P(\neg p|s,k,n)} = \frac{P(s|k,p)P(n|p)P(k|p)}{P(s|k,\neg p)P(n|\neg p)P(k|\neg p)} \qquad (4)$$

Equation (4) calculates the posterior probability ratio of the case where the detected phoneme chunk is actually the correct phone, to where detected phoneme chunk is a false positive.

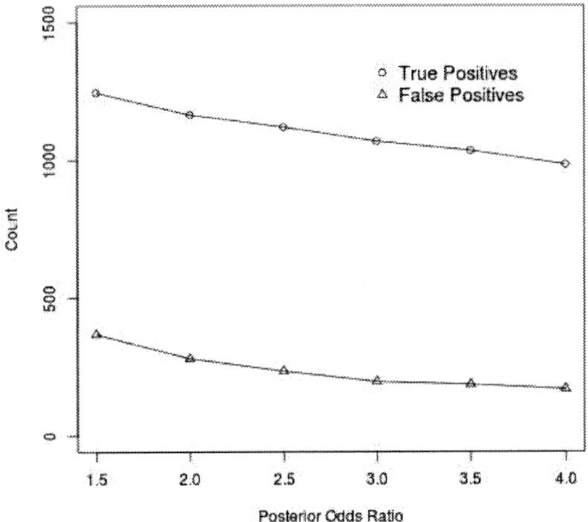

Figure 12: Posterior ratio vs true positives and false positives for /p/

4   Experimental Results

As this approach focuses on confidence scoring for a detected phone, it is the precision that has to be tested. Models $P(k|p)$, $P(k|\neg p)$, $P(s|k,p)$, $P(s|k,\neg p)$, $P(n|p)$, and $P(n|\neg p)$ are built from d_m. For chunk size $k \geq 10$, where the number of instances are less for $\neg p$, data is pooled together and the skew normal distribution is fit. This makes sense as for $k \geq 10$, the average softmax probability of the phoneme chunk varies gradually, as is shown in Fig 7. Testing is done on the subset d_3. Fig 12 plots the posterior ratio vs true positives and false positives for a selected phoneme /p/.

Each point (x, y) in the true positive curve means the following. For posterior odds ratio greater than x, there are y instances of the

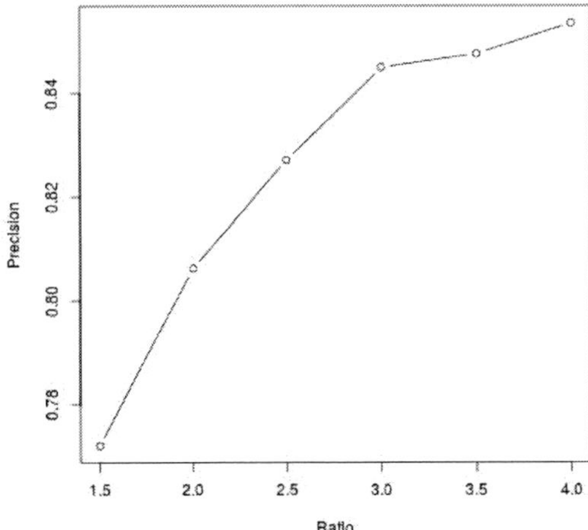

Figure 13: Phoneme /p/ precision

phoneme chunk /p/ recognized which are true positives. And each point (x, y) in the false positive curve means, for the posterior odds ratio greater than x, there are y instances of phoneme chunk /p/ detected which are false positives. The result is the aggregate of all the chunk sizes together. As false positives decreases, true positives also decreases. Fig 13 plots the precision of phoneme /p/. As the threshold of posterior ratio increases, the precision also increases, but at the expense of true positives. Based on the use case, the best operating point can be selected.

The difference between this approach and a direct posterior based confidence scoring approach (Wang et al., 2009) is in the additional assumptions made on the softmax probability. Characteristics of the posteriors for the true positive and false positives, associated with a phoneme, is incorporated into the probabilistic framework. The focus here is on the precision of the phoneme detection.

5   Conclusion

A new probabilistic approach is presented which provides a confidence score to a phoneme chunk detected by the frame classifier. Predictor variables like the phoneme chunk size, number of distinct phonemes in an adjacent window to the phoneme chunk, the average softmax probability of the phoneme chunk, are explored. A full probabilistic model is specified with conditional independence assumptions to make the distributions simple. The distributions are learned from real-world data. Benchmarking of the approach is done with the sole focus on precision.

This probabilistic model is suitable for adding new variables if the likelihood of new variable value conditioned on various phonemes can be computed. More variables derived independently from acoustic phonetics, time domain, or spectrum, can be easily added to the model. As long as the variables are meaningful and with proper conditional independence assumptions, the confidence score can be calculated without expensive computation.

In this paper, the focus is solely on the precision. This helps in calibrating the confidence scoring mechanism for a certain type of utterances like confirmations in an IVRS system, where a mis-recognition is very expensive. In the future, we aim to make a confidence scoring mechanism with an overall goal of improving recall, which suits a host of other applications like recognition from a list of words. Another area of improvement is to use the confidence score of a phoneme chunk to calculate the confidence score of another chunk, possibly in the same word. This requires a language model at the phonetic level to model the short-range dependencies.

References

Adelchi Azzalini. 2013. *The Skew-Normal and Related Families*. Institute of Mathematical Statistics Monographs. Cambridge University Press.

Giulia Bernardis and Hervé Bourlard. 1998. Improving posterior based confidence measures in hybrid hmm/ann speech recognition systems. In *ICSLP*.

J Duchateau, Kris Demuynck, and Patrick Wambacq. 2002. Confidence scoring based on backward language models. volume 1, pages 221–224.

Po-Sen Huang, Kshitiz Kumar, Chaojun Liu, Yifan Gong, and Li Deng. 2013. Predicting speech recognition confidence using deep learning with word identity and score features. In *Acoustics, Speech, and Signal Processing, ICASSP-2013*, pages 7413–7417.

Timothy J. Hazen, Joseph Polifroni, and Stephanie Seneff. 2002. Recognition confidence scoring and its use in speech understanding systems. *Computer, Speech and Language*, 16:49–67.

Hui Jiang. 2005. Confidence measures for speech recognition: A survey. *Speech Communication*, 45:455–470.

Thomas Kemp and Thomas Schaaf. 1997. Estimating confidence using word lattices. *Proceedings of Eurospeech*, pages 827–830.

Hamed Ketabdar. 2010. Improving posterior based confidence measures using enhanced local posteriors. *2010 18th European Signal Processing Conference*, pages 2007–2011.

Akinobu Lee, Kiyohiro Shikano, and Tatsuya Kawahara. 2004. Real-time word confidence scoring using local posterior probabilities on tree trellis search. In *International Conference on Acoustics, Speech, and Signal Processing*, volume 1, pages 793–796.

Richard Rose, B.H. Juang, and Chin-Hui Lee. 1995. A training procedure for verifying string hypotheses in continuous speech recognition. *Acoustics, Speech, and Signal Processing, IEEE International Conference on*, 1:281–284.

Bernhard Rueber. 1997. Obtaining confidence measures from sentence probabilities. In *EUROSPEECH-1997*, pages 739–742.

T. Schaaf and T. Kemp. 1997. Confidence measures for spontaneous speech recognition. In *Proceedings of ICASSP 97 Volume 2*, pages 875–878.

Dong Wang, Javier Tejedor, Joe Frankel, Simon King, and Jose Colas. 2009. Posterior-based confidence measures for spoken term detection. In *Proceedings of the 2009 IEEE International Conference on Acoustics, Speech and Signal Processing*, ICASSP '09, pages 4889–4892.

M. Weintraub, F. Beaufays, Z. Rivlin, Y. Konig, and A. Stolcke. 1997. Neural - network based measures of confidence for word recognition. In *Proceedings of the 1997 IEEE International Conference on Acoustics, Speech, and Signal Processing (ICASSP '97)-Volume 2*, pages 887–890.

Frank Wessel, Klaus Macherey, and Hermann Ney. 1999. A comparison of word graph and n-best list based confidence measures. In *Proceedings of Eurospeech*, pages 315–318.

Dong Yu, Jinyu Li, and Li Deng. 2011. Calibration of confidence measures in speech recognition. *Trans. Audio, Speech and Lang. Proc.*, 19(8):2461–2473.

A Crowdsourcing-based Approach for Speech Corpus Transcription
Case of Arabic Algerian Dialects

Ilyes Zine, Mohamed Cherif Zeghad, Soumia Bougrine and Hadda Cherroun
Laboratoire d'Informatique et Mathématique (LIM)
Université Amar Telidji Laghouat, Algérie
{i.zine,m.zeghad,sm.bougrine,hadda_cherroun}@lagh-univ.dz

Abstract

In this paper we describe a corpus annotation project based on crowdsourcing technique that performs orthographic transcription of KALAM'DZ corpus (Bougrine et al., 2017c). This latter is a speech corpus dedicated to Arabic Algerian dialectal varieties. The recourse to crowdsourcing solution is deployed to avoid time and cost consuming solutions that involves experts. Since Arabic dialects have no standard orthographic, we have fixed some guidelines that helps crowd to get more normalized transcriptions. We have performed experiments on a sample of 10% of KALAM'DZ corpus, totaling 8.75 hours. The quality control of the output transcription is ensured within three stages: Pre-qualification of crowd, online filtering and in lab validation and revision. A baseline resource is used to evaluate both first stages. It consists on 5% of the targeted dataset transcribed by well trained transcribers. Our results confirm that the crowdsourcing solution is an effective approach for speech dialect transcription when we deal with under-resourced dialects. Before the validation of the well trained transcribers the accuracy of transcriptions reached 74.38. In addition, we present a set of best practices for crowdsourcing speech corpus transcription.

1 Introduction

The transcription task is the process of language representation in written form. The source can either be speech or a text in another writing system. Transcribed Speech Corpora are crucial for both developing and evaluating NLP systems such speech recognition. Such corpora have to respond to NLP communities expectations and allow to be exploited in machine learning based solutions.

For many languages, the state of the art of NLP systems have achieved accurate mature situation thanks to large and well designed corpora. On the other extreme, there are few corpora for Arabic (Surowiecki, 2004). Moreover, very few attempts have been considered for Algerian Arabic dialect (Mansour, 2013). Recently, KALAM'DZ corpus (Bougrine et al., 2017c) has been developed to cover the Arabic dialectal varieties of Algeria. This corpus is collected using web-based sources. Despite its important size, about more than 104 hours, very few annotations are available. In fact, only dialect and speaker annotations are provided. In this paper, we investigated a crowdsourcing-based approach to transcribe its speeches. Transcribing dialectal speeches is a very challenging task as dialects have no linguistic rules and a recourse to experts transcription is time and cost consuming.

The rest of this paper is organized as follows. In the next section, we review some related work that have dealt with speech corpus transcription for Arabic. In Section 3, we give brief glance to Algerian dialects linguistic properties. In Section 4 we describe the target corpus KALAM'DZ. Section 5 is dedicated to our crowdsourcing solution, in which we explain the designed crowdsourcing project and the deployed quality control strategy. A list of best practices based on these crowdsourcing experiments is compiled in Section 6.

2 Related Work

The existing speech corpora annotated by orthographic transcripts, could be classified into two major groups: Pre-transcribed and Post-transcribed speech corpus. In fact, pre-transcribed speech datasets are mostly collected by recording audio files directly from a set of text files prepared to be uttered by various speakers. While, post-transcribed corpora represent speech datasets collected from Internet or by recording sponta-

Corpus	Transcription Type	Language	Details
A-SpeechDB (2005)	Automatic + Manual Revision	MSA	20 hours of continuous speech, 30% of females and 70% of males
NetDC (2004)	Manual transcription by experts	MSA	Using Transcriber tool (1998),22 hours of broadcast news speech
Fisher (2004)	Manual transcription by experts	Levantine Arabic Dialect	250 hours of telephone conversations, Using AMADAT tool
CallHome (1997)	Manual transcription by experts	Egyptian Arabic Dialect	120 telephone conversations
SAAVB (2008)	Manual transcription by experts	Saudi Dialect	96 hours distributed among 60 947 files
STAC (2015)	Manual transcription by experts	Tunisian Dialect	5 hours, Using Praat tool (2001)
MD-ASPC (2013)	Pre-transcribed	MSA, Gulf, Egypt, Levantine	32 hours
Aljazeeras Corpus (2015)	Manual transcription using crowdsourcing	Egyptian, Levantine, Gulf, Maghrebi	Using CrowdFlower
Alg-Daridjah (2016)	Manually transcribed	Arabic Algerian dialects	4h30mn, 6213 utterances
MGB-2 (2016)	Manually transcribed	MSA, Egyptian, Levantine, Gulf, Maghrebi	1200 hours, 70% of the speech is MSA, and the rest is in different Dialectal Arabic
MGB-3 (2017)	Manually transcribed	Egyptian dialectal Arabic	16 hours extracted from 80 YouTube videos

Table 1: Details on Corpora Transcription Approaches

neous/random conversations. Thus, the second category requires a transcription process.

Regarding transcribing approaches, we can classify them according to the used method into two categories: manual and semi-automatic transcription. This latter way is usually used to transcribe a non-colloquial language such as English, French or Modern Standard Arabic (MSA). The transcription process is achieved into two passes. By the first pass, an Automatic Speech Recognition (ASR) is used in order to generate a rough transcription that is manually reviewed in the second pass. On the other hand, manual transcription, is divided according to the transcriber level into two classes: experts or non-expert (crowd).

In this literature review, we focus on transcribed Arabic Speech corpora and their related transcription process. Let us note that the major Arabic dialects corpora are available through the Linguistic Data Consortium (LDC) as well as European Language Resources Association (ELRA) catalogues. Table 1 summarizes the reviewed transcribed speech corpora.

A-SpeechDB[1] is an MSA speech database suited for training acoustic models. The transcriptions are automatically generated. In addition, each transcribed sentence is augmented by a manually revised version (2005). NetDC[2] (Network of Data Centers) (Choukri et al., 2004), is an Arabic broadcast news speech corpus. It is dedicated to the Modern Standard Arabic from the Middle East region. The corpus is transcribed manually using *Transcriber*[3] software (Barras et al., 1998).

As regards LDC Catalogue, we can review Fisher Levantine Arabic[4] and CallHome[5] Egyptian Arabic projects. Fisher Levantine Arabic corpus contains a collection of 2000 telephone calls of 9400 speakers from the Northern, Southern and Bedwi dialects of Levantine Arabic (Maamouri et al., 2004). The transcription was done by experts using Arabic Multi-Dialectal Transcription Tool (AMADAT). Besides, the colloquial corpus called CallHome Egyptian Arabic is transcribed manually by Gadalla et al. (1997).

Saudi Accented Arabic Voice Bank (SAAVB) is dedicated to Saudi Arabic dialect. It is a very rich corpus in terms of its speech sound content and speaker diversity within the Saudi Arabia (Alghamdi et al., 2008). The transcription was done manually by experts using their own transcription interface.

Zribi et al. (2015) have built a Spoken Tunisian Arabic Corpus (STAC). It is transcribed manually by experts using Praat[6] tool (Boersma and Van Heuven, 2001). The transcription was done respect to OTTA an Orthographic Transcription of Tunisan dialect (Zribi et al., 2013).

Almeman et al. (2013) have built a Multi-Dialect Arabic Speech Parallel Corpus (MD-

---

[1]Code product: ELRA catalogue ELRA-S0315.
[2]Codè product: ELRA catalogue ELRA-S0157

[3] www.transcriber.com
[4]LDC Catalogue No. LDC2007T04
[5]LDC Catalogue No. LDC97T19
[6]www.praat.org

ASPC). It contains written MSA prompts translated to dialects and then recorded. This one is an illustration of pre-transcribed speech corpora.

Wray et al. (2015) have transcribed a speech dataset collected from programs uploaded to Aljazeeras website. The transcription is performed by a crowdsourcing technique through the Crowd-Flower platform.

Bougrine et al. (2016) have build an Arabic speech corpus for Algerian dialects, by recording 109 native speakers from 17 different provinces. The transcription was done manually by authors.

The Arabic Multi-Genre Broadcast (MGB-2) Challenge used recorded programs from 10 years of Aljazeera Arabic TV channel (Ali et al., 2016; Khurana and Ali, 2016). These programs were manually captioned on their Arabic website[7] with no timing information (Ali et al., 2016). Thus, an alignment was required for the manual captioning in order to produce speech segments for training speech recognition (Khurana and Ali, 2016). Furthermore, the Arabic MGB-3 Challenge (Ali et al., 2017), unlike Arabic MGB-2 Challenge, emphasizes dialectal Arabic using a multi-genre collection of Egyptian YouTube videos. The speech transcription was done manually using Transcriber tool, without a strict guidelines for standardizing DA orthography.

We observed that most reviewed transcribed corpora did not use crowdsourcing for speech transcription. Plus, Algerian Dialect has not received any attention.

3 Algerian Dialects

Algeria is a large country, administratively divided into 48 provinces. Its first official language is Modern Standard Arabic (MSA). However, Algerian dialects are widely the predominant means of communication.

Algerian Arabic dialects resulted from two Arabization processes due to the expansion of Islam in the 7th and 11th centuries, which lead to the appropriation of the Arabic language by the Berber population. According to both Arabization processes, Algerian Arabic dialects can be divided into two major groups: Pre-Hilālī and Bedouin dialect. Both dialects are different by many linguistic features (Gibb et al., 1986; Caubet, 2000). Bougrine et al. (2017b) give a preliminary version

of an hierarchy structure for Arabic Algerian dialects (Figure 1).

Algerian dialect is considered among the most complex Arabic dialects with a lot of linguistic phenomena. For the current purpose, let us focus on some lexical, morphological and syntactic properties. Algerian DA vocabulary is mostly issued from MSA with many phonological alteration and many borrowed words from other languages, such as Turkish, French, Italian, and Spanish due to the deep colonization. In addition, code switching is omnipresent especially from French (Harrat et al., 2016; Saadane and Habash, 2015; Bougrine et al., 2017c).

Algerian DA morphology is similar to MSA excepts for some features. Some variations make Algerian DA morphology simpler than MSA. Essentially in some aspects of inflection and inclusion system, by eliminating several clitics and rules. Whereas negation in Algerian DA, including other Arabic dialects, is more complex than MSA. It is expressed by the circum-clitic negation ما and ش surrounding the verb with all its clitics or the indirect object pronouns (Harrat et al., 2016; Saadane and Habash, 2015).

As regards Algerian DA syntax, the words order of a declarative sentence is relatively flexible and all orders are allowed. The speaker begins the phrase with what he wants to highlight (Harrat et al., 2016). But the most commonly used order is the SVO order (Subject-Verb-Object) (Souag, 2006).

For more details on Algerian linguistic features refer to Embarki (2008); Saadane and Habash (2015); Harrat et al. (2016).

4 Targeted Corpus

Few speech corpora for Algerian Dialectal varieties are available (Bougrine et al., 2016, 2017c). For this study purpose, we have chosen KALAM'DZ corpus (Bougrine et al., 2017c). KALAM'DZ is a large speech corpus dedicated to Algerian Arabic dialectal varieties (Bougrine et al., 2017c). It covers eight major Arabic dialects spoken in Algeria. This corpus is collected from web sources namely YouTube, Online Radio stations, and TV channels. The size of the corpus is about 104 hours with 4881 speakers. All annotations are extracted from the related web sources metadata which are namely the ti-

---

[7] www.aljazeera.net

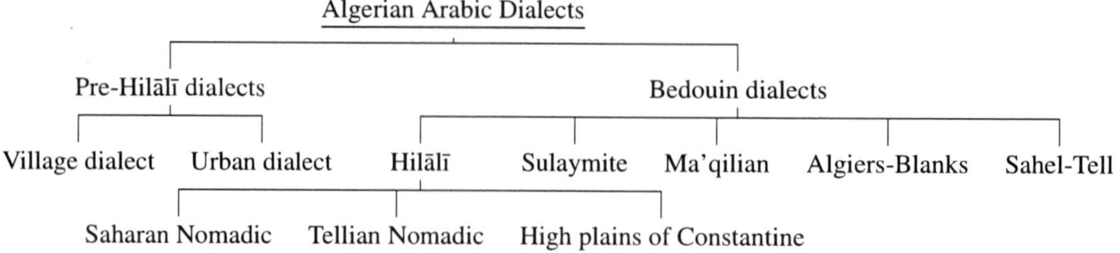

Figure 1: Hierarchy Structure for Algerian Dialects.

tle, category, location from where the source is posted, and the identity of the publisher. In addition, speaker gender is detected automatically by VoiceID tool. Concerning the dialect annotation, they are performed thanks to a crowdsourcing solution (Bougrine et al., 2017a).

In the current crowdsourcing task, we consider more than 8.75h hours to be transcribed. It contains 5122 speech segments with an average size of 6.2 seconds. Table 2 gives the distribution of speeches per Algerian dialect.

Sub-Dialect	# Segments	Duration (hour)
Hilālī-Saharan	1495	2.00
Sulaymite	1268	2.25
Algiers-blanks	1445	2.50
Ma'qilian	914	2.00
Total	**5122**	**8.75**

Table 2: Distribution of the Targeted Sample per Dialect.

5 Transcription Project

In order to transcribe the part of KALAM'DZ corpus, we have relied on crowdsourcing solution. To make these annotations scalable and of high quality, we have followed the crowdsourcing engineering process defined by Sabou et al. (2014). It suggests designing the system in four stages: project definition, data preparation, project execution, and data aggregation & evaluation. The project is baptized SPEECH2TEXT'DZ.

5.1 Project Definition

In this stage, we define the crowdsourcing task as well as the choice of crowdsourcing genre. As a basic task:" The contributor will be asked to listen to a short audio segment then write what they have heard exactly using Arabic letters and some shortcuts". The latter are deployed to facilitate the task and avoid contributor workload.

In order to make more interaction, users will be paid. Funding crowdsourcing projects is still not a common practice within the Algerian research community. Thus, we decided to go with a modest paid-for crowdsourcing. Where a user can collect points with a variable rate per task. These points can be used for mobile phones recharging.

5.2 Data Preparation

In this second stage, we build the project user and management interfaces. In order to collect crowdsourced transcripts, we have developed our own crowdsourcing platform[8] due to many constraints. Indeed, our targeted communities presence in crowdsourcing platforms as client is very modest. In addition to the administration profile, two roles are allowed: Transcriber and Well-Trained Transcriber (WTT). The *transcribers* are the crowd that can submit transcriptions. While WTT are users with more privileges. They are allowed to control transcribers' submissions. They are mainly lab members.

Concerning the transcriber interface, we have designed a form containing a text editor frame where the crowd transcribes the given speech segment, a set of shortcuts to help the crowd, and a link to a video that demonstrates the transcription guidelines. Our task is restricted mainly to Algerian users for that the form is written in Arabic. The management interface allows WTT validating and revising transcribers' output.

5.3 Project Execution

This is the main phase of any crowdsourcing project. In this step we performed three jobs: recruit contributors, train/retain contributors and manage/monitor crowdsourcing tasks.

---

[8]`www.speech2text-dz.com`

Publishing and advertising for attracting and retaining a large number of contributors is a key of success of any crowdsourcing system. We have decided to follow a simple strategy to advertise our platform. Social networks are always a good choice; we have gone with Facebook as preferable way for our targeted community.

Given that dialectal Arabic lacks a standardized orthography, we have defined an Orthographic Transcription Guideline that help to deliver a normalized transcription as much as possible. Our designed guideline is inspired from Saadane and Habash (2015) and Wray et al. (2015). In fact, we have designed some rules based on the Conventional Orthography for Dialectal Arabic (CODA) due to Habash et al. (2012) and adapted for Algerian dialect by Saadane and Habash (2015). Some other rules are added following the recommendations for crowdsourcing Arabic speech transcription due to Wray et al. (2015). This guideline is delivered through a video demonstration. Among these rules:

- The transcription is done in Arabic Script.

- To have a normalized spelling, the crowd has to transcribe colloquial words as close as possible to appropriate MSA spelling.

- In order to facilitate future potential Part-Of-Speech (POS) tagging task; foreign words, named entities, places and proper names should be transliterated in Arabic and guarded by some predefined tags. For example: [علم : مكان الجزائر] ([Named Entity: Place Algeria]) is used to tag that [الجزائر] is a proper noun indicating Algeria country.

- For more uniform transcription, a given spoken form is always written the same way.

- To be more faithful when transcribing; all non-speech sounds should be transcribed. For instance music, noise, breathing, laughs, they have to use respectively the predefined tags [موسيقى] [ضجيج] [تنفس] [ضحك].

Quality Control

A front-end verification process makes sure that transcribers respect the given guideline. In fact, two JavaScript functions are deployed, one function forces transcribers to type using only Arabic letters, and the second function to make sure that no spamming data are collected by disabling Copy/Paste functionality.

In order to ensure the quality control of the output transcriptions, we have acted in three stages: *Transcriber Pre-qualification*, *Online Filtering*, and *WTT revision*.

For the two first stages, we use an in lab transcripts as a *Baseline Resource* (BR) coupled with a mechanism of *Transcriber Trusting*. BR resource contains 256 transcribed utterances which represents 5% of the targeted sample. In brief, the mechanism works as follows. Initially, an arbitrary score of 50% is assigned to any new transcriber. This score changes every time that the transcriber has to pass a trusting control by means of transcribing a speech segment belonging to BR. In fact, his transcript is confronted to the corresponding BR one. The comparison is done by means of Levenshtein distance and similar tests.

Now, let us explain how the control quality is performed:

- Within the *Pre-qualification* stage, the transcriber should go through a trust test. In fact, they have to perform 5 successful transcripts. Then, he will be allowed working. Otherwise the transcriber is invited to check the guideline once again, and every transcriber has 3 attempts before suspending their account.

- Once trusted, this is not for ever, the *Online Filtering* stage is activated. In fact, a verification process is launched after every 5 submitted transcripts. Where the system ask the transcriber to transcribe one speech among BR. Here also users are invited to check the guideline once again, if their scores are lowered. Users with score higher than or equal to 70% will be considered as a trusted transcriber so he will be tested every 10 transcriptions instead of 5.

- In parallel, the *WTT revision* step is launched. It is added to get more accurate transcriptions. In fact, the well trained transcribers, mainly the authors and lab members, reviewed the transcriptions submitted by users with score less than 70%. If the task needs a bit revision they performed it. Otherwise, they list the task again. Figure 2 shows WTT interface to validate/revise transcriptions.

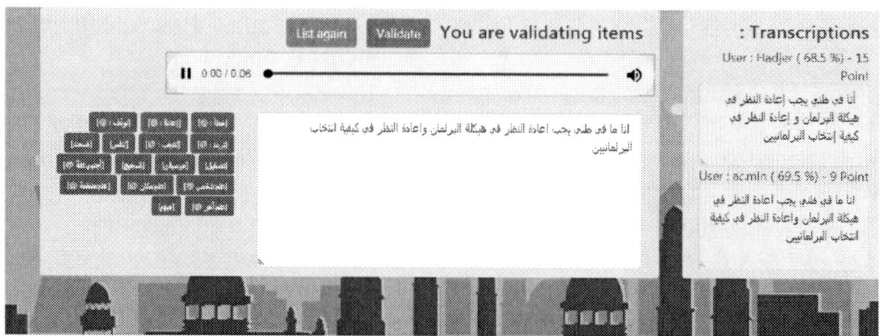

Figure 2: WTT Review and Validate Transcriptions Page

5.4 Project Data Evaluation and Aggregation

SPEECH2TEXT'DZ project was launched on May 2018. Contributors were invited to participate.

Total duration	51 Days
Number of crowd	208
Number of transcription	5335
Number of audio transcribed twice	277
Number of audio transcribed more than twice	312
Average Transcriptions per user	25.65
Guideline video views per day	33
Average Transcription time	3min 21s

Table 3: Global Statistics about the Project Execution.

After 51 days of web application hosting, more than 208 users registered. According to Google Analytics tool and our platform administration page we have got some statistics and details regarding user participation and behaviors. Table 3 gives global statistics about the project execution. In average a time of 3min 21s is needed for one transcription. This fact, shows that the transcription task is very challenging despite that utterance size is about 6.2s in average. This is also confirmed by the fact that in average a user transcribes less than 26 speeches. .

In order to ensure transcription quality, all works took less than 20 seconds are treated as malicious work and been consequently eliminated. Moreover and as explained, WTT can validate and review users transcriptions and list a task again if it is needed.

For evaluating the crowdsourcing solution, we consider the transcription quality by the crowd transcribers before the WTT revision stage. Table 4 shows the distribution of users according to their achieved scores and the related number of transcribed utterances.

Scores show that the well transcribed utterances were performed by less than 21 crowds. While the 73 transcribers reached a score between 60% and 80%.

The overall precision Pr achieved is computed using the following formula:

$$Pr = \frac{\sum_{i=1}^{NT} \#Utt_i * Score_i}{N}$$

Where N is the total number of transcribed utterances, NT the number of transcribers, $\#Utt_i$ and $Score_i$ are respectively, the number of transcribed utterances and the average score of a user i. Accordingly, we have got a precision about 74.38%. which can be considered as an acceptable result according to the challenging dialect transcription task.

Let us mention that after the WTT revision step all the transcription are considered as well transcribed according to the defined guideline.

Figure 3 illustrates a sample of transcriptions confronted to the well-trained transcribers' ones. We have observed that the most common mistakes and errors are due to the misunderstanding of guideline or also from the fact that users ignore watching the video tutorial that demonstrates how to transcribe and use the platform. Also some users misuse the defined tags, for example instead of using the tag [تردد] they used [تعجب].

%	55 <	55–60	60–70	70–80	> 80
# Users	33	81	39	34	21
# Transcribed Utterances	1136	1011	1186	936	1086

Table 4: Users Score Quality Rates and Transcriptions Distribution by Score.

Expert	بينما الواقع نتاع الرياضة [تردد] واش نقلك ؟ شباب طموح جدا جدا داير دورة رياضية
Crowd	بينما لواقع تاع رياض وشن نقلك شباب طموح جدا [عادة : جداً] دار دورة رياضا
Crowd	بينما لواقع نتاع رياضا واشن نقلك شباب طموح جدا [إعادة] دير دورة رياضا
Expert	كاين بزاف مواطنين مازالو ينيروا على الشموع [صحيح]
Crowd	كاينة بزاف مواطنين مزالو ينيرو على شموع
Crowd	كاينا بزاف مواطنين مزلو ينرو على شمع
Expert	[تردد : ال] الموال راه عندو مصاريف يصرفها على هذي الشاه ما محي يلحقها لوقت العيد حتان !
Crowd	الموال راه عندو مصاريف يصرفها على هذي الشاه ما محي يلحقها لوقت العيد حتى
Crowd	[تردد : ال] الموال راه عندو مصاريف يصرفها على هذي الشاه ما محي يلحقها لوقت العيد [توقف : حتان]

Figure 3: A Sample of Expert vs. Crowd Transcriptions.

6 Best Practices

Based on the experiments of this crowdsourcing-based solution and the resented results, we have dedicated some rules for a good validation of dialect transcription :

- Dialect speech transcription is a hard task, for that the size of the speech segments must be managed.

- Daily observation must be done to check the progress of completed tasks to recall new users when it needed.

- A part of quality control must be implemented on the project to avoid malicious work and get accurate result.

- The online filtering stage is very important to ensure quality control and avoid useless workload.

- The time of launching calls must be considered to get a large participation.

7 Conclusion and Future Work

For many researchers and institutions, crowdsourcing has become a popular method in NLP for lowering time and cost comparing to expert requirements. In this paper, we have investigated a paid crowdsourcing solution in order to transcribe a part of the speech utterances of KALAM'DZ corpus. We have followed two strategies to ensure the control quality of users transcriptions. First a predefined guideline is provided in order to help and train the crowd to deliver as normalized transcriptions as possible. The second control quality strategy is ensured using three control stages: Pre-qualification of transcribers, online filtering and revision step.

The results show that using crowdsourcing with a well tuned quality control mechanisms is an effective way for speech dialect transcription. In fact, the reached transcription results shows that the precision of the transcripts is more than 74.38% according to a baseline resource.

In addition, we have determined a list of best practices for crowdsourcing-based solutions for corpus transcription.

This crowdsourcing-based solution has proved its accuracy, in an ongoing work we are enlarging the dataset to be transcribed by improving the crowd recruitment strategy.

As future work, we plan to extend the usage of crowdsourcing in order to cover further annotation and validation to KALAM'DZ corpus such start POS tagging the sentences to build a treebank-like resource.

References

Mansour Alghamdi, Fayez Alhargan, Mohammed Alkanhal, Ashraf Alkhairy, Munir Eldesouki, and Ammar Alenazi. 2008. Saudi Accented Arabic Voice Bank. *Journal of King Saud University - Computer and Information Sciences*, 20:45–64.

Ahmed Ali, Peter Bell, James Glass, Yacine Messaoui, Hamdy Mubarak, Steve Renals, and Yifan Zhang. 2016. The MGB-2 Challenge: Arabic Multi-Dialect Broadcast Media Recognition. In *2016 IEEE Spoken Language Technology Workshop (SLT)*, pages 279–284. IEEE.

Ahmed Ali, Stephan Vogel, and Steve Renals. 2017. Speech Recognition Challenge in the Wild: Arabic

MGB-3. In *2017 IEEE Automatic Speech Recognition and Understanding Workshop (ASRU)*, pages 316–322. IEEE.

Khalid Almeman, Mark Lee, and Ali Abdulrahman Almiman. 2013. Multi Dialect Arabic Speech Parallel Corpora. In *2013 1st International Conference on Communications, Signal Processing, and their Applications (ICCSPA)*, pages 1–6. IEEE.

Claude Barras, Edouard Geoffrois, Zhibiao Wu, and Mark Liberman. 1998. Transcriber: a Free Tool for Segmenting, Labeling and Transcribing Speech. In *First international conference on language resources and evaluation (LREC)*, pages 1373–1376.

Paul Boersma and Vincent Van Heuven. 2001. Speak and unSpeak with PRAAT. *Glot International*, 5(9/10):341–347.

Soumia Bougrine, Hadda Cherroun, and Ahmed Abdelali. 2017a. Altruistic Crowdsourcing for Arabic Speech Corpus Annotation. *Procedia Computer Science*, 117:137 – 144.

Soumia Bougrine, Hadda Cherroun, and Djelloul Ziadi. 2017b. Hierarchical Classification for Spoken Arabic Dialect Identification using Prosody: Case of Algerian Dialects. *CoRR*, abs/1703.10065.

Soumia Bougrine, Hadda Cherroun, Djelloul Ziadi, Abdallah Lakhdari, and Aicha Chorana. 2016. Toward a Rich Arabic Speech Parallel Corpus for Algerian sub-Dialects. In *The 2nd Workshop on Arabic Corpora and Processing Tools 2016 Theme: Social Media*, pages 2–10. European Language Resources Association (ELRA).

Soumia Bougrine, Aicha Chorana, Abdallah Lakhdari, and Hadda Cherroun. 2017c. Toward a Web-based Speech Corpus for Algerian Arabic Dialectal Varieties. In *Proceedings of the Third Arabic Natural Language Processing Workshop*, pages 138–146. Association for Computational Linguistics.

Dominique Caubet. 2000. Questionnaire de dialectologie du Maghreb (d'après les travaux de W. Marçais, M. Cohen, GS Colin, J. Cantineau, D. Cohen, Ph. Marçais, S. Lévy, etc.). *Estudios de Dialectología Norteafricana y Andalusí (EDNA)*, 5:73–92.

Khalid Choukri, Mahtab Nikkhou, and Niklas Paulsson. 2004. Network of data centres (NetDC): BNSC - an Arabic broadcast news speech corpus. In *Proceedings of the Fourth International Conference on Language Resources and Evaluation (LREC'04)*, pages 889–892. European Language Resources Association (ELRA).

European Language Resources Association (ELRA). 2005. A-SpeechDB ID: ELRA-S0315. `http://catalog.elra.info/en-us/repository/browse/ELRA-S0315/`. Accessed: 2018-10-30.

Mohamed Embarki. 2008. Les dialectes arabes modernes : état et nouvelles perspectives pour la classification géo-sociologique. *Arabica*, 55(5):583–604.

Hassan Gadalla, Hanaa Kilany, Howaida Arram, Ashraf Yacoub, Alaa El-Habashi, Amr Shalaby, Krisjanis Karins, Everett Rowson, Robert MacIntyre, Paul Kingsbury, David Graff, and Cynthia McLemore. 1997. CALLHOME Egyptian Arabic Transcripts. *Linguistic Data Consortium, Philadelphia.*

Hamilton Alexander Rosskeen Gibb, Johannes Hendrik Kramers, Évariste Lévi-Provençal, Bernard Lewis, Charles Pellat, Joseph Schacht, et al. 1986. *The Encyclopaedia of Islam*, new edition, volume 1, chapter Algeria. E. J. Brill, Leiden.

Nizar Habash, Mona Diab, and Owen Rambow. 2012. Conventional Orthography for Dialectal Arabic. In *Proceedings of the Language Resources and Evaluation Conference (LREC), Istanbul*, pages 711–718. European Language Resources Association (ELRA).

Salima Harrat, Karima Meftouh, Mourad Abbas, Khaled-Walid Hidouci, and Kamel Smaili. 2016. An Algerian dialect: Study and Resources. *International journal of advanced computer science and applications (IJACSA)*, 7(3):384–396.

Sameer Khurana and Ahmed Ali. 2016. QCRI advanced transcription system (QATS) for the Arabic Multi-Dialect Broadcast media recognition: MGB-2 challenge. In *2016 IEEE Spoken Language Technology Workshop (SLT)*, pages 292–298. IEEE.

Mohamed Maamouri, Tim Buckwalter, and Christopher Cieri. 2004. Dialectal Arabic Telephone Speech Corpus: Principles, Tool Design, and Transcription Conventions. In *NEMLAR International Conference on Arabic Language Resources and Tools, Cairo*, pages 22–23. Linguistic Data Consortium (LDC).

Mohamed Abdelmageed Mansour. 2013. The Absence of Arabic Corpus Linguistics: A Call for Creating an Arabic National Corpus. *International Journal of Humanities and Social Science*, 3(12):81–90.

Houda Saadane and Nizar Habash. 2015. A Conventional Orthography for Algerian Arabic. In *Proceedings of the Second Workshop on Arabic Natural Language Processing*, pages 69–79. Association for Computational Linguistics.

Marta Sabou, Kalina Bontcheva, Leon Derczynski, and Arno Scharl. 2014. Corpus Annotation through Crowdsourcing: Towards Best Practice Guidelines. In *Proceedings of the Ninth International Conference on Language Resources and Evaluation (LREC'14)*, pages 859–866. European Language Resources Association (ELRA).

Mostafa Lameen Souag. 2006. *Explorations in the Syntactic Cartography of Algerian Arabic*. Ph.D. thesis, University of London, School of Oriental and African Studies, London.

James Surowiecki. 2004. *The wisdom of crowds*, first edition. Anchor Books, New York.

Samantha Wray, Hamdy Mubarak, and Ahmed Ali. 2015. Best Practices for Crowdsourcing Dialectal Arabic Speech Transcription. In *Proceedings of the Second Workshop on Arabic Natural Language Processing*, pages 99–107. Association for Computational Linguistics.

Inès Zribi, Mariem Ellouze, Lamia Hadrich Belguith, and Philippe Blache. 2015. Spoken Tunisian Arabic Corpus "STAC": Transcription and Annotation. *Research in computing science*, 90:123–135.

Inès Zribi, Marwa Graja, Mariem Ellouze Khmekhem, Maher Jaoua, and Lamia Hadrich Belguith. 2013. Orthographic Transcription for Spoken Tunisian Arabic. In *International Conference on Intelligent Text Processing and Computational Linguistics*, pages 153–163. Springer-Verlag Berlin Heidelberg.

Sample Size in Arabic Authorship Verification

Hossam Ahmed

Leiden University Institute for Area Studies
Witte Singel 25, 2311 BZ, Leiden, The Netherlands
`h.i.a.a.ahmed@hum.leidenuniv.nl`

Abstract

Authorship Verification aims at identifying whether a document of questionable authorship is created by a specific author, given a number of documents known to have been written by that author. This type of authorship analysis uses feature engineering of feature sets extracted from large documents. Given the nonlinear morphology and flexible syntax of Arabic, feature extraction in large Arabic texts requires complex preprocessing. The requirement of large training and testing documents is also impractical for domains where large documents are available in print, given the scarcity of reliable Arabic OCR. This problem is approached by investigating the effectiveness of using an author profiling-based approach on a small set of shorter documents. The findings show that it is possible to outperform the state-of-the-art authorship verification method by using a small set of training documents. It is also found that an increase in the size of the training or testing corpus does not correlate with improving the accuracy of the authorship verification method.

1   Introduction

Authorship Verification (AV) is a type of authorship analysis task where a document of questionable attribution is judged as to whether it is written by a certain author, given a number of documents known to be written by that author. AV tasks are often compared to Authorship Attribution (AA) tasks, where a document of unknown attribution is attributed to one of a number of candidate authors. AV has a number of applications in forensic linguistics and literary studies in areas where an AA task cannot answer the problem at hand. For example, while an AA task is appropriate in some cases of plagiarism detection, an AV task can better suite a situation where the text is not written by any of the candidate authors, or when there is only one candidate author.

This paper examines the effect of small sample size on the accuracy of AV tasks. Specifically, it addresses the following question: is it possible to use small testing and training datasets without significant accuracy sacrifices in an Arabic AV task? Recent developments in AV (and AA) have achieved high rates of accuracy using various Machine Learning (ML) techniques and feature configurations. Current research (c.f. section 2) achieves accurate AV results using relatively large training and testing corpora. A smaller training and/or testing set is, of course, advantageous. For one thing, a smaller data size allows for more efficient processing. For another, in real-life situations, there may not be plenty of large texts available for the AV task. Either the question document or the authentic corpus could be of small size. In a situation specific to Arabic literary studies, a great deal of documents is only available in non-machine readable format, and in typeface that does not allow for efficient OCR. Digitizing large texts for the purpose of automatic AV is, then, an unduly expensive procedure. In this paper I examine the effects of using a small corpus for training or testing documents on the accuracy of predicting AV in different domains in Modern Standard Arabic (MSA) through a number of AV experiments.

This paper is organized as follows: section 2 outlines a brief review of literature on AV, Arabic AV and AA, and how sample size is handled in the relevant literature. Section 3 describes the corpus and features used in the experiments. Section 4 describes the verification method. Section 5 describes the procedure of the two experiments conducted. Section 6 outlines the results and I discuss their implications in 7. Section 8 is the conclusion.

2 Related Work

Statistical methods in AA have been the subject of much recent research. Ouamour and Sayoud (2013) show that ML methods (specifically SVM) perform better than purely statistical AA tasks. Howedi and Mohd (2014) and Altheneyan and Menai (2014) use naïve Bayes to test AA in Classical Arabic texts. Other ML algorithms used vary from Linear Discriminant Analysis (LDA) (Shaker, 2012) to Naive Bayes. Altakrori et al. (2018) examine a variety of ML algorithms (Naive Bayes, SVM, Decision Trees, Random Forests, and cosine distance) to examine Arabic AA in Twitter data. In terms of feature selection, successful features used include rare word unigrams (Ouamour and Sayoud, 2013), function words (Shaker, 2012), and function word and punctuation (García-Barrero et al., 2013). Altakrori et al. (2018) examine a large variety of features (character, word, and sentence counts; average word and sentence lengths, ratios of characters, short words, blank lines; punctuation, and diacritics; as well as function words).

As far as AA is concerned, a survey of Arabic AA by Ouamour and Sayoud (2018) shows that Manhattan Distance and SMO-SVM give best accuracies. It has been possible to achieve high accuracy using small text datasets. García-Barrero et al. (2013) use 650-word document samples written in MSA and Ouamour and Sayoud (2018) use 10 books (10 extracts each) of 550 average word length, achieving 90% accuracy using Manhattan Distance.

2.1 Authorship Verification in Arabic

While AA and AV share much of task characteristics, the essential difference is the lack of negative evidence. AA is essentially a classification problem, where a Question Document is put in the class of the author to which it is most similar. In AV, however, available data comes from only one author. Although this scenario is more likely to happen in real-world applications (e.g. a section of a text being added from another source), it is much more difficult to characterize and solve than an AA problem. Available data is only a corpus of work by a single author, and a single document of questionable attribution to that author (Stamatatos, 2009).

To handle the challenge of the absence of negative evidence, two approaches are generally followed (Halvani et al., 2017). In the Imposter Method, a supplementary dataset of documents not written by the same author as the authentic documents, converting the problem into an AA problem. Altakrori et al. (2018) implicitly follow this approach for Arabic Twitter posts. Although their stated scenario is that of law enforcement, they frame the AV problem as determining the true author of tweets from a list of suspects. It is likely in that context that law enforcement needs to determine the attribution of a tweet to a single individual one at a time, as the true author may not be any of the suspects. The second approach is Author Profiling. In that approach, features form documents of known authorship are extracted and used to calculate a profile of the author. The question document is then tested against that profile. If it is similar to the profile beyond a certain threshold, it is deemed authentic. Successful similarity measures in AV include Manhattan Distance (Halvani et al., 2016; Burrows, 2002), or compression-based distance (Halvani et al., 2017). Halvani et al. (ibid) note that the second approach is more computationally efficient, as only the dataset of known documents is processed. Ahmed (2017) argues that the performance of imposter-based systems relies on the selection of the supplementary dataset, which can be contentious. To determine a similarity threshold, Halvani et al., (2017; 2016) use Equal Error Rate (ERR) for English (Halvani et al., 2017) and a number of other languages (Halvani et al., 2016), ERR is a similarity value where false positives and false negatives are equal. False positives are determined from a supplementary set of negative data. For the English, Spanish, and Greek, Jankowska et al. (2014) use the area under ROC curve to determine the threshold. For Arabic, Ahmed (2018, 2017) uses a simpler Gaussian curve and dispenses with supplementary negative data altogether.

There has been limited research on Arabic AV, all of which uses author profiling techniques and datasets of varied length. Elewa (2018) examines AV of disputed Hadith (sayings of Prophet Mohammed) as related to the distribution of lexical features (token length, token-type ratio, n least/most common tokens). It uses training and testing sets of 20 hadiths each, averaging about 150 words each. With such small text size, the author uses multivariate analysis to manually notice relations rather than Machine Learning. Ahmed (2018) uses an array of feature n-grams (tokens, stems, trilateral roots, Part-of-Speech tags, diacritics), a similarity measure based on Manhattan Distance (Burrows, 2002), and a similarity threshold based on simple probability to investigate their use in AV in Classical Arabic on a small corpus with large document sizes (11,000 – 400,000 tokens). Although the model achieves high accuracy (87.1%), the size of the training and testing documents, as well as the type of preprocessing needed to extract the best performing feature (stem bigrams) make the task computationally expensive and unsuitable for online processing. Furthermore, such huge document size in the training corpus, while may be realistic for Classical Arabic heritage work, is uncommon in modern Arabic. All the studies above are concerned with Classical Arabic. This is the first study to investigate Modern Standard Arabic genres.

3 Corpus

To test the accuracy of an AV task in Modern Standard Arabic (MSA) with small sample sizes, a corpus taken from a number of domains is compiled. Five MSA domains are selected: fiction, nonfiction, economics, politics, and opinion columns. For each domain, texts written by 10 authors are used for training and testing. Table 1 details the composition of the corpus.

Choice of the authors and text has been governed by copyright considerations, as well as the availability of a sufficient number of texts produced by the same author to allow for training and testing at different sample sizes. Whenever possible, authors coming from the same country (Egypt) have been selected to control for cross-dialectal variation.

3.1 Feature Selection

To establish a suitable baseline for evaluation, the same features used in Ahmed (2018) have been selected. It is also the highest performing approach we are aware of for Arabic AV (albeit Classical Arabic, as opposed to MSA in this experiment). Classical Arabic and Modern Standard Arabic share essentially the same grammar (syntax and

Author	Documents	Source
Fiction		
Ali Al-Jaarim	10	
Abdul Aziz Baraka Sakin	10	
Nicola Haddaad	10	
Nawaal Al-Saadaawi	10	Hindawi Foundation repository `www.hindawi.org`
Georgi Zidaan	10	
Non-fiction		
Abbas Al-Aqqaad	11	
Ismail Mazhar	10	
Salama Moussa	10	
Fouad Zakareyya	10	
Zaki Naguib Mahmoud	10	
Economics		
Musbah Qutb	10	`www.almasryalyoum.com`
Mohammed Abd Elaal	10	
Bissan Kassab	10	`www.madamasr.com`
Waad Ahmed	10	
Yumn Hamaqi	10	`www.ik.ahram.org.eg`
Politics		
Alaa Al-Aswani	10	`www.dw.com`
Wael Al-Semari	10	`www.youm7.com`
Danadarawy Al-Hawari	10	`www.youm7.com`
Belal Fadl	11	`www.alaraby.co.uk`
Salma Hussein	10	`www.shorouknews.com`
Columnists		
Ashraf Al-Barbari	11	
Emad Eldin Hussein	10	
Fatima Ramadan	10	`www.shorouknews.com`
Mostafa Kamel El Sayyed	10	
Sara Khorshid	10	
Total	**253**	

Table 1: Corpus used.

morphology). However, hundreds of years of language change have contributed to a greatly expanded lexicon. Additionally, it does not follow naturally that MSA authors make the same choices when it comes to selecting among available structures (e.g. using Verb-first vs. noun-first sentence types). However, as this is the best

Domain	Avg. size
Columnists	802
Economics	820
Fiction	1,159
Nonfiction	1,108
Politics	850

Table 2: average document size per domain.

available benchmark available for Arabic, it allows for an acceptable starting point.

A secondary, yet welcome, information that this experiment can provide is identify whether an AV technique used in Classical Arabic is also applicable to MSA, which may attest to studies related to language change and historical linguistics.

Specifically, the feature set used in this paper consists of n-grams (n = 1 − 4) of the following features:

- **Token**: individual words separated by spaces. They may include proclitics and enclitics.

- **Stem**: a token without proclitics or enclitics.

- **Root**: the triliteral root from which the word is derived.

- **Diacritics**: each token is vocalized, then letter characters are removed.

- **Part of Speech**: each document is tagged for POS using MADAMIRA tagset (Pasha et al., 2014).

3.2 Preprocessing and Feature Extraction

For pre-processing, documents are downloaded as plain text (UTF-8 encoding). Fiction and non-fiction documents are downloaded as epub and converted to plain text. Front matter of each document is removed (title, author name, name and URL of the web site, etc.). Documents longer than 1,000 words are truncated. Documents consisting of fewer than 1,000 words are used in their entirety. Table 2 shows average document size per domain. For books (fiction and non-fiction), a slice of 1,000 words is taken from the middle of each book. This decision is taken to avoid the possibility of repeated sections typical of a given author across works (for example, a repeated preface in non-fiction, or list of characters in a work of fiction). White spaces are normalized to single space, and punctuation marks are removed.

For feature extraction, tokens are defined as strings of characters separated by space. Roots, POS tags, and diacritics are generated using MADAMIRA version 2.1 with default settings. MADAMIRA output files are processed using Regular Expressions to extract relevant features to separate plain-text files.

4 Method

The purpose of this paper is to determine the effect of document size on the accuracy of AV tasks. To do so, two experiments are carried out. The first experiment uses the dataset in its entirety to determine which specific feature n-gram ensembles yield best results (i.e. highest accuracy) for each of the five domains. This experiment is motivated by the fact that the feature set used in Ahmed (2018) is tested in Classical Arabic, and should not be taken for granted that the same feature configuration will perform equally well in MSA, or similarly across genres. The second experiment uses the best performing feature for each domain and examines the change in AV accuracy with progressively smaller training set size. Linear regression analysis of the results of each experiment is conducted to estimate whether there is correlation between document or corpus size and accuracy.

4.1 Verification Method

Each verification task is divided into a number of problems. Each problem consists of a question document and a set of known documents.

In the training step, the known documents are used to calculate a similarity threshold. In the testing step, similarity between the question document and the training set is calculated. The question document is deemed authentic if its similarity value is higher than the threshold. The verification method is similar to that used in Ahmed (2018), with the difference that the current experiment uses the entire set of features, not only the most frequent n%.

4.2 Training, testing, and evaluation

For each domain, input to the training phase is a set of strings representing the feature in question known to be attributed to a given author. N-grams of appropriate value for n are generated using NLTK (Bird et al., 2009), and relative (normalized) frequencies of the features described in the section

Feature Selection are calculated, also using NLTK. Output of the training phase is a similarity value threshold for an authentic document.

Similarity is calculated using Manhattan Distance between a document X and a corpus of known documents Y:

$$dist(X,Y) = \sum_{j=1}^{n} |X_j - Y_j| \quad (1)$$

where X_j and Y_j are the normalized frequencies of feature j. Distance is then converted into a similarity score:

$$Sim(X,Y) = \frac{1}{dist(X,Y)} \quad (2)$$

Similarity Threshold θ is calculated by determining Sim for each document in the training set in relation to the reset of the training documents, creating a confidence interval for all the training documents. θ is then calculated as the upper bound of the interval at $p<0.005$.

Testing and evaluation are done by calculating *Sim* for each test document. Accuracy is calculated as the number of correct answers divided by the total number of documents tested.

Although the aim of this paper is to evaluate the effectiveness of using different sample sizes, a task that essentially does not require a baseline, an accuracy of 87.1% will be used as a guiding baseline. This accuracy is the best accuracy achieved in the relevant literature (Ahmed, 2018), albeit coming from a different register (MSA).

5 Experiments

5.1 Experiment 1: Best performing ensembles

In order to be able to plot AV accuracies against document size, it is necessary to identify best performing feature ensemble (feature + ngram). Although previous literature (Ahmed, 2018) suggests that stem bigrams are the most successful feature combinations, it should not be taken for granted that the feature combination that has been successful for Classical Arabic is also the best performer across domains in MSA.

To select the best performing feature-n-gram ensemble for each domain, the AV task described in the previous section is implemented on the full size of the corpus. For each domain, the accuracy of each feature ensemble is evaluated using the

Domain	Features	Accuracy
Columnists	Stem bigrams	80%
	Token unigrams	80%
	Diacritic unigram	80%
Economics	Root bigrams	76.8%
Fiction	Diacritic bigrams	84%
Nonfiction	Stem unigrams	81.57%
Politics	Token unigrams	84.53%

Table 3: Best performing feature ensemble per domain.

leave-one-out method. Table 3 shows the best performing feature combination for each domain.

The results of experiment 1 show that with a test document size averaging 850 – 1000 tokens, best performing features vary by MSA domain. None of the domains achieved an accuracy close to the baseline, although the two domains that score lowest accuracy (economics and columnists) have the lowest document average size.

5.2 Experiment 2: Document Size Effects

There are three factors in play for determining size effects in AV: the size of the question document, the number of training documents, and the size of the training set overall. Experiment 2 examines all three variables.

For Experiment 2, the training and testing procedure for Experiment 1 is replicated 6 times, using only the highest performing features as indicated in Experiment 1, and with varying sizes of the training set $S \in \{5, 6, 7, 8, 9, 10\}$ documents. The result of the experiment is an ordered set (Q, T, R), where Q is the size of the question document, T is the size of the combined training set, and R (1, 0) is the result of the verification process. R = 1 if the correct prediction is made, and R = 0 if an incorrect prediction is made. Accuracy is calculated for values of Q in intervals demarked by $Q \in \{0, 500, 600, 700, 800, 900, 1000, 1100, 1200\}$, and for $T \in \{0, 5000, 6000, 7000, 7500, 8000, 8500, 9000, 11000\}$. Two datapoints are excluded (fiction T = (8000, 8500) and nonfiction T = (7000, 7500)) as outliers. Each of the two datapoints consist of one document and have R = 0%. Linear regression analysis between accuracy and relevant size variable is then conducted using SPSS.

Domain	Features	Training set (documents)	Accuracy
Columnists	Stem bigrams	5	**87.84%**
		6	87.45%
		7	85.10%
		8	84.71%
		9	81.57%
		10	80.00%
Economics	Root bigrams	5	**90.00%**
		6	88.00%
		7	86.00%
		8	84.00%
		9	81.20%
		10	78.40%
Fiction	Diacritic bigrams	5	**89.20%**
		6	86.80%
		7	84.80%
		8	84.00%
		9	83.00%
		10	84.00%
Nonfiction	Stem unigrams	5	**89.80%**
		6	87.84%
		7	87.45%
		8	84.71%
		9	83.14%
		10	81.57%
Politics	Token unigrams	5	**90.59%**
		6	87.06%
		7	85.49%
		8	85.49%
		9	83.92%
		10	83.53%
Baseline	**Stem bigrams**	**19**	**87.1%**

Table 4: Best performing feature ensemble per domain.

6   Results

Table 4 shows the results of testing the verification method using the leave-one-out method on a training corpus of 5 – 10 documents, and using the best-performance features identified in Experiment 1. In all five domains, the verification method performs best at S = 5 training documents. Regression Analysis shows a strong correlation coefficient of -0.931, with p<0.005 (c.f. Figure 1).

Regression analysis to identify correlation between the accuracy of the verification method and the total size of the training set in tokens is conducted. As Figure 2 shows, there is a moderate positive correlation of 0.492, with p<0.05 (p = 0.003).

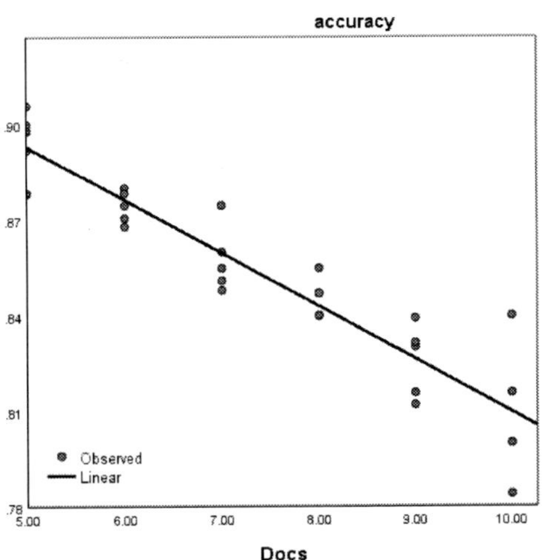

Figure 1: Number of training docs – accuracy correlation.

Regression analysis between accuracy of the verification method and the size of the test document in tokens does not show any significant correlation between the two variables (coefficient of correlation = 0.132, p = 0.48).

7   Discussion

The results of Experiment 2 show that a training set with a smaller number of documents outperforms one with a larger number of documents.

In every domain, a training set of five authentic documents outperforms the baseline of 87.1% in classical Arabic. This finding is consistent with Altakrori et al.'s (2018) observation for AA that fewer candidate authors generally contribute to better performance. The finding in this paper extends the scope of that statement to Modern Standard Arabic AV number of training documents.

Another informative finding of the experiment is the lack of significant correlation between the size of the question document and AV task performance. The implication of this finding in Digital Humanities and literary studies is that if the suspect document is an entire book, there is no need to digitize the whole document. This is especially useful for Arabic given the vast amount of print resources, and lack of reliable affordable OCR.

A rather unexpected result from Experiment 2 is the positive correlation between training set size in

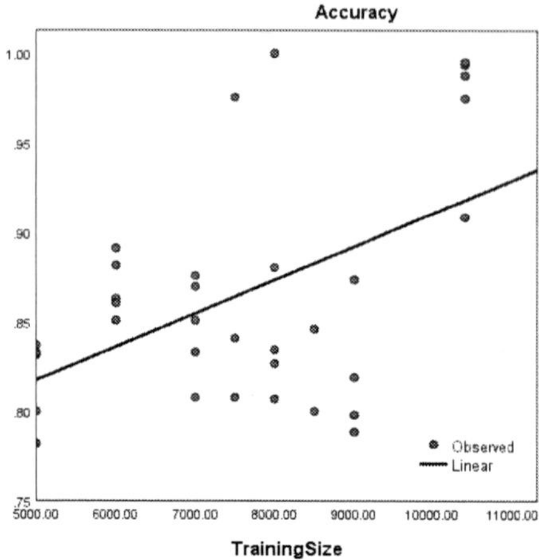

Figure 2:   Training set size – accuracy correlation.

tokens on the one hand and accuracy on the other. If there is significant strong negative correlation between the number of documents in the training set, one would expect negative or no correlation between the sum of those training documents and accuracy. One could rule this result out as coincidence, but this is unlikely, given a low p-value (0.003). A possible explanation for this result could be the difference in average document size of the fiction and nonfiction corpora. The higher average document size in these two domains means that all the observations related to those two domains are clustered towards the upper bound of the word count, including their highest accuracy observations; the results with fewer training documents (e.g. S = 5) for fiction and non-fiction are in the same band for larger S for other domains. Indeed, this seems to be the case. When the regression analysis is repeated excluding measurements for fiction and non-fiction, regression for the remaining three genres show no statistical significance.

8   Conclusion and future work

This paper shows that high AV accuracy can be achieved using relatively small sample size for the training corpus (5 documents). It also shows that for document size < 1000 words, having a larger training or testing sample does not affect the performance of AV. The findings of this paper are of particular interest in the context of literary and journalistic analysis.

There are a number of areas that future research can cover. First, this paper shows that smaller training sets result in improved accuracy, when applied to the set of features that perform best on experiment 1 (full training set). Future research can investigate if other feature ensembles can outperform the ones tested in experiment 2, but were not considered here because of steeper degradation in accuracy at training set size S = 10. The accuracies reported here rely in part on the accuracy of feature extraction as well as on the distance measure used (Delta, (Burrows, 2002)). The accuracy of the feature extraction using MADAMIRA is around 96%, depending on the feature extracted (Pasha et al., 2014). As better morphological analyzers ae developed, future research should consider the effects of better feature extraction on the selection of features to be used. Additionally, other distance measures should be considered, in addition to Manhattan Distance. Finally, It is unclear if high AV accuracy based on this method can be achieved in other domains where document sizes are necessarily shorter, such as online product reviews and social media communications. Nonlinguistic features such as punctuation and non-Arabic characters were also not investigated. I leave these questions for future research.

References

Hossam Ahmed. 2017. Dynamic Similarity Threshold in Authorship Verification: Evidence from Classical Arabic. *Procedia Computer Science*, 117:145–152.

Hossam Ahmed. 2018. The Role of Linguistic Feature Categories in Authorship Verification. *Procedia Computer Science*, 142:214–221.

Malik H Altakrori, Benjamin C M Fung, Steven H H Ding, Abdallah Tubaishat, M H Altakrori, S H H Ding, and Farkhund Iqbal. 2018. Arabic Authorship Attribution: An Extensive Study on Twitter Posts. *ACM Trans. Asian Low-Resour. Lang. Inf. Process*, 18(1):51.

Alaa Saleh Altheneyan and Mohamed El Bachir Menai. 2014. Naïve Bayes classifiers for authorship attribution of Arabic texts. *Journal of King Saud University - Computer and Information Sciences*, 26(4):473–484.

Steven Bird, Ewan Klein, and Edward Loper. 2009. *Natural language processing with Python: analyzing text with the natural language toolkit*. O'Reilly Media, Inc.

John Burrows. 2002. "Delta": a measure of stylistic difference and a guide to likely authorship. *Literary and Linguistic Computing*, 17(3):267–

287.

Abdelhamid Elewa. 2018. Authorship verification of disputed Hadiths in Sahih al-Bukhari and Muslim. *Digital Scholarship in the Humanities.*

David García-Barrero, Manuel Feria, and Maria Teresa Turell. 2013. Using function words and punctuation marks in Arabic forensic authorship attribution. In Rui Sousa-Silva, Rita Faria, Núria Gavaldà, and Belinda Maia, editors, *Proceedings of the 3rd European Conference of the International Association of Forensic Linguists,* pages 42–56, Porto, Portugal. Faculdade de Letras da Universidade do Porto.

Oren Halvani, Christian Winter, and Anika Pflug. 2016. Authorship verification for different languages, genres and topics. *Digital Investigation,* 16:S33–S43.

Oren Halvani, Christian Winter, and Lukas Graner. 2017. Authorship Verification based on Compression-Models.

Fatma Howedi and Masnizah Mohd. 2014. Text Classification for Authorship Attribution Using Naive Bayes Classifier with Limited Training Data. *Computer Engineering and Intelligent Systems,* 5(4):48–56.

Magdalena Jankowska, Evangelos Milios, and Vlado Kešelj. 2014. Author Verification Using Common N-Gram Profiles of Text Documents. *Proceedings of COLING 2014, the 25th International Conference on Computational Linguistics*:387–397.

Siham Ouamour and Halim Sayoud. 2013. Authorship Attribution of Short Historical Arabic Texts Based on Lexical Features. In *2013 International Conference on Cyber-Enabled Distributed Computing and Knowledge Discovery,* pages 144–147.

Siham Ouamour and Halim Sayoud. 2018. A Comparative Survey of Authorship Attribution on Short Arabic Texts.

Arfath Pasha, Mohamed Al-badrashiny, Mona Diab, Ahmed El Kholy, Ramy Eskander, Nizar Habash, Manoj Pooleery, Owen Rambow, and Ryan M Roth. 2014. MADAMIRA : A Fast , Comprehensive Tool for Morphological Analysis and Disambiguation of Arabic. *Proceedings of the 9th Language Resources and Evaluation Conference (LREC'14)*:1094–1101.

Kareem Shaker. 2012. *Investigating features and techniques for Arabic authorship attribution.* Ph.D. thesis, Heriot-Watt University.

Efstathios Stamatatos. 2009. A survey of modern authorship attribution methods. *Journal of the American Society for Information Science and Technology,* 60(3):538–556.

A folksonomy-based approach for profiling human perception on word similarity

GuanI Wu
Department of Statistics,
University of California, Los Angeles
guani@g.ucla.edu

Ker-Chau Li
Department of Statistics,
University of California, Los Angeles
ISS, Academia Sinica
kcli@stat.sinica.edu.tw

Abstract

Automatic assessment of word similarity has long been considered as one important challenge in the development of Artificial Intelligence. People often have a big disagreement on how similar a pair of words is. Yet most word similarity prediction methods, taking either the knowledge-based approach or the corpus-based approach, only attempt to estimate an average score of human raters. The distribution aspect of similarity for each word-pair has been methodologically neglected, thus limiting their downstream applications in Natural Language Processing. Here, utilizing the category information of Wikipedia, we present a method to model similarity between two words as a probability distribution. Our method leverages unique features of folksonomy. The success of our method in describing the diversity of human perception on word similarity is evaluated against the rater dataset WordSim-353. Our method can be extended to compare documents.

1 Introduction

Making machine understand human language is one of the ultimate goals in the development of Artificial Intelligence (Christopher D. Manning, 2015). In order to reach the goal, many different Natural Language Processing (NLP) tasks were designed. Among them, one of the fundamental upstream tasks is to automatically assess similarities between words. The performance of this task has directly impacts on many downstream NLP applications such as Question Answering, Information Retrieval, Topic Modeling, and Text Clustering (Sandhya and Govardhan, 2012; Nathawitharana et al., 2016; Wei et al., 2015), etc.

Methods automatically assessing word similarity generally fall into two categories, knowledge-based and corpus-based approaches (Harispe et al., 2015). The corpus-based approach was founded on the maxim "You should know a word by the companies it keeps (Firt, J. R., 1957), which has shown remarkable performance on different word-similarity tests. Landauer et al. proposed Latent Semantic Analysis (LSA) that employs singular value decomposition to generate vectors as word representations (Thomas K Landauer et al., 1998). Since then, many methods were proposed to generate word vectors. Bengio et al. published a series of papers using neural network techniques (Yoshua Bengio et al., 2003). The team of Tomas Mikolov proposed the continuous bag of words (CBOW) and skip grams (also known as Word2vec) (Tomas Mikolov et al., 2013) and Jeffrey et al. proposed GloVe (Pennington et al., 2014). These methods need to be fed with a large corpus to train models in order to generate word vectors. To obtain a similarity score between two words, the dot product of the two word vectors is computed.

Instead of the dependence on which corpus to use, the knowledge-based approach requires a pre-existing knowledge base. WordNet is the most common knowledge base employed by the majority of methods developed in this realm. WordNet collects over 150,000 English words, and organizes them into cognitive synonyms (synsets). These synsets are connected through conceptual, semantic and lexical relations such as hyponyms, hypernyms, meronyms, holonyms (George A. Miller, 1995). Wu and Palmer proposed a method that exploited ontology/taxonomy to compute similarity scores based on Least Common Subsumer (LCS) (Zhibiao Wu and Martha Palmer, 1994). Many methods based on LCS, known as the edge-counting-based approach, were proposed (T. Slimani et al., 2006; Yuhua Li et al., 2003; Hadj Taieb et al., 2014). Another type of knowledge base approach used features of words to assess the similarities (Amos Tversky, 1977; Andrea Rodriguez and Max J Egenhofer, 2003; Euripides G.M. Petrakis et al., 2006).

The performance of computed similarity has to be evaluated against human raters, but human raters often display considerable disagreement in assigning similarity scores. As an example, see Figure 1 for the distribution of 16 raters' scores assigned to the pair of *life* and *lesson* from **WordSim-353** (Finkelstein et al., 2002). Such rating disagreements are quite common. However, most word-similarity methodologies attempt to estimate only the "average" score of human rating. The distribution aspect has been methodologically neglected, thus limiting their downstream applications in NLP.

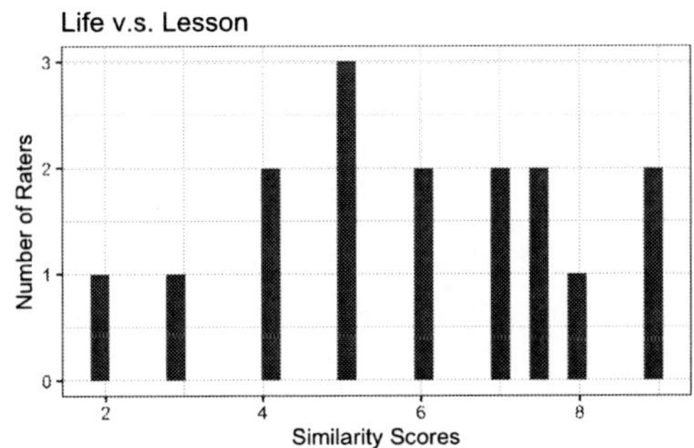

Figure 1: The histogram of similarity scores assigned by 16 raters to the pair of *life* and *lesson*.

2 Rater Disagreement on Word-Similarity

WordSim-353 is composed of two datasets: **WordSim-353.1**, a list of 153 word-pairs rated by 13 persons, and **WordSim-353.2**, a list of 200 word-pairs rated by 16 persons. We computed the Pearson correlation coefficient and the weighted Cohen's kappa coefficient for the similarity scores between any two raters. The results are shown in Figure 2 and Figure 3 after we ordered raters by hierarchical clustering. Rater disagreement on word-similarity is evident.

The important message we like to deliver is two-fold. First, the computer-imputed single similarity score has grossly simplified the human behavior. Second, using average rater score to evaluate the performance of different word-similarity prediction algorithms is itself a problematic evaluation approach.

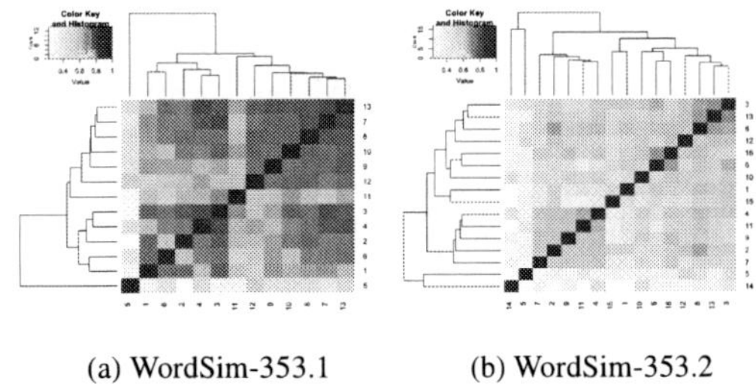

(a) WordSim-353.1   (b) WordSim-353.2

Figure 2: Weighted Cohen's kappa coefficient matrices for WordSim-353.1 and WordSim-353.2.

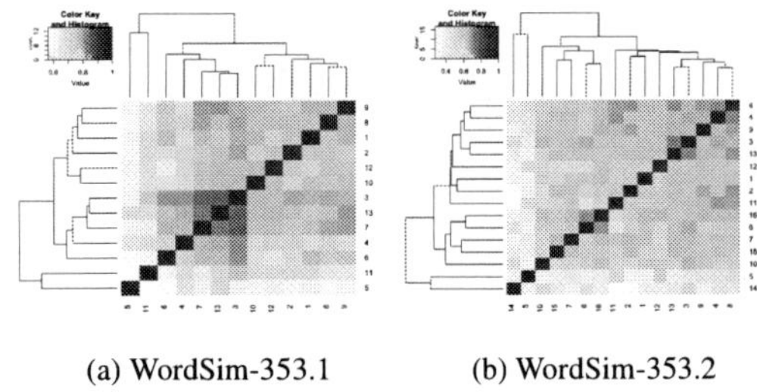

(a) WordSim-353.1   (b) WordSim-353.2

Figure 3: Pearson correlation matrices for WordSim-353.1 and WordSim-353.2.

3 Leveraging Folksonomy for Distribution Quantification of Word Similarity

To reflect the more realistic human behaviors, we propose that in lieu of assigning a single similarity score, a better computer task would be to assign a probability distribution to each word-pair, $(p_0, p_1, \ldots, p_d, \ldots, p_\delta)$, where p_d denotes the probability of similarity score d, and δ is the highest allowable score. To evaluate the performance of a computer algorithm, we should employ common statistical criteria that are designed for the distribution against distribution comparison.

3.1 Category Information of Wikipedia

Wikipedia organizes the categories of articles via folksonomy, which is a collaborative tagging system allowing users to tag articles with multiple category notions (Aniket Kittur and Ed H. Chi, Bongwon Suh, 2009). Links between categories do not impose any specification on relations such as *is-a*, *is-part-of*, *is-an-example-of*, etc. Figure 4 illustrated how Wikipedia category is organized into a Directed Acyclic Graph (DAG). It is typical to find multiple roots linking to the title of an article.

In contrast to the traditional centralized classification, folksonomy may directly reflect the diversity of article contributors in their personal styles of vocabulary management, which in turn are influenced by a variety of factors including cultural, social or personal bias. At this writing, about 70,000 editors—from expert scholars to casual readers—regularly edit Wikipedia. (March 2, 2019 https://en.wikipedia.org/wiki/Wikipedia:About)

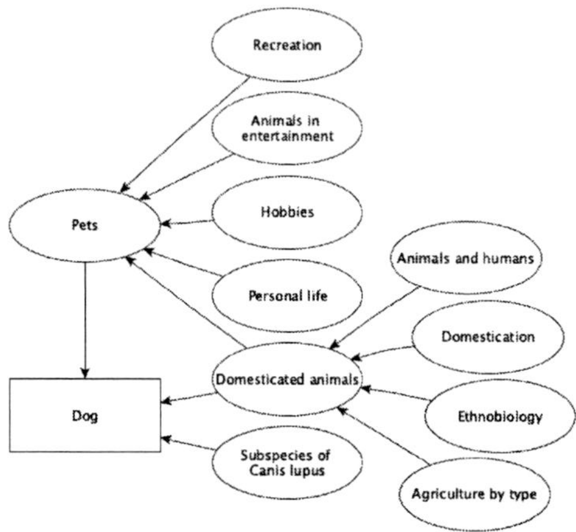

Figure 4: An example of Wikipedia category structure, where rectangle indicates a title of an article, and ellipses are categories. The graph is drawn based on the data downloaded from https://wiki.dbpedia.org/dataset-36.

3.2 Distribution Quantification of Word-Similarity

We propose a method to assign a probability distribution to a pair of words (W_1, W_2). First, we find the set of conceptual paths $X = \{X_1, \ldots, X_N\}$ linking to W_1, and also find the set of conceptual paths $Y = \{Y_1, \ldots, Y_M\}$ linking to W_2. We delete paths in X that are disconnected from any path in Y, and vice versa. We then compute a similarity score c_{ij} for each path pair (X_i, Y_j) to generate a matrix as shown in Table 1. The probability of similarity score d, denoted by p_d, is set to be the proportion of path pairs with $c_{ij} = d$.

We propose Equation 1 to calculate the similarity score for (X_i, Y_j).

$$sim(C_i, C_j) = 1 - \frac{(K_i + K_j)}{L_i + L_j} \propto L_i + L_j - K_i - K_j \quad (1)$$

As illustrated by Figure 5, L_i is the number of

X / Y	X_1	X_2	$\ldots$	X_N
Y_1	c_{11}	c_{12}	$\ldots$	c_{1N}
Y_2	c_{21}	c_{22}	$\ldots$	c_{2N}
$\vdots$	$\ldots$	$\ldots$	$\ddots$	$\vdots$
Y_M	c_{M1}	c_{M2}	$\ldots$	c_{MN}

Table 1: Matrix of Similarity Degrees Between Sets of Conceptual Paths.

nodes on the path from C_i to its root node R_i, and L_j is the number of nodes on the path from C_j to its root node R_j. K_i is the number of nodes on the path from C_i to C_k, and K_j is the number of nodes on the path from C_j to C_k.

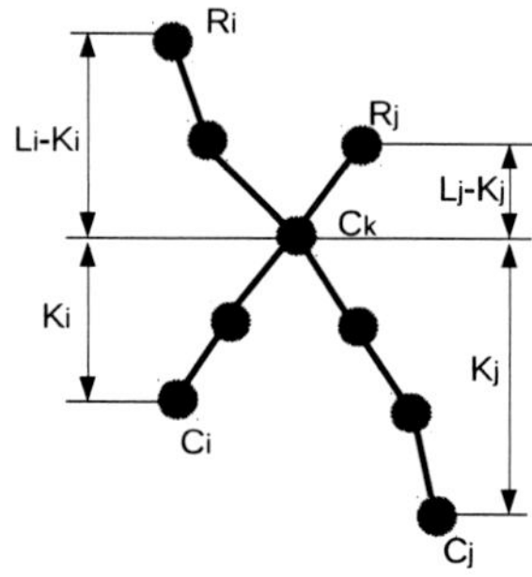

Figure 5: Calculating similarity between two conceptual paths via node counting.

In our implementation, we set L_i and L_j as constants and let $L_i = L_j = L$. There are two reasons. First, nodes that are too far away from C_i, C_j are often un-informative. Second, due to the large number of conceptual paths in X and Y, we must alleviate computational complexity. This leads to

$$c_{ij} = 2L - K_i - K_j \quad (2)$$

3.3 Implementation

Since there are over one million categories contained in Wikipedia, it would be a challenge to collect data directly from Wikipedia. Fortunately, DBpedia has collected and organized Wikipedia data in a way easier for us to use (Auer et al., 2007). We downloaded two datasets, *article-categories* and *skos-categories*; the former keeps the links between articles and categories, and the latter stores links between categories. Since the downloaded databases are stored in Triplestore format, *subject-predicate-object*, we set up Apache Jena Fuseki as an in-house SPARQL server for access by our main program. Figure

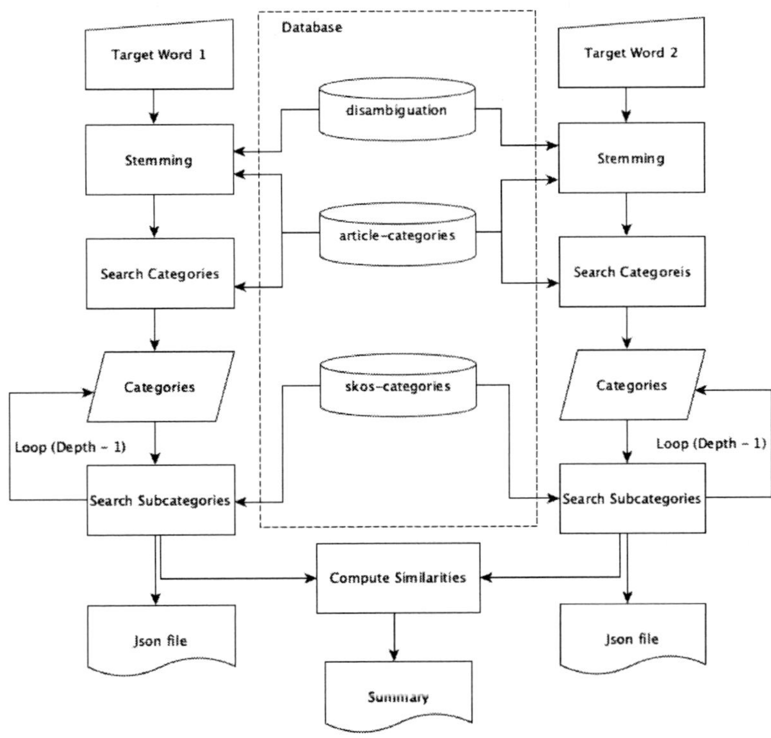

Figure 6: The flowchart of main program.

6 illustrated how we implement our method. After inputing a pair of target words (W_1, W_2), the program will start with stemming the words, and check if they can be found in *article-categories*. If not, the program will search the disambiguation database and return a category closest to the target word. After stemming, the program sends the linked categories as the input to Search Subcategories. This phase recursively searches superior categories of given categories until the search reaches the maximum number of depth we set initially. Once the search is done, the system generates a plain file in Jason format for displaying the output as a taxonomy-like graph on the website. Through the same procedure, the program generates the other plain file in the same format for the other target word. Finally, we use the distribution quantification method described earlier to generate the probability distribution $(p_0, p_1, \ldots, p_d, \ldots, p_\delta)$ for (W_1, W_2).

We developed a website to implement our method, http://ws.stat.sinica.edu.tw/wikiCat. Given a pair of words, it provides a summary table and two taxonomy-like graphs for the input words as shown in Figure 7. Every node in the graph represents a category, and it can be clicked to show its superior categories hidden underneath. The column "Proportions" gives the similarity distribution for the query (Life, Lesson). Compared to Figure 1, the agreement with the human raters is quite good. The time for executing a query varies around 2 seconds to 30 seconds.

4 Experiment

We use WordSim-353 to evaluate the performance of our method. We set $L = 5$ in order to be consistent with the scale used in WordSim-353 (from 0 to 10), so that our program will yield a probability distribution $(p_0, p_1, ..., p_{10})$ for each word-pair(W_1, W_2). To see how our probability distribution agrees with the score distribution of WordSim-353 raters, Kolmogorov-Smirnov statistic (K-S statistic) between two distributions is used. We perform the following procedure 1000 times to get a p-value. A p-value smaller than 0.05 indicates significant disagreement between the two distributions.

1. Simulating 13 (16, respectively) scores from

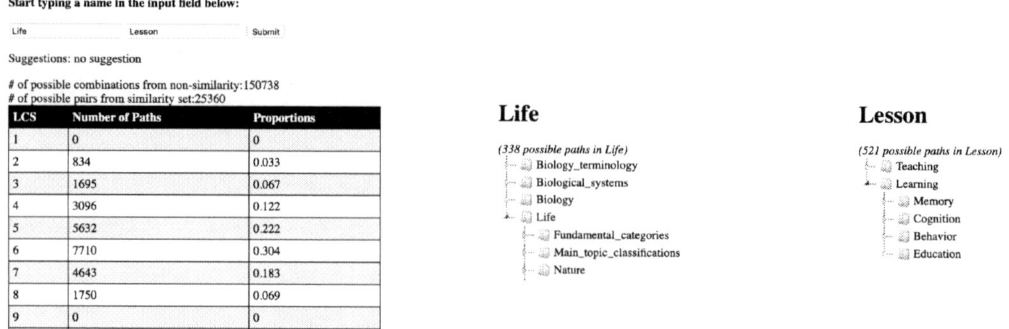

LCS	Number of Paths	Proportions
1	0	0
2	834	0.033
3	1695	0.067
4	3096	0.122
5	5632	0.222
6	7710	0.304
7	4643	0.183
8	1750	0.069
9	0	0
10	0	0

Figure 7: A screen shot of the developed website.

the distribution $(p_0, p_1, ..., p_{10})$ for the word pair (W_1, W_2) from WordSim-353.1 (from WordSim-353.2, respectively).

2. Computing Kolmogorov-Smirnov distance between $(p_0, p_1, ..., p_{10})$ and the distribution of simulated scores.

After 1000 simulations, the p-value for (W_1, W_2) is given by the proportion of times that the observed K-S statistic exceeds the simulated K-S distance. As it turns, around 50% of word-pairs showed agreement between human rating and our computer rating (Figure 8). Given that the raters of WordSim-353 were from a generation before the inception of Wikipedia, we consider this result supports the potential of our folksonomy-based approach in reflecting human judgment diversity. Figure 9 showed some cases that our folksonomy-based method agreed very well with human rating.

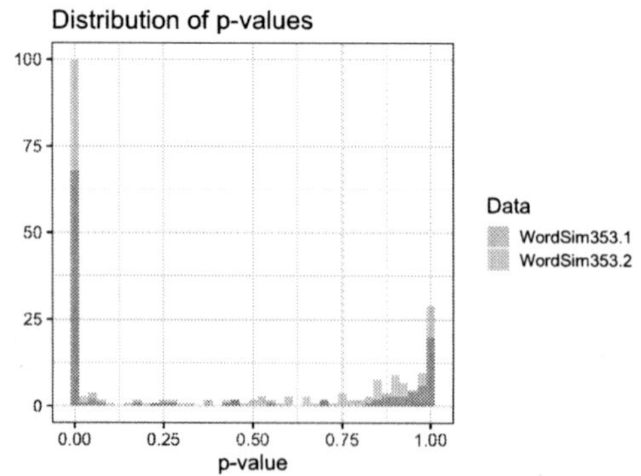

Figure 8: Histograms of p-values for WordSim-353.1 and WordSim-353.2. 53.59% of word-pairs have p-values greater than 0.05 in WordSim-353.1 and 48% in WordSim-353.2.

We further split the word pairs into two groups, AG (agreement, word pairs with p-value > 0.05) and DIS (disagreement, word pairs with p-value < 0.05). We examined the variance of human rater scores for each word-pair and plot the distribution for AG group and DIS group separately for comparison (Figure 10). We found AG group of word pairs tend to have larger variance than the DIS group. This indicates our approach may overestimate the degree of divergence in human rating, provided that the small group of raters participating WordSim-353 did not under-represent the true diversity of human behavior.

5   Application in Document Similarity Comparison

Our method can be extended for comparing documents. As a word can be mapped to multiple conceptual paths, a document will be mapped to an even bigger set of conceptual paths. As an example, we select three documents (*talk.politics.178908*, *talk.politics.178860* and *sci.med.59319*) from The 20 Newsgroups dataset (Lang, 1995). We further employed tf-idf (term frequency-inverse document frequency) (Salton and McGill, 1986) to extract the feature words of documents. Only top 10 words with highest tf-idf were kept (Table 2). We merge conceptual paths of these words to form a bigger set of representative conceptual paths for each document. Then we applied the same procedure as described in 3.2 to yield a probability distribution of similarity scores between two documents.

In this example, we set $L = 4$ to yield a probability distribution $(p_0, p_1, \ldots, p_8)$ for comparing two documents as shown in Table 3. Here PP is *talk.politics.178908* v.s. *talk.politics.178860*,

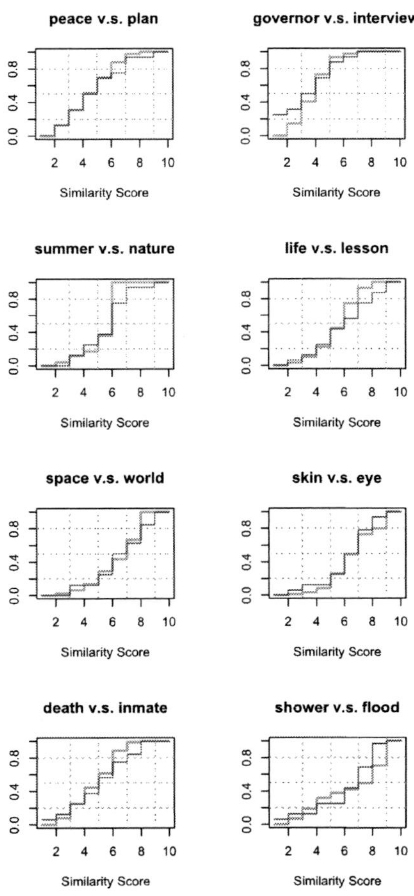

Figure 9: Eight cases that our method agreed well with human rating. The red lines are CDF by human rating and the blue lines are CDF by our folksonomy-based method.

talk.politics 178908	talk.politics 178860	sci.med 59319
president	oath	widex
masks	garrett	resound
attorney	gain	aids
federal	ingres	programmable
gas	nixon	hearing
reno	powers	loss
yesterday	office	ear
departments	personal	ahead
janet	monetary	sloping
children	indictment	reprogramed

Table 2: Lists of top 10 words with highest tf-idf scores.

PM1 is *talk.politics.178908* v.s. *sci.med.59319* and PM2 is *talk.politics.178860* v.s. *sci.med.59319*. Evidently, the probability distributions for (*talk.politics.178908, sci.med.59319*)

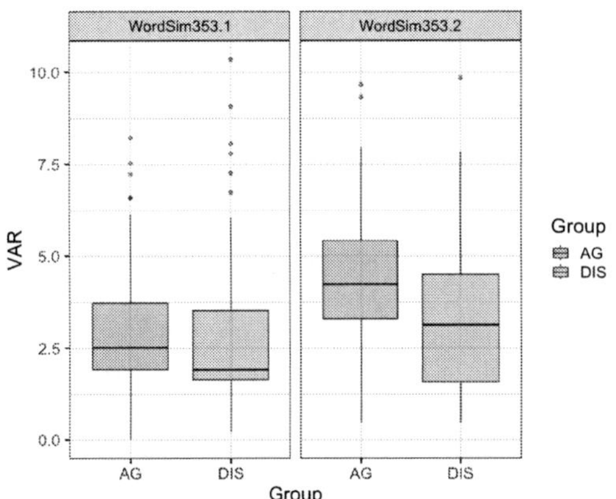

Figure 10: Boxplots for variances of similarity scores across 13 raters (WorSim-353.1) and 16 raters (WordSim-353.2). Word-pairs are split into two groups, AG (agreement, $p > 0.05$) and DIS (disagreement, $p < 0.05$).

	PP	PM1	PM2
0	0	0	0
1	0	0	0
2	0.1236742	0.2240363	0.2725498
3	0.1616162	0.3133787	0.3924248
4	0.1674242	0.245805	0.2225693
5	0.1511995	0.2126984	0.1124561
6	0.1440657	0.004081633	0
7	0.1337121	0	0
8	0.1183081	0	0

Table 3: Probability distributions of document similarity for comparing *talk.politics.178908*, *talk.politics.178860* and *sci.med.59319*.

and (*talk.politics.178860, sci.med.59319*) have low probabilities on high similarity scores (6, 7, 8). In contrast, we observe relatively higher probabilities being assigned to high similarity scores for (*talk.politics.178908, talk.politics.178860*).

6 Conclusion

Human perception on word similarity can be very discordant. Against the common trend of assigning a single score of similarity by most computer algorithms, we request a new computer task of assigning a probability distribution of similarity for each word pair. Leveraging the rich information embroidered behind the principle of free expression and empowered by user diversity of folksonomy, we design an approach that exploited the category tagging system of Wikipedia articles to perform the task. The good performance of our method is illustrated against two word similarity datasets with scores assigned by human raters. Our way of using Wikipedia (via folksonomy) is very different from many others; for example, the method of Explicit Semantic Analysis (Gabrilovich and Markovitch, 2007) treated articles in Wikipedia as a document corpus and produced only a single similarity score. For future works, we plan to modify our word similarity scoring formula by path-dependent weight adjustment for broadening the application in document comparison. It would also be worthwhile to apply our method to other languages for comparing the possible differences between languages in assigning similarity distributions.

Acknowledgments

This work was supported in part by grants from Academia Sinica, Taiwan, AS-104-TP-A07 and National Science Foundation, USA, NSF, DMS-1513622, and by MIB, Institute of Statistical Science, Academia Sinica. The content is solely the responsibility of the authors and does not necessarily represent the official views of NSF.

References

Amos Tversky. 1977. Features of Similarity. *Psycological Review*, 84(4):327–352.

Andrea Rodriguez and Max J Egenhofer. 2003. Determining Semantic Similarity among Entity Classes from Different Ontologies. *IEEE Transactions on Knowledge and Data Engineering*, 15(2):442–456.

Aniket Kittur and Ed H. Chi, Bongwon Suh. 2009. What's in Wikipedia?: mapping topics and conflict using socially annotated category structure. In *The SIGCHI Conference on Human Factors in Computing Systems*, pages 1509–1512.

Sören Auer, Christian Bizer, Georgi Kobilarov, Jens Lehmann, Richard Cyganiak, and Zachary Ives. 2007. DBpedia: A Nucleus for a Web of Open Data. In *Proceedings of the 6th International The Semantic Web and 2Nd Asian Conference on Asian Semantic Web Conference*, ISWC'07/ASWC'07, pages 722–735, Berlin, Heidelberg. Springer-Verlag.

Christopher D. Manning. 2015. Computational Linguistics and Deep Learning. *Computational Linguistics*, 41(4):701–707.

Euripides G.M. Petrakis, Giannis Varelas, Angelos Hliaoutakis, and Paraskevi Raftopoulou. 2006. X-Similarity: Computing Semantic Similarity between concepts from different ontologies. *Journal of Digital Information Management*, 4(4):233–237.

Lev Finkelstein, Evgeniy Gabrilovich, Yossi Matias, Ehud Rivlin, Zach Solan, Gadi Wolfman, and Eytan Ruppin. 2002. Placing search in context: The concept revisited. *ACM Trans. Inf. Syst.*, 20(1):116–131.

Firt, J. R. 1957. A Synopsis of Linguistic Theory 1930-55. *Studies in Linguistic Analysis(special volume of the Philological Society)*, pages 1–32.

Evgeniy Gabrilovich and Shaul Markovitch. 2007. Computing semantic relatedness using wikipedia-based explicit semantic analysis. In *Proceedings of the 20th International Joint Conference on Artifical Intelligence*, IJCAI'07, pages 1606–1611, San Francisco, CA, USA. Morgan Kaufmann Publishers Inc.

George A. Miller. 1995. WordNet: a lexical database for English. *Communications of the ACM*, 38(11):39–41.

Mohamed Ali Hadj Taieb, Mohamed Ben Aouicha, and Abdelmajid Ben Hamadou. 2014. Ontology-based Approach for Measuring Semantic Similarity. *Eng. Appl. Artif. Intell.*, 36(C):238–261.

Sébastien Harispe, Sylvie Ranwez, Stefan Janaqi, and Jacky Montmain. 2015. Semantic Similarity from Natural Language and Ontology Analysis. *Synthesis Lectures on Human Language Technologies*, 8(1):1–254.

Ken Lang. 1995. Newsweeder: Learning to filter netnews. In *Proceedings of the Twelfth International Conference on Machine Learning*, pages 331–339.

Nilupulee Nathawitharana, Damminda Alahakoon, and Daswin De Silva. 2016. Using semantic relatedness measures with dynamic self-organizing maps for improved text clustering. *2016 International Joint Conference on Neural Networks (IJCNN)*, pages 2662–2671.

Jeffrey Pennington, Richard Socher, and Christopher D. Manning. 2014. GloVe: Global Vectors for Word Representation. In *Empirical Methods in Natural Language Processing (EMNLP)*, pages 1532–1543.

Gerard Salton and Michael J McGill. 1986. Introduction to modern information retrieval.

Nadella Sandhya and A. Govardhan. 2012. Analysis of Similarity Measures with WordNet Based Text Document Clustering. In *Proceedings of the International Conference on Information Systems Design and Intelligent Applications 2012 (INDIA 2012) held in Visakhapatnam, India, January 2012*, pages 703–714. Springer Berlin Heidelberg.

T. Slimani, B. Ben Yaghlane, and K. Mellouli. 2006. A New Similarity Measure based on Edge Counting. In *World Academy of Science, Engineering and Technology*, volume 17, pages 232–236.

Thomas K Landauer, Peter W. Foltz, and Darrell Laham. 1998. An Introduction to Latent Semantic Analysis. *Discourse Processes*, 25:259–284.

Tomas Mikolov, Kai Chen, Greg Corrado, and Jeffrey Dean. 2013. Efficient Estimation of Word Representations in Vector Space. In *Workshop at International Conference on Learning Representations*.

Tingting Wei, Yonghe Lu, Huiyou Chang, Qiang Zhou, and Xianyu Bao. 2015. A semantic approach for text clustering using WordNet and lexical chains. *Expert Systems with Applications*, 42(4):2264–2275.

Yoshua Bengio, Réjean Ducharme, Pascal Vincent, and Christian Janvin. 2003. A neural probabilistic language model. *The Journal of Machine Learning Research*, 3:1137–1155.

Yuhua Li, Zuhair A. Bandar, and David McLean. 2003. An Approach for Measuring Semantic Similarity between Words Using Multiple Information Sources. *IEEE Transactions on Knowledge and Data Engineering*, 15(4):871–882.

Zhibiao Wu and Martha Palmer. 1994. Verbs semantics and lexical selection. In *ACL 94 Proceedings of the 32nd annual meeting on Association for Computational Linguistics*. Association for Computational Linguistics Stroudsburg.

Automatic Diacritization as Prerequisite Towards the Automatic Generation of Arabic Lexical Recognition Tests

Osama Hamed
Language Technology Lab
University of Duisburg-Essen
osama.hamed@uni-due.de

Torsten Zesch
Language Technology Lab
University of Duisburg-Essen
torsten.zesch@uni-due.de

Abstract

The automatic generation of Arabic lexical recognition tests entails several NLP challenges, including corpus linguistics, automatic diacritization, lemmatization and language modeling. Here, we only address the problem of automatic diacritization, a step that paves the road for the automatic generation of Arabic LRTs. We conduct a comparative study between the available tools for diacritization (Farasa and Madamira) and a strong baseline. We evaluate the error rates for these systems using a set of publicly available (almost) fully diacritized corpora, but in a relaxed evaluation mode to ensure fair comparison. Farasa outperforms Madamira and the baseline under all conditions.

1 Introduction

Lexical recognition tests are widely used to assess vocabulary knowledge. LRTs are based on the assumption that recognizing a word is sufficient for 'knowing' the word (Cameron, 2002). In such tests, the participants are being shown a list of items, containing words and nonwords. Their task is based on word recognition approach, i.e. they have to say 'Yes' when the item is word and 'No' otherwise – see Figure 1.

In the past LRTs were manually generated, as in LexTALE[1] and other LexTALE-like tests (Lemhöfer and Broersma, 2012). However, for the repetitive testing as used in formative assessment (Wang, 2007), LRT's test stimuli need to be generated automatically using natural language processing (NLP) techniques. The automatic generation of LRTs involves two NLP tasks: (i) a simple task: words selection from a corpus, and (ii) a complex task: nonwords generation. Some researchers have recently proposed an approach to

generate nonwords automatically using character n-gram language models as obtained from Brown corpus (Hamed and Zesch). They applied their approach to English, and considered word selection using frequency per million word.

We want to generalize their approach to other languages, and more specifically Arabic, which is both interesting and challenging language. Creating Arabic lexical recognition tests is a task that entails a lot of NLP challenges regarding automatic diacritization, corpus linguistic, morphological analysis e.g. lemmatization and language modeling.

While there exist well-established lexical recognition tests for English, and other European languages like German and Dutch (Lemhöfer and Broersma, 2012), French and Spanish, for many under-resourced languages, like Arabic, a lot of challenges still remain. We are aware of very few studies for Arabic, like (Ricks, 2015; Baharudin et al., 2014). Both studies were conducted without any diacritical marks, which means that the respondent claims to know the most frequent diacritized form of a word. Although some researchers have recently shown that the diacritical marks play a vital role in improving the difficulty of Arabic LRTs (Hamed and Zesch, 2017), they did not automate the whole process.

In this paper, we address one of these NLP challenges by taking a closer look on the different approaches for Arabic automatic diacritization, a dominant step in the design process of Arabic tests and especially the role of lexical diacritics that are a defining feature of Arabic word sense. Next, we provide some background on lexical recognition tests, followed by the entailed NLP challenges.

---

[1]The Lexical Test for Advanced Learners of English

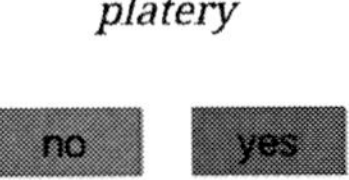

Figure 1: Example of a lexical recognition test as Yes/No question.

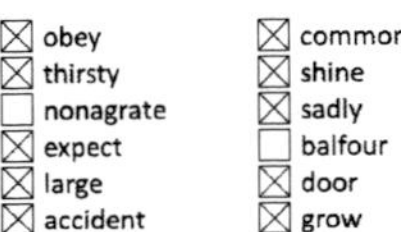

Figure 2: Example of a lexical recognition test in checklist format.

2 Related Work

The lexical recognition tests are typically used to measure the size of vocabulary, i.e. they only measure the breadth of vocabulary knowledge, but not the depth or quality (Schmitt, 2014). As described by Read (2004), breadth is used to "refer to any vocabulary measure that requires just a single response to each target word, by indicating whether the word is known or not". LRTs have two presentation formats: Yes/No question format, or checklist format – as show in Figures 1, 2.

2.1 Arabic LRTs

We are aware of a limited set of studies on Arabic lexical recognition tests.

– Test of Arabic Vocabulary (TAV) Baharudin et al. (2014) developed the *Test of Arabic Vocabulary* that uses 40 words selected from a book by panel of experts, but no nonwords. Thus, the test is vulnerable to test-wiseness or overconfidence (just answering 'yes' for each item).

– Test of Arabic Checklist Ricks (2015) developed a checklist-format test with 40 words and 20 nonwords (following the format introduced with LexTALE). Words were randomly selected from the Buckwalter/Parkinson frequency dictionary (Buckwalter and Parkinson, 2014), but excluding dialectal words. Nonwords were manually created using letters substitution approach.

Importance of Diacritics for LRTs In a recent studies (Hamed and Zesch, 2017, 2018), the researchers added a new parameter to Ricks's test. They constructed a diacritized test, where they partially diacritized the test stimuli (words and nonwords) and applied a form of relaxation that

drops some diacritics. It was shown that diacritics play a vital role in words recognition, especially for beginner and intermediate learners. Hamed and Zesch (2018) demonstrated the impact of diacritization on increasing the difficulty of Arabic LRTs.

3 NLP Challenges

Three Arabic NLP challenges are entailed in the automatic generation of Arabic LRTs.

3.1 Diacritized Text Availability

LRT is a corpus-based assessment. To obtain a reliable frequency count, we typically need a large set of diacritized text. However, the currently available diacritized corpora are limited to religion related texts (Classical Arabic) such as the Holy Quran[2], RDI[3] and Tashkeela (Zerrouki and Balla, 2017) or newswire genres available in Penn Arabic Treebanks (PATB) from the Linguistic Data Consortium (LDC). Below we shed the light on the limitations of available corpora.

- **Religious Text** As we are trying to build education application that measure language proficiency. We need text that cover a variety of themes like: politics, economics, health, science and technology, sports, arts, culture and religion.

- **ATB** Which is limited in terms of size with less than 570k tokens and in terms of diversity with 87,160 unique surface forms (excluding numerals). In comparison, the AFP news corpus has approximately 765,890 unique tokens (Cole et al., 2001). Moreover, ATB often uses inconsistent diacritizations (Darwish et al., 2017).

Such a huge corpus can be crawled from the internet, lemmatized and diacritized accordingly.

3.2 Lemmatization

Lemmatization is the process of grouping together the different inflected forms of a word, so they can be analyzed as a single item (a.k.a the lemma). The lemma (aka the dictionary citation form) is a conventionalized choice using one of the word forms to stand for the set (Habash, 2010). Typically, the lemmas are written without any clitics

---

[2] http://tanzil.net/download/
[3] http://www.rdi-eg.com/RDI/TrainingData/

and without any sense (meaning indices). For example, the lemma of a verb is the third person masculine singular perfective form e.g. اتصل /AtSl/; while the lemma for a noun is the masculine singular form e.g. بيت /bayt/.[4]

Lemmas are usually presented in the LRTs for English and other European languages . Following standard practice for frequency lists in English and other languages, Buckwalter and Parkinson (2014) adopt the lemma as the organizing principle in their frequency dictionary. Lemmatization is difficult because Arabic is a morphology rich language and its words are highly inflected and derived (Aqel et al., 2015). We are aware of a well-established research that compares the available lemmatization tools. For example, Darwish and Mubarak (2016) have shown that Farasa outperforms or equalizes state-of-the-art Arabic segmenters like Madamira (Pasha et al., 2014). Next, we investigate the performance of Arabic diacritization tools.

3.3 Diacritization

The Arabic script contains two classes of symbols for writing words: letters and diacritics (Habash, 2010). Diab et al. (2007) grouped the diacritical marks into three categories: vowels (Fatha /a/, Damma /u/, Kasra /i/ and Sukun to indicate the no presence of any vowel), nunations or Tanween (Fathatan, Dammatan, Kasratan) and Shadda (gemination or a consonant doubling). The following examples show the appearance of all diacritics on the Arabic letter "د" /d/ grouped by categories: short vowels (دَ /da/, Damma دُ /du/, Kasra دِ /di/ and Sukun دْ /do/), Tanween (دًا /daN/, دٌ /duN/ and دٍ /diN/) and Shadda (دّ /dd/) respectively. Diacritization is the task of restoring missing diacritics automatically in languages that are usually written without diacritics like Arabic and Hebrew. We are not going to reinvent the wheel, instead we are going to evaluate the existing and freely available diacritization tools and report the best performing one. We are aware of two tools: MADAMIRA and Farasa. Next, we provide some

Corpus	Description	Availability	# of words
Quran	Religious	Free	78 K
RDI	Religious	Free	20 M
Tashkeela	Religious	Free	60 M
PATB	News	Commercial	1 M

Table 1: Summary of diacritized corpora.

background on Arabic automatic diacritization.

4 State of the Art Overview

We shortly describe the diacritized datasets, and give an overview of the results that have so far been obtained on different corpora using the standard evaluation metrics.

4.1 Datasets

Table 1 summarizes the existing diacritized corpora, we conduct our experiments using Free corpora.

4.2 Evaluation Metrics

Two standard evaluation metrics are used almost exclusively to measure the system performance, in terms of error rates on the character and word levels. Namely, diacritization error rate (DER) and word error rate (WER). The smaller the error rates, the better the performance.

Case Endings In the diacritized version of the LRTs, the test stimuli are typically shown with lexical diacritics and without syntactic diacritics (a.k.a. case endings). Thus, we are going to report a variant of the above two mentioned metrics that ignore the word's last letter, denoted as **DER-1** and **WER-1**.

4.3 Results Overview

The existing diacritization approaches can be grouped into four main categories: statistical, sequence labeling, morphological analysis, and hybrid approaches (Metwally et al., 2016). Although there are several models within each approach, we only shed the light on one tool (not necessarily the the best performing one). A detailed review can be found in (Azmi and Almajed, 2015).

Statistical For example, the approach by Hifny (2012) is using an n-gram language model.

Sequence Labeling Some researchers have proposed handling the problem as a sequence labeling problem in which every letter of the word may be

---

[4]If no masculine is possible, then the feminine singular.

tagged with any of the possible diacritics. For example, recurrent neural networks model (Abandah et al., 2015).

Morphological Analysis   For example, the system by Habash et al. (2009) is based on MADA, the tool for the morphological analysis and disambiguation of Arabic.

Hybrid   Usually, the hybrid approach combines multiple-layers, each is utilizing one single approach. For example, the Rashwan et al. (2011) combines the unfactorized system (dictionary-based system) and a morphological analyzer.

Table 2 gives an overview of the reported results from the literature. The results are grouped by the corpus that was used for testing in order to allow for a fair comparison. Most numbers are still not directly comparable as they were obtained using different test sets. As most of the systems from the literature are not freely available, we have no way of directly comparing them. In this paper, we establish a comparative study that only includes the systems that are freely available along with the freely available corpora under a controlled settings.

5   Experimental Setup

The experiments are carried out using DKPro TC, the open-source UIMA-based framework for supervised text classification (Daxenberger et al., 2014). All the experiments were conducted as ten-fold (1 part testing, 9 parts training) cross validation reporting the average over the ten folds.

5.1   Used Data

Because of the commercial availability of LDC's PATB datasets, our experimental data are drawn from the Quran, Tashkeela (CA) and RDI (contemporary writing). Table 3 shows the statistics for these three sub-datasets (punctuation marks are not counted).

Data Preprocessing   The files from Tashkeela and RDI contain Quranic symbols or English alphabets and numerics respectively. In order to prepare them for training and testing purposes, the following preprocessing steps are performed: (i) convert them from HTML to plain text files that have one sentence per line. (ii) clean the files by removing the Quranic symbols and words written in non Arabic letters. (iii) normalize the Arabic

text by removing the extra white spaces and the Tatweel.

5.2   Sequence Labeling Baseline

This treats diacritization as a sequence labeling (multi-class text classification) problem and proposed a baseline solution using conditional random fields (Lafferty et al., 2001).

Given a sentence (set of non-diacritized words) separated using white-space delimiter, each word in the sentence is a sequence of characters, and we want to label each letter with its corresponding labels from the diacritics set D = $(d_1, ..., d_N)$. We represent each word as input sequence X = $(x_1, ..., x_N)$, where we need to label each consonant in X with the diacritics that follow this consonant. Thus, the diacritization of X sequence is to find its labeling sequence Y, of word length and derived from D. A word might have more than one valid labeling. For the word "ktAb" (كتاب) X = (k, t, A, b), Y_1 = (i, a, o, u) and Y_2 = (i, a, o, a) are examples of two possible labeling.

Our features are character n-grams language model (LM) in sequence labeling approach. The features extractor selects the character-level features relevant to diacritics from annotated corpora. It collects the diacritics on previous, current and following character and up to the 6th character.

5.3   Diacritization Tools

We are aware of a few tools that can be tested with thousands of words, enhanced or integrated with Java Frameworks.

MADAMIRA   A fast, comprehensive tool for morphological analysis and disambiguation of Arabic (Pasha et al., 2014). It is the successor of MADA (Habash et al., 2009).

Our experiments are carried out using the SAMA enabled version of Madamira *v2.1*. Madamira reported the accuracy of 86.3 and 95.3 for full and partial diacritization using an MSA blind test set. Madamira was used to diacritize the test sequences from the three corpora: Quran, Tashkeela (CA) and RDI. As the resulting diacritized text is encoded using Buckwalter transliteration, it is necessary to decode it into Arabic text. We compare the mapped Arabic text with gold sequence and calculating the different evaluation metrics.

Farasa   A fast and accurate text processing toolkit for Arabic text (Darwish and Mubarak,

Corpus	Test Size (10^3)	Approach	All Diacritics		Ignore Last	
			DER	**WER**	**DER-1**	**WER-1**
	52	Morphological (Habash et al., 2009)	4.8	14.9	2.2	5.5
ATB (Parts 1–3)	52	Hybrid (Rashwan et al., 2011)	3.8	12.5	**1.2**	**3.1**
	37	RNN (Abandah et al., 2015)	**2.7**	**9.1**	1.4	4.3
Quran	76	RNN (Abandah et al., 2015)	**3.0**	**8.7**	**2.0**	**5.8**
Tashkeela	1902	Statistical (Hifny, 2012)	-	8.9	-	**3.4**
	272	RNN (Abandah et al., 2015)	**2.1**	**5.8**	**1.3**	3.5
Tashkeela+RDI	199	Hybrid (Bebah et al., 2014)	7.4	21.1	3.8	7.4

Table 2: List of Arabic Diacritization Systems.

ID	Corpus	# words (10^3)	∅ chars per word	Words / sentence
Q	Quran	78	4.25	12.6
R	RDI	297	4.47	34.1
T	Tashkeela	4,926	4.11	14.7

Table 3: Statistics of corpora sub-datasets used in this study.

2016).

We did not find any reported published results for Farasa diacritizer. We use Farasa to diacritize test sequence from the three corpora. We compare the resulting diacritized text with gold sequence and calculate the different metrics.

5.4 Evaluation Metrics

The evaluation was conducted across the character and word levels. For the Arabic LRTs, the test stimuli are not fully diacritized, instead they conform to specific diacritization (no default diacritics, no case-endings) settings. Thus, the different error rates are reported in relaxed mode, not in strict mode:

Strict Mode Whenever a letter has a set of diacritics in the gold standard, the tools are expected to predict exactly this set. This means that we punish tools that only provide a partial diacritization, e.g. by not returning some default diacritics. For example (قال) /qAl/ instead of (قَال) /qaAl/.

Relaxed Mode Whenever a letter has a set of diacritics in the gold standard, we do not expect the tool to predict exactly this set. Which means that we do not punish the tools on a letter that does not hold a diacritic. Instead, we only count for the letters that holds diacritic. This assumption remains

valid only for words that are labeled with at least one diacritic by the diacritization tool (i.e. the tool is punished if no-diacritics are provided).

The following pre/post-processing steps are applied on the text to do the comparison in relaxed mode.

- **Comply to Default Diacritics** It is important to note that both Madamira and Farasa ignore the default diacritics, so that we normalize the gold sequence in such a way that also ignores the default diacritics to ensure fair comparison.

- **Sukun Removal** Some writing styles use the Sukun diacritic to mark un-diacritized letters and some styles leave such letters without any diacritic. To overcome these differences when computing the error rates, we discard the Sukun to neglect it in our evaluation.

5.5 Making Results Comparable

In Table 4, we show the average number and ratio of diacritics per letter for the gold standard and all systems used in our experiments. It shows that Madamira and Farasa both assign about the same amount of diacritics on average, but substantially fewer than the gold standard. This means that both tools are especially punished by the strict evaluation. These findings motivate us to do the evaluation using the *relaxed mode*. This requires us to normalize the ratio of letters with diacritics in the gold standard, training and output texts.

Table 5 shows the results in relaxed mode. The error rates are generally as expected. Farasa diacritizer outperforms all other methods in all conditions. The performance of Madamira with the Quran is lower than its performance with RDI and

Approach	Avg.			Ratio		
	Quran	RDI	Tashkeela	Quran	RDI	Tashkeela
Gold	.84	.83	.83	.78	.77	.77
Seq. Labeling	.82	.78	.78	.77	.74	.74
Madamira	.55	.59	.61	.51	.54	.56
Farasa	.58	.58	.61	.55	.54	.58

Table 4: Average number of diacritics per letter (Avg.), and the ratio of letters with diacritics (Ratio).

Tashkeela, and it outperforms the baseline with RDI and Tashkeela under all conditions. Farasa gets its best WER with RDI corpus, and outperforms almost at the same levels with Quran and Tashkeela. Madamira also performs almost on the same level with RDI and Tashkeela.

As most of the systems from the literature are not freely available, we have no way of directly comparing our results with those approaches unless they have the same settings. Only Farasa comes closer to the DER and DER-1 numbers by (Abandah et al., 2015) in Table 2 when text is drawn from the Quran. If we ignore the sample size, it can be clearly seen that the results of Farasa in relaxed mode are on the same level under (DER and DER-1) and outperforms the results approached by Bebah et al. (2014) under (WER and WER-1). The error rates are relatively high, we expect a certain level of overfitting on the domain (due to free words order) to play a role and that our results are closer to the actual performance that can be expected from existing tools.

Recall that Madamira reported an accuracy of 86.3% when evaluated using a blind MSA test set from the PATB. Madamira performs better in the relaxed mode (there is a slight difference). For instance, on average it shows a 74%, 80% and 80% WERs with the Quran, RDI and Tashkeela respectively. On the other hand, Farasa reported an accuracy of 86% with the three corpora.

6 Conclusion and Future Work

Arabic LRTs are corpus-based assessments that make use of diacritized words counts in a huge corpus. The lack of diacritized Arabic resources is one of the main challenges entailed in the automatic generation of Arabic LRTs. This paper approached the lack of diacritized Arabic resources via automatic diacritization. We presented a comparative study between the publicly available tools for diacritization. The evaluation experiments are conducted using diacritized text from the Quran,

Tashkeela and RDI corpora, but in a relaxed evaluation mode to ensure fair comparison and suit the design of Arabic LRTs. Farasa outperforms Madamira under all conditions. In future work, we want to investigate the creation of dialectal Arabic lexical recognition tests automatically.

References

Gheith Abandah, Alex Graves, Balkees Al-Shagoor, Alaa Arabiyat, Fuad Jamour, and Majid Al-Taee. 2015. Automatic diacritization of arabic text using recurrent neural networks. *International Journal on Document Analysis and Recognition (IJDAR)*, 18(2):183–197.

Afnan Aqel, Sahar Alwadei, and Mohammad Dahab. 2015. Building an Arabic Words Generator. *International Journal of Computer Applications*, 112(14).

Aqil Azmi and Reham Almajed. 2015. A survey of automatic arabic diacritization techniques. *Natural Language Engineering*, 21(03):477–495.

Harun Baharudin, Zawawi Ismail, Adelina Asmawi, and Normala Baharuddin. 2014. TAV of Arabic language measurement. *Mediterranean Journal of Social Sciences*, 5(20):2402.

Mohamed Bebah, Chennoufi Amine, Mazroui Azzeddine, and Lakhouaja Abdelhak. 2014. Hybrid approaches for automatic vowelization of arabic texts. *arXiv preprint arXiv:1410.2646*.

Tim Buckwalter and Dilworth Parkinson. 2014. *A frequency dictionary of Arabic: Core vocabulary for learners*. Routledge.

Lynne Cameron. 2002. Measuring vocabulary size in English as an additional language. *Language Teaching Research*, 6(2):145–173.

Andy Cole, David Graff, and Kevin Walker. 2001. Arabic newswire part 1 corpus (1-58563-190-6). *Linguistic Data Consortium (LDC)*.

Kareem Darwish and Hamdy Mubarak. 2016. Farasa: A New Fast and Accurate Arabic Word Segmenter. In *Proceedings of the Tenth International Conference on Language Resources and Evaluation (LREC 2016)*, Paris, France. European Language Resources Association (ELRA).

Kareem Darwish, Hamdy Mubarak, and Ahmed Abdelali. 2017. Arabic diacritization: Stats, rules, and hacks. In *Proceedings of the Third Arabic Natural Language Processing Workshop*, pages 9–17.

Johannes Daxenberger, Oliver Ferschke, Iryna Gurevych, Torsten Zesch, et al. 2014. DKPro TC: A Java-based Framework for Supervised Learning Experiments on Textual Data. In *ACL (System Demonstrations)*, pages 61–66.

Corpus	Approach	All Diacritics		Ignore Last	
		DER	WER	DER-1	WER-1
Quran	Seq. Labeling	15.1	22.0	7.6	13.5
	Madamira	14.5	26.4	10.2	15.6
	Farasa	**7.8**	**14.0**	**5.0**	**6.8**
RDI	Seq. Labeling	16.7	28.0	13.6	12.0
	Madamira	12.5	20.4	8.6	10.2
	Farasa	**8.3**	**13.8**	**5.0**	**5.1**
Tashkeela	Seq. Labeling	24.0	35.4	15.0	22.0
	Madamira	12.4	20.3	8.5	10.1
	Farasa	**8.3**	**13.9**	**5.0**	**5.1**

Table 5: Error rates in relaxed evaluation mode.

Mona Diab, Mahmoud Ghoneim, and Nizar Habash. 2007. Arabic diacritization in the context of statistical machine translation. In *Proceedings of MT-Summit*.

Nizar Habash. 2010. Introduction to Arabic natural language processing. *Synthesis Lectures on Human Language Technologies*, 3(1):1–187.

Nizar Habash, Owen Rambow, and Ryan Roth. 2009. MADA + TOKAN: A toolkit for Arabic tokenization, diacritization, morphological disambiguation, POS tagging, stemming and lemmatization. In *Proceedings of the 2nd international conference on Arabic language resources and tools (MEDAR), Cairo, Egypt*, pages 102–109.

Osama Hamed and Torsten Zesch. Generating Nonwords for Vocabulary Proficiency Testing.

Osama Hamed and Torsten Zesch. 2017. The Role of Diacritics in Designing Lexical Recognition Tests for Arabic. In *3rd International Conference on Arabic Computational Linguistics (ACLing 2017)*, Dubai, UAE. Elsevier.

Osama Hamed and Torsten Zesch. 2018. The role of diacritics in increasing the difficulty of Arabic lexical recognition tests. In *Proceedings of the 7th workshop on NLP for Computer Assisted Language Learning*, Stockholm, Sweden. LiU Electronic Press.

Yasser Hifny. 2012. Smoothing techniques for arabic diacritics restoration. In *12th Conference on Language Engineering*, pages 6–12.

John Lafferty, Andrew McCallum, and Fernando Pereira. 2001. Conditional random fields: Probabilistic models for segmenting and labeling sequence data.

Kristin Lemhöfer and Mirjam Broersma. 2012. Introducing LexTALE: A quick and valid lexical test for advanced learners of English. *Behavior Research Methods*, 44(2):325–343.

Aya S Metwally, Mohsen A Rashwan, and Amir F Atiya. 2016. A multi-layered approach for arabic text diacritization. In *Cloud Computing and Big Data Analysis (ICCCBDA), 2016 IEEE International Conference on*, pages 389–393. IEEE.

Arfath Pasha, Mohamed Al-Badrashiny, Mona Diab, Ahmed El Kholy, Ramy Eskander, Nizar Habash, Manoj Pooleery, Owen Rambow, and Ryan Roth. 2014. Madamira: A fast, comprehensive tool for morphological analysis and disambiguation of arabic. In *LREC*, pages 1094–1101.

Mohsen Rashwan, Mohamed Al-Badrashiny, Mohamed Attia, Sherif Abdou, and Ahmed Rafea. 2011. A stochastic arabic diacritizer based on a hybrid of factorized and unfactorized textual features. *Audio, Speech, and Language Processing, IEEE Transactions on*, 19(1):166–175.

John Read. 2004. Plumbing the depths: How should the construct of vocabulary knowledge be defined. *Vocabulary in a second language*, pages 209–227.

Robert Ricks. 2015. The Development of Frequency-Based Assessments of Vocabulary Breadth and Depth for L2 Arabic.

Norbert Schmitt. 2014. Size and depth of vocabulary knowledge: What the research shows. *Language Learning*, 64(4):913–951.

Tzu-Hua Wang. 2007. What strategies are effective for formative assessment in an e-learning environment? *Journal of Computer Assisted Learning*, 23(3):171–186.

Taha Zerrouki and Amar Balla. 2017. Tashkeela: Novel corpus of Arabic vocalized texts, data for auto-diacritization systems. *Data in Brief*, 11:147–151.

Expanding English and Chinese Dictionaries by Wikipedia Titles

Wei-Ting Chen, Yu-Te Wang and Chuan-Jie Lin
Department of Computer Science and Engineering
National Taiwan Ocean University
{10757025, 00557025, cjlin}@ntou.edu.tw

Abstract

This paper introduces our preliminary work in dictionary expansion by adding English and Chinese Wikipedia titles along with their linguistic features. Parts-of-speech of Chinese titles are determined by the majority of heads of their Wikipedia categories. Proper noun detection in English Wikipedia is done by checking the capitalization of the titles in the content of the articles. Title alternatives will be detected beforehand. Chinese proper noun detection is done via interlanguage links and POS. The estimated accuracy of POS determination is 71.67% and the accuracy of proper noun detection is about 83.32%.

Keywords—dictionary expansion, proper nouns, parts-of-speech, Wikipedia

1   Introduction

Dictionaries play an important role in many NLP researches. A dictionary contains a list of words. It can be used to provide candidates in Chinese word segmentation. If a dictionary also collect phrases, it can help to detect syntactic units when doing syntax parsing. Some dictionaries provide information about parts-of-speech or semantics, which is important for POS tagging and many other NLP applications (Harabagiu and Hickl, 2006; Allam and Haggag, 2012; Liu *et al.*, 2016).

A major issue of using dictionaries is the expansion of unknown words. This issue is especially important in Chinese word segmentation. If the dictionary does not recognize many new words, it is impossible to segment an input sentence correctly. It might be easy to collect unknown words from the Internet such as Wikipedia, but their parts-of-speech or other important linguistic features are not easy to be determined, because their sources are not designed for NLP purposes.

In NLP domain, there have been many researches about extracting information from Wikipedia in different aspects and methods. Popular researches include knowledge base expansion (Ji and Grishman, 2011), Wikipedia article similarity measurement by the hierarchy of categories (Ponzetto and Strube, 2007; Witten and Milne, 2008), infobox completion (Wu and Weld, 2008), and so on. Many NLP applications used Wikipedia as a resource, such as improving machine translation by Wikipedia interlanguage links (Jones *et al.*, 2008; Nguyen *et al.*, 2009), measuring document similarity (Nakamura *et al.*, 2014), word sense disambiguation (Hoffart *et al.*, 2011), annotating Wikipedia entries in documents (Kulkarni *et al.*, 2009), and question answering (Buscaldi and Rosso, 2006; Waltinger *et al.*, 2011), including answer-type decision by Wikipedia (Huang *et al.*, 2008; Chen *et al.*, 2016).

This paper proposes methods to expand English and Chinese dictionaries by adding titles of Wikipedia articles, for they are new and constantly maintained. Note that many of them are indeed multi-word phrases. Methods to add linguistic features to these new words, such as parts-of-speech, and proper nouns, are also discussed.

This paper is organized as follows. Section 2 describes how we preprocess data in Wikipedia. Section 3 introduces our approach to determine parts-of-speech. Section 4 proposes methods to decide whether a title is a proper noun or not. Section 5 shows the experimental results and Section 6 concludes the paper.

2   Preprocessing Wikipedia Data

Wikipedia is a collaborative encyclopedia contributed by real users around the world. It contains millions of Chinese pages and tens of millions of English pages. However, not all pages are main encyclopedia articles, such as the pages listed as follows. They should be discarded beforehand.

(1) **Removing administration pages:** An administrative page usually has a title containing a semicolon but not followed by a whitespace, such as "Help:Category" in English Wikipedia or "使用說明:分類" in Chinese Wikipedia. These are not main articles hence should be removed.

(2) **Removing disambiguation pages:** A disambiguation page defines an ambiguous term by providing a list of Wikipedia articles as reference. For example, the term "blue" may refer to a color "Blue", a movie "Three Colors: Blue", or many other meanings provided in the page "Blue (disambiguation)". These are not main articles hence should be removed.

(3) **Removing list pages:** A list page provides a list of Wikipedia articles concerning a specific topic, such as "List of Game of Thrones characters". We think the titles of these pages are not suitable for dictionaries and discard them. The title of an English list page usually starts with "List of" or "Lists of". A Chinese list page is often categorized under "xxx 索引" (*index*) or "xxx 列表" (*list*).

(4) **Pending redirect pages:** Redirect pages often link titles to an authoritative and highly correlated page, sometimes these titles are paraphrases. For example, both "US" and "USA" redirect to the page "United States". These pages are not included in our work described in this paper. In the future, if we can determine whether the title of a redirect page is a paraphrase to a main page, we can add this title into our dictionary and share the same linguistic features as its authoritative title.

After removing these pages, all other titles will be added into our dictionaries. The following sections propose methods to decide their linguistic features.

3 Parts-of-Speech Determination

Our first challenge is to determine the part-of-speech of each Wikipedia title. POS information is not explicitly given in Wikipedia but is essential for many NLP techniques.

The solution might be easier in English, because it is a convention to write the title of an encyclopedia article in its nominal form. For example, the editors tend to create an article named "humiliation" rather than "to humiliate". However, its corresponding Chinese title "羞辱" is a verb.

Since most of the English titles are nouns, we can determine the part-of-speech of a title by deciding whether this title is in singular or plural form (NN vs. NNS) or a common noun or proper noun (NN vs. NNP). This process is not the main focus of this paper thus will not be discussed here.

Chinese Wikipedia titles may have parts-of-speech other than nouns. In Chinese, many verbs and adjectives can be nominalized without inflection, such as the previous example "羞辱". These words only have parts-of-speech of verbs in Academia Sinica Lexicon[1], a standard Chinese lexicon, and will be not tagged as Nv (nominalized verb) until being nominalized in sentences. Therefore, there are many possible POS candidates for Chinese titles.

Besides, as defined in the Academia Sinica Lexicon, there are 44 different parts-of-speech in Chinese. We only consider open classes, i.e. nouns, verbs, and adjectives, to be POS candidates of new terms. A complete list is shown in Table 1.

POS	Meaning
A	Non-predicative adjective
Na	Common Noun
Nb	Proper Noun
Nc	Place Noun
Nd	Time Noun
VA	Active Intransitive Verb
VAC	Active Causative Verb
VB	Active Pseudo-transitive Verb
VC	Active Transitive Verb
VCL	Active Verb with a Locative Object
VD	Ditransitive Verb
VE	Active Verb with a Sentential Object
VF	Active Verb with a Verbal Object
VG	Classificatory Verb
VH	Stative Intransitive Verb
VHC	Stative Causative Verb
VI	Stative Pseudo-transitive Verb
VJ	Stative Transitive Verb
VK	Stative Verb with a Sentential Object
VL	Stative Verb with a Verbal Object

Table 1: Open Classes of Chinese Parts-of-Speech.

[1] http://ckip.iis.sinica.edu.tw/CKIP/engversion/20corpus.htm

Our approach to decide a Chinese title's POS is counting the parts-of-speech of the heads of the title's categories. As another convention, Wikipedia categories are often written in noun phrases, too. The heads of these phrases are often (but not always) hypernyms of the Wikipedia title. For example, the term "自燃" (*spontaneous combustion*) belongs to the category "燃燒" (*burning*) and hence is a verb in Chinese. Similarly, the term "自由滑" (*free skating*) is a verb because it belongs to the category "花式滑冰" (*figure skating*) whose head "滑冰" (*skating*) is a verb in Chinese.

Since Chinese is a head-final language, i.e. the head of a phrase appears at the end of that phrase, we segmented the Wikipedia category labels by the Academia Sinica Lexicon and treated the last words as the heads.

The same approach might be able to predict a title's semantic class as well, because the most frequent head is highly related to its semantic class. Take the term "飆風特攻" (Point Break) as an example. Heads of 16 of its Chinese categories are "電影" (*movie*). 6 of them are hyponyms of "movie", including "驚悚片" (*thriller film*) and "動作片" (*action movie*). Only 2 heads are not related to "movie". We can say that the semantic class of "飆風特攻" is "movie". As we have also observed some counter examples, this idea will be explored more fully in the future.

4 Proper Noun Identification

Our second challenge is to identify proper nouns from these Wikipedia titles. Some Wikipedia articles are about proper nouns (such as "United Nations") and some are not (such as "Rainbow"). As we know that proper nouns carry more information than common nouns, it will be great if the information of proper nouns can be added into a dictionary.

Proper nouns can be identified based on two features. One feature is infobox template or category type. The other is the distribution of capitalization. We will discuss these two features in the following sections.

4.1 Finding Proper Nouns by Special Categories

Some classes of Wikipedia articles can be easily decided by their categories and infoboxes. We use the following rules to collect articles in special categories and decide their properness.

(1) **Person names:** If an article uses an infobox template which belongs to the category of "people and person infobox templates" (in English Wikipedia) or "人物信息框模板" (in Chinese Wikipedia), its title is considered as a person name.

(2) **Location names:** If an article uses an infobox template which belongs to the category of "geography and place infobox templates" (in English Wikipedia) or "地理和場所信息框模板" (in Chinese Wikipedia), its title is considered as a location name.

(3) **Letters and numbers:** Pages about alphabets of a language, numbers, dates, and domain names are NOT proper nouns. They belong to some specific categories and can be easily identified.

When we say that an article belongs to Category B, we mean that this article belongs to a category that is Category B itself or B's descendant in the Wikipedia category hierarchy.

4.2 Finding Proper Nouns by Capitalization

Proper nouns in English are usually capitalized. However, it is not that straightforward because a) titles of Wikipedia articles do not always appear in the content, and b) words at the beginning of sentences are also capitalized.

To deal with the first issue, we find that the absent titles may be mentioned by using different words or phrases. These alternatives can be found by several ways as discussed later.

To identify proper-noun titles, we define a set of rules to classify them into several groups. The main feature in the grouping rules is the frequency of a title being capitalized in its article. The majority in a group defines its likelihood of having proper nouns as members.

Title Alternatives

In the case that a title does not appear in the article by itself, we need to find its alternatives by the following methods before counting the frequency of capitalized cases.

(1) Removing phrases after punctuations
Sometimes an additional phrase is attached to a title with a punctuation for the purpose of

disambiguation. Such a phrase is not part of a name and should be removed.

> **Arena, North Dakota** (*alternative: "Arena"*)
> Arena is an extinct town in Burleigh County, North Dakota. The GNIS classifies it as…

(2) Removing parenthesized phrases
Sometimes a parenthesized string is attached to a title for the purpose of disambiguation. Such a phrase is not part of a name and should be removed.

> **Android (robot)** (*alternative: "Android"*)
> An android is a humanoid robot or synthetic organism designed to look and act like…

(3) Detecting boldfaced phrases in the lead sections
A lead section[2] of a Wikipedia article *"serves as an introduction to the article and a summary of its most important contents."* If the author wants to use a different string to substitute the title, he or she will introduce this phrase in the lead section in boldface.

> **Namhansan** (*alternative: "Namhan Mountain"*)
> **Namhan Mountain** is a 460 m peak in Gyeonggi-do province, South Korea…

If there are two or more boldfaced phrases in the lead section, we choose the one which appears the most times in the article, or the most similar one (by edit distance) if tied. In the following example, the title "Halahala" does not appear in the article at all, but "Halāhala" appears many times, hence being chosen as the title's alternative.

> **Halahala** (*alternative: "Halāhala"*)
> **Halāhala** (Sanskrit हलाहल) or **kālakūṭa** (Sanskrit कालकूटं, literally: 'black mass' or 'time puzzle') is the name of a poison…

Grouping Rules

For each title (or its alternative if the original title does not appear in the article), we first count the times it is being capitalized or lowercased, at the beginning or in the middle of a sentence. But it does not count if the target title appears in a longer Wikipedia title. For example, the article of the term "football" contains the sentence *"In 1888, the Football League was founded in England, becoming the first of many professional football*

competitions."* The capitalized phrase *"the Football League"* is another Wikipedia title. So the term "football" only counts once, as "being lowercased in the middle of a sentence".

According to the times of a title being capitalized in its article, we define 10 groups as follows. The grouping rules are applied in order. One title can only belong to one group. A title which does not match any rule will remain unclassified.

G00: If a title has one capital letter which is not at its beginning, such as the capital 'M' in the title "HiM", it belongs to this group and is considered as a proper noun. Note that a title only being uppercased in its article also belongs here. An example is the title "Lindauer Dornier" in the sentence *"Lindauer DORNIER GmbH is a family-owned business…"*

G01: If a single-word title has ever been capitalized inside (not at the beginning of) a sentence, such as "Animalia" in the sentence *"Julia MacRae Books published an Animalia colouring book in 2008"*, it belongs to this group and is considered as a proper noun.

G02: If a single-word title is more often lowercased than capitalized inside its article, it belongs to this group and is considered as a common noun. An example is the title "Chuckwagon" which is found 4 times capitalized but 20 times lowercased inside its article. It is a type of wagon so it is just a common noun.

G03: If a single-word title is only lowercased in its article, it belongs to this group and is considered as a common noun.

G04: If a single-word title is only capitalized in its article but all at the beginning of sentences, it belongs to this group. Following the majority rule, i.e. most of the observed titles in this group are proper nouns, they are considered as proper nouns.

G05: If a single-word title does not appear in its article at all, it belongs to this group.

<hr>

[2] https://en.wikipedia.org/wiki/Wikipedia:Manual_of_Style/Lead_section

Following the majority rule, they are considered as common nouns.

G06: If a multi-word title contains a lowercased content word, it belongs to this group and is considered as a common noun. An example is the title "Ames test", where "test" is a content word but lowercased.

G07: If a multi-word title is capitalized at least once in its article, such as the title "First Women's Bank of California" in the sentence *"The First Women's Bank of California was a local Los Angeles bank dedicated to…"*, it belongs to this group and is considered as a proper noun.

G08: If a multi-word title appears in its article but written in lowercase, such as the title "Push Stick" in the sentence *"The purpose of a push stick is to help the user…"*, it belongs to this group and is considered as a common noun.

G09: A multi-word title does not appear in its article, but its head is often capitalized inside the article, it is considered as a proper noun.

4.3 Finding Proper Nouns by Interlanguage Links and POS

Because Chinese does not have capitalization, our first approach to identify Chinese proper nouns is via interlanguage links which connect Wikipedia articles discussing the same topic but in different languages. If a Chinese article links to an English article in the groups G00 ~ G09, the Chinese title joins that group and can be classified as its majority.

However, half of the Chinese articles do not link to any English articles. We need to look for other solutions in the future.

5 Experiments

The experimental data are dumped files of English Wikipedia and Chinese Wikipedia on 2019/2/1. After removing administrative, disambiguation, and list pages, there are totally 5,679,503 English Wikipedia main articles and 995,294 Chinese Wikipedia main articles. After further identifying person names, location names, letters and numbers, 3,905,050 English and 839,174 Chinese articles are waited to be processed as shown in Table 2.

5.1 Parts-of-Speech Determination for Chinese Titles

To observe the correctness of POS determination, we chose 21,211 Chinese titles which have appeared and been manually POS-tagged in ASBC (Academia Sinica Balanced Corpus) (Chen *et al.*, 1996) and have category labels in Wikipedia. Note that they may have more than one POS in ASBC. Methods introduced in Section 3 were used to predict POS sets for these Chinese titles.

We made three different observations. If only top 1 choice counted, there were 11,459 correct guessing with an accuracy of 54%. If any match in the POS sets counted, 15,201 correct guessing made an accuracy of 71.67%. It means that the guessed POS sets were efficient candidates for further verification in the future.

One major type of the errors is that categories tend to be nouns. For example, the term "羞辱" (humiliation) is a verb in Chinese, but its categories are "道德" (morality), "情緒" (emotions), and "性行為" (sexual acts), which are all nouns in Chinese.

5.2 Proper Noun Detection in English

3,905,050 English main articles were grouped by the rules introduced in Section 4. There were still 125,924 articles left as unclassified.

To evaluate the accuracy of proper noun detection, we randomly selected a small subset in

Type	English	Chinese
Main pages	5,679,503	995,294
Person names	1,505,094	49,592
Location names	263,805	100,586
Letters & numbers	5,554	5,942
To be processed	3,905,050	839,174

Table 2: Pre-Determined Wikipedia Pages.

Group	Articles	Proper	Subset	Acc.
G00	330,569	Y	101	84.16%
G01	450,022	Y	107	80.37%
G02	22,947	N	103	100.0%
G03	24,490	N	103	96.12%
G04	150,090	Y	110	91.82%
G05	46,764	N	103	56.31%
G06	957,198	N	162	82.72%
G07	1,581,486	Y	222	83.33%
G08	470	N	107	83.18%
G09	238,037	Y	108	84.62%
noG	125,924	N	108	83.33%

Table 3: English Proper Noun Detection Accuracy.

each group and assessed by human. The performance is shown in Table 3. The estimated overall accuracy is about 83.32%.

One type of the errors is that a common-noun title appears inside a proper name but the proper name is not a Wikipedia title, such as "chuckwagon" in the name "the American Chuckwagon Association". If the title does not appear many times, it will be misclassified as a proper noun.

Another type of the errors is the inconsistent capitalization of the writers. For example, the term "East Bradford Township" is the name of a township in US, but the authors of this Wikipedia article also use "East Bradford township" to refer to this area, and the term is misclassified as a common noun.

5.3   Proper Noun Detection in Chinese

Only 554,892 of 839,174 Chinese articles can be mapped to English articles via interlanguage links. 85,302 of them map to person names, 42,727 to location names, and 4,323 to letters or numbers. 410,258 are grouped into G00 ~ G09 and 292,268 of them are classified as proper nouns.

6   Conclusion

This paper depicts our preliminary work of dictionary expansion by adding Wikipedia titles. The parts-of-speech of Chinese titles are decided by the voting of heads of their categories. English proper nouns are identified by cases of capitalization, while Chinese ones are identified via interlanguage links. These methods achieved an accuracy of 71.67% in POS determination and 83.32% in English proper noun detection.

More modern methods will be experimented in the future. Sentences containing Wikipedia titles will be POS-tagged to decide the titles' POS. Their semantic classes and properness can be determined by deep learning.

Acknowledgments

This research was funded by the Taiwan Ministry of Science and Technology (grant: MOST 106-2221-E-019-072.)

References

Ali Mohamed Nabil Allam and Mohamed Hassan Haggag. 2012. The question answering systems: a survey. *International Journal of Research and Reviews in Information Sciences (IJRRIS)*, 2(3):211-221.

David Buscaldi and Paolo Rosso. 2006. Mining knowledge from Wikipedia for the question answering task. In *Proceedings of the 5th International Conference on Language Resources and Evaluation (LREC 2006)*, pages 727-730.

Keh-Jiann Chen, Chu-Ren Huang, Li-ping Chang, and Hui-Li Hsu. 1996. Sinica Corpus: design methodology for balanced corpora. In *Proceeding of the 11th Pacific Asia Conference on Language, Information and Computation*, pages 167-176.

Po-Chun Chen, Meng-Jie Zhuang, and Chuan-Jie Lin. 2016. Using Wikipedia and semantic resources to find answer types and appropriate answer candidate sets in question answering. In *Proceedings of the Open Knowledge Base and Question Answering (OKBQA) Workshop, the 26th International Conference on Computational Linguistics (COLING 2016)*, pages 1-10.

Sanda Harabagiu and Andrew Hickl. 2006. Methods for using textual entailment in open-domain question answering. In *Proceedings of the 21st International Conference on Computational Linguistics and the 44th annual meeting of the ACL*, pages 905-912.

Johannes Hoffart, Mohamed Amir Yosef, Ilaria Bordino, Hagen Fürstenau, Manfred Pinkal, Marc Spaniol, Bilyana Taneva, Stefan Thater, and Gerhard Weikum. 2011. Robust disambiguation of named entities in text. In *Proceedings of the Conference on Empirical Methods in Natural Language Processing (EMNLP '11)*, pages 782-792.

Zhiheng Huang, Marcus Thint, and Zengchang Qin. 2008. Question classification using head words and their hypernyms. In *Proceedings of the Conference on Empirical Methods in Natural Language Processing (EMNLP '08)*, pages 927-936.

Heng Ji and Ralph Grishman. 2011. Knowledge base population: successful approaches and challenges. In *Proceedings of the 49th Annual Meeting of the Association for Computational Linguistics: Human Language Technologies (HLT '11)*, pages 1148-1158.

Gareth J.F. Jones, Fabio Fantino, Eamonn Newman, and Ying Zhang. 2008. Domain-specific query translation for multilingual information access using machine translation augmented with dictionaries mined from Wikipedia. In *Proceedings of CLIA 2008 - 2nd International Workshop on Cross Lingual Information Access, the 3rd International Joint Conference on Natural Language Processing (IJCNLP 2008)*, pages 34-41.

Sayali Kulkarni, Amit Singh, Ganesh Ramakrishnan, and Soumen Chakrabarti. 2009. Collective annotation of Wikipedia entities in web text. In *Proceedings of the 15th ACM SIGKDD*

International Conference on Knowledge Discovery and Data Mining (KDD '09), pages 457-466.

Chi-Ting Liu, Shao-Heng Chen, and Chuan-Jie Lin. 2016. Learning textual entailment classification from a Chinese RITE dataset specialized for linguistic phenomena. In *Proceedings of IEEE 17th International Conference on Information Reuse and Integration (IRI), IEEE International Workshop on Empirical Methods for Recognizing Inference in Text (EMRITE)*, pages 506-512.

Tatsuya Nakamura, Masumi Shirakawa, Takahiro Hara, and Shojiro Nishio. 2014. Semantic similarity measurements for multi-lingual short texts using Wikipedia. In *Proceedings of the 2014 IEEE/WIC/ACM International Joint Conferences on Web Intelligence (WI) and Intelligent Agent Technologies (IAT)*, pages 22-29.

Dong Nguyen, Arnold Overwijk, Claudia Hauff, Dolf R. B. Trieschnigg, Djoerd Hiemstra, and Franciska de Jong. 2009. WikiTranslate: query translation for cross-lingual information retrieval using only Wikipedia. *Evaluating Systems for Multilingual and Multimodal Information Access*, 5706:58-65.

Simone Paolo Ponzetto and Michael Strube. 2007. Knowledge derived from Wikipedia for computing semantic relatedness. *Journal of Artificial Intelligence Research (JAIR)*, 30:181-212.

Ulli Waltinger, Alexa Breuing, and Ipke Wachsmuth. 2011. Interfacing virtual agents with collaborative knowledge: open domain question answering using Wikipedia-based topic models. In *Proceedings of the 22nd International Joint Conference on Artificial Intelligence (IJCAI-11)*, pages 1896-1902.

Ian Witten and David Milne. 2008. An effective, low-cost measure of semantic relatedness obtained from Wikipedia links. In *Proceeding of AAAI Workshop on Wikipedia and Artificial Intelligence: an Evolving Synergy*, pages 25-30.

Fei Wu and Daniel S. Weld. 2008. Automatically refining the Wikipedia infobox ontology. In *Proceedings of the 17th International Conference on World Wide Web (WWW '08)*, pages 635-644.

Production of the Voicing Contrast by Greek Children with Cochlear Implants

Georgia A. Koupka, Areti Okalidou
University of Macedonia
Thessaloniki. Greece
georgiakoupka@gmail.com
okalidou@uom.edu.gr

Katerina Nicolaidis
Aristotle
University of Thessaloniki,
Greece
knicol@enl.auth.gr

Ioannis Konstantinidis, Georgios Kyriafinis
AHEPA Hospital
1stOtorhinolaryngology Clinic,
Thessaloniki, Greece
{orlcln, orlcln}@med.auth.gr

Abstract

Previous research has documented variability in speech production by speakers with CI. With reference to stop production, VOT duration has been reported to differ for children with Cochlear Implants (CI) and normal hearing (NH) in different languages. As the voicing contrast differs across languages, it is important to examine VOT production in the speech of individuals with CI in different languages. The Greek stop consonant inventory consists of voiceless unaspirated stops and prevoiced stops at the bilabial, dental and velar places of articulation. In this study, VOT duration is examined for voiceless and voiced word initial stops in the context of the vowel /a/ produced by 24 Greekspeaking children with CI and 24 agematched children with NH. Results showed a tendency for longer VOT duration for the voiceless stops produced by the children with NH than with CI and longer prevoicing for the children with CI compared to their NH peers.

1 Introduction

Past research on children with profound hearing loss reported that variation in certain acoustic characteristics, such as the voicing contrast in stop consonants, impacts negatively on their speech intelligibility (Metz et al., 1990; Monsen, 1983). The speech intelligibility of children with profound hearing loss has greatly improved following cochlear implantation (Lane et al., 1995). Yet, a lot of variability in production has been observed, often attributed to several factors, such as the age of onset of hearing loss, the age of cochlear implantation (Dunn et al., 2014; Geers et al., 2003; Fryauf-Bertschy et al., 1997) but also to factors relevant to limitations of cochlear implant technology such as inadequate processing of the spectral and fine temporal structure of speech (Oxenham and Kreft, 2014; Zeng et al., 2008; Rubinstein, 2004).

A cue of fine acoustic contrast is Voice Onset Time (VOT), defined as the temporal interval between the moment of the release of the stop and the onset of glottal pulsing. It takes positive values when the stop release precedes the onset of voicing and negative values when the stop release occurs after the onset of voicing. Values clustering at 0 ms indicate simultaneous release of the articulatory closure and the onset of vocalic voicing (Lisker and Abramson, 1964).

Previous research has shown that VOT duration differs in children with CI as compared to children with NH. (Scarbel et al., 2013) reported longer VOT durations for voiceless stops and shorter VOT values for voiced stops for French speaking children with CI compared to NH controls. They interpreted their findings to suggest exaggeration of the voicing contrast between voiced and voiceless stops by children with CI. (Aksoy et al., 2017) examined variation in VOT duration as a function of the duration of cochlear implantation. They reported VOT values for children with CI with 1 up to 8 years of implantation. Overall, shorter VOT durations were reported for all voiceless and voiced consonants for children with 1-3 years of

CI use. They also reported that longer implant use resulted in VOT durations that were closer to the NH controls.

As the voicing contrast differs across languages, it is important to examine VOT production in the speech of individuals with CI in different languages. This study aims to provide insights on VOT production by children with CI by examining data from Greek.

The Greek stop consonant inventory consists of voiceless unaspirated stops /p, t, k/ and pre-voiced stops /b, d, g/ (Arvaniti, 1999). Several studies have reported VOT duration for adult speakers of Greek (see Arvaniti, 2007 for a review) but there are few studies for children (Okalidou et al., 2010; Tsiartsioni, 2011; Chionidou and Nicolaidis, 2015). (Okalidou et al., 2010) reported VOT values ranging approximately between -140ms to -60ms for voiced stops and 10 to 50ms for voiceless stops for Greek children whose ages ranged from 2;0 to 4;0 The same study reported that Greek speaking children acquire an adult-like two-way voicing contrast, i.e. between the pre-voiced and the voiceless unaspirated stops, at all places of articulation (bilabial, dental, velar) by ages 2;62;11 (3035 months). (Tsiartsioni, 2011) examined VOT duration for Greek-speaking and English speaking children aged 10, 13 and 16 years old. VOT duration ranged between 11.98 ms to 12.85 ms for /p/, 14.29 ms to 14.83 ms for /t/, 28.89 ms to 31.86 ms for /k/, -95.90 ms to -98.68 ms for /b/, -91.40 ms to -99.99 ms for /d/ and -85.08 ms to -103.42 for /g/ for Greek. VOT duration ranged between 51.9 ms to 67.98 ms for /p/, 66.12 ms to 79.16 ms for /t/, 60 ms to 82.06 ms for /k/, -0.14 ms to -28.88 ms for /b/, -0.14 ms to -22.66 ms for /d/ and 5.72 ms to -21.10 for /g/ for English. (Chionidou and Nicolaidis, 2015) reported VOT mean values of 17 ms for [p], 17 ms for [t] and 37 ms for [k] for Greek children whose ages ranged from 8;2 to 12;6.

Furthermore previous research has examined several parameters that may have an effect on VOT production, including place of articulation, stress, and the following vowel. For voiceless stops, as articulation moves from the bilabial to the velar place of articulation the duration of VOT increases, e.g. for English (Peterson and Lehiste, 1960; Klatt, 1975; Volaitis and Miller, 1992; Cho and Ladefoged, 1999; Whiteside and Marshall, 2001; Morris et al., 2008), for Greek (Fourakis,

1986; Nicolaidis, 2002), for German (Lein et al., 2016), for Spanish (Schmidt and Flege, 1996), for Hungarian (Gósy and Ringen, 2009), for Cantonese (Tse, 2005), for Armenian and Korean (Cho and Ladefoged, 1999). On the other hand, prevoicing is longer for bilabials and dentals than velars in various languages (e.g. Helgason and Ringen, 2008 for Standard Swedish). Stress has not been found to influence the VOT duration of voiceless stops. Voiced stops tend to have longer VOT values in unstressed syllables but this difference has not been found to be statistically significant for English (Abramson and Lisker, 1964). Typically, the VOT of voiceless stops is longer when a high vowel follows than in the context of a low vowel (Lisker and Abramson, 1964, 1967; Klatt, 1975; Smith, 1978; Port and Rotunno, 1979; Morris et al., 2008; Nicolaidis, 2002).

In this study, the VOT duration of the Greek stop consonants /p, t, k, b, d, g/ in word initial position will be measured. The research questions are: a) Are there any differences in the VOT duration between Greek-speaking children with CI and NH? b) Are there any differences in VOT duration as a function of place of articulation for Greek-speaking children with CI compared to children with NH? To our knowledge, there has been no previous study examining VOT production for Greekspeaking children with CI. The study of VOT production is of theoretical and clinical importance. Clinically, the onset of voicing is usually used for the evaluation of developmental maturation of neuro-motor coordination (DiSimoni, 1974; Eguchi, 1969; Zlatin and Koenigsknecht, 1976) and constitutes an essential part of the evaluation of speech production in people with hearing loss (Monsen, 1976).

2 Method

2.1 Participants

Twenty four children with CI and twenty four age- and gender-matched children with NH participated in the study. The participants ages ranged from 2;8 to 13;3. Post-implant age ranged from 1;11 months to 11;5 (23-137 months). All participants were monolingual native speakers of Greek. In an attempt to avoid any additional effect of mental health, the Raven Test was administered; the scores for both groups ranged from 90 to 135 which is within normal limits. The speakers of the control group did not have any hearing or speech problems as reported by their parents. Signed consent was obtained from the parents of all participants.

2.2 Material

The speech material consisted of Greek disyllabic and trisyllabic real words with word initial voiceless and voiced stops /p, t, k, b, d, g/. Stops were followed by the vowel /a/, e.g. ('papa, 'bala, 'tafos, 'dama, ka'fes, ga'raz). Stress placement was on the first or second syllable.

2.3 Procedure

A word naming task was carried out and each target word was produced at least three times in random order by all participants.

Data acquisition took place at the Cochlear Implant Center of the 1stOtorhinolaryngology Clinic of AHEPA Hospital in Thessaloniki. Data was recorded in a sound-proof booth with a SONY PCM D50 digital recorder.

2.4 Measurements

PRAAT was used for the measurement of VOT duration (www.praat.org). For voiceless stops, VOT was measured from the stop burst to the onset of the first glottal cycle and formant structure on the acoustic waveform and spectrogram respectively. For the voiced stops, VOT was measured from the first glottal cycle of the stop to the stop burst. A total of 864 tokens were produced (48 children x 6 words x 3 repetitions).

Our data didnt follow a normal distribution and violated the principle of homogeneity based on the Levenes test. Thus, non-parametric tests Mann-Whitney U test and Wilcoxon, were used for the analyses. Differences between the two groups (CI/NH) were measured.

Due to the wide range in the age of the participants, there was not homogeneity in the sample. So, further analyses were carried out on participants separated in four age subgroups by chronological age: the first group consisted of children from 2 to 4 years old (4 children in total, 2 with CI & 2 with NH), the second group ranged from 5 to 7 years old (18 children in total, 9 with CI & 9 with NH), the third group ranged from 8 to 10 years old (16 children in total, 8 with CI & 8 with NH) and the last group ranged from 11 to 13 years old (10 children in total, 5 with CI & 5 with NH).

Category	Child groups		P value	U
	NH	CI		
[voiceless]*	18.22	15.30	0.012	167.5
[voiced]	-89.45	-106.08	0.059	195.0

*p<0.05

Table 1: Mean VOT values for voiced and voiceless Greek stops produced by children with CI and with NH, n=48.

Category	Child groups		P value	U
	NH	CI		
voiceless				
[p]	15.14	12.08	0.075	201.5
[t]	12.19	9.14	0.091	205.5
[k]	27.33	24.68	0.126	214.0
voiced				
[b]	-105.97	-129.85	0.070	200.5
[d]*	-94.69	-121.10	0.009	164.5
[g]	-67.68	-67.31	0.789	274.0

*p<0.05

Table 2: Mean VOT values, p and U values for voiced and voiceless Greek stops produced by children with CI and NH as a function of place of articulation, n=48.

3 Results

All participants with CI and NH Table 1 presents mean VOT durations of the Greek voiceless and voiced stops (pooled for place of articulation) produced by all participants with CI and NH. For the voiceless stops, a statistically significant difference was found in overall VOT duration between the two groups; VOT duration was shorter in the stop productions of children with CI as compared to NH controls, p=0.012, d=-0.3586. For the voiced stops, children with CI showed longer mean prevoicing values as compared to their NH peers; however, the difference was not statistically significant. Table 2 presents mean VOT values for the stops at each place of articulation Group comparisons for each place of articulation, for the voiced and voiceless categories revealed a statistically significant difference only for the voiced alveolar stop /d/ , U=164.5, p=0.009 (d=0.36762). In particular, mean VOT for /d/ was significantly longer for the children with CI than NH. Longer VOT was also found for /b/ for the same group; however it did not reach statistical significance. VOT duration for /g/ was similar

	R				SD	
	NH		CI		NH	CI
	Min	Max	Min	Max		
p	5	22	5	26	5.936	5.328
t	6	34	0	18	5.731	4.485
k	14	42	13	63	8.515	11.729
b	-191	-65	-404	-34	31.579	69.070
d	-153	-60	-323	0	25.341	63.097
g	-119	-29	-180	0	26.494	48.410

Table 3: Range and Standard Deviation values for voiced and voiceless Greek stops produced by children with CI and NH n=48.

for the two groups. In addition, there was a tendency for the VOT of /p, t, k/, to be shorter for the children with CI than NH although differences did not reach statistical significance. Table 3 presents the range and standard deviation values for all the stops measured.

With reference to the influence of place of articulation, a tendency for longer VOT duration for the voiceless velar stops /k/ is observed, in agreement with previous literature (Okalidou et al., 2010; Tsiartsioni, 2011; Chionidou and Nicolaidis, 2015). This is evident for both groups. For the voiced consonants, a decrease in VOT duration is evident from /b/ to /d/ to /g/ for both groups, (cf. (Tsiartsioni, 2011) for children with NH); additional statistical analyses are needed to confirm the place of articulation effect.

Group A: 2-4 years old A comparison between the two groups shows shorter VOT values for voiceless and voiced consonants for children with CI. However, no statistically significant differences were found (Table 4) (p=0.333, U=0.000, for /p/, p=0.667, U=1.000, for /t/, p=0.667, U=1.000, for /k/, p=0.667, U=1.000, for /b/, p=1.000, U=2.000, for /d/, p=0.667, U=1.000, for /g/).

Group B: 5-7 years old A comparison between the two groups shows shorter VOT values for the voiceless and longer for the voiced consonants except for the voiced velar /g/ for children with CI. However, no statistically significant differences were found (Table 4) (p=0.279, U=21.000 for /p/, p=0.195, U=19.000 for /t/, p=0.065, U=14.000 for /k/, p=0.798, U=29.000 for /b/, p=0.083, U=15.000 for /d/, p=0.328, U=22.000 for /g/).

Group C: 8-10 years old A comparison between the two groups shows shorter VOT values for the voiceless and longer for the voiced for children CI. However, no statistically significant differences were found (Table 4) (p=0.297, U=28.000 for /p/, p=1.000, U=40.500 for /t/, p=0.863, U=38.500 for /k/, p=0.063, U=19.000 for /b/, p=0.161, U=24.000 for /d/, p=0.730, U=36.000 for /g/).

Group D: 11-13 years old A comparison between the two groups shows shorter VOT values for the voiceless consonants and longer for the voiced, except for the voiceless velar /k/, for children with CI. However, no statistically significant differences were found (Table 4) (p=0.548, U=9.000 for /p/, p=0.095, U=4.500 for /t/, p=0.1.000, U=12.000 for /k/, p=0.056, U=3.000 for /b/, p=0.095, U=4.000 for /d/, p=0.095, U=4.000 for /g/).

4   Discussion

Many studies have measured VOT in different languages but there is relatively limited literature for VOT duration in Greek especially with reference to children. This study contributes to current knowledge by providing VOT data for Greek-speaking children with cochlear implants.

Our results have shown significantly shorter VOT duration for the voiceless stops (pooled for place of articulation) when produced by children with CI compared to NH controls. Further analyses for each consonant separately showed that there was a tendency for shorter VOT values to be produced by children with CI for all voiceless consonants; however this difference did not reach statistical significance. With reference to the voiced stops, significantly longer prevoicing was produced for /d/ by children with CI. A similar tendency was observed for /b/ but this difference was not statistically significant.

Further analyses per age group showed that for the voiceless consonants there is a tendency for shorter VOT values produced by children with CI in all age groups. For the voiced consonants there is a tendency for longer VOT values produced by children with CI in all but the first age group (2-4 years of age). This may relate to ongoing developmental changes for this group (cf. Okalidou et al., 2010).

Differences in VOT values were observed as a function of place of articulation. Both groups

		[p]	[t]	[k]	[b]	[d]	[g]
Age Group							
1	NH	14.67	11.83	26.33	-146	-104.67	-77
(n=4)	CI	8.5	6.5	19.17	-127.17	-98.5	-65.33
2	NH	14.46	11.29	28.54	-117.88	-104.46	-74.83
(n=18)	CI	11.17	8.12	19.63	-140.17	-148.58	-51.33
3	NH	15.30	10.37	27.19	-97.89	-94.37	-64.33
(n=16)	CI	11.56	9.70	26.56	-132.81	-106.78	-68.11
4	NH	16.13	17.07	26.07	-85.47	-75.67	-58.53
(n=10)	CI	15.93	10.80	31.60	-109.07	-111.93	-92.20

Table 4: Mean VOT values for voiced and voiceless Greek stops produced by children with CI and NH /, for the age groups 1, 2, 3 & 4.

(CI/NH) present the same pattern in VOT for the different places of articulation. For children in all subgroups, there was a tendency for the VOT duration of voiceless stops to increase from bilabials/dentals to velars, which is consistent with previous studies reporting longer VOT duration the further back the closure is produced (Peterson and Lehiste, 1960; Klatt, 1975; Fourakis, 1986; Volaitis and Miller, 1992; Cho and Ladefoged, 1999; Whiteside and Marshall, 2001; Nicolaidis, 2002; Morris et al., 2008). For voiced consonants, there was a tendency for the VOT duration to decrease from bilabials to dentals to velars which is also in agreement with previous studies (Helgason and Ringen, 2008).

5 Conclusion

Overall our results showed a tendency for longer VOT duration for the voiceless stops produced by children with NH than CI and longer prevoicing for the children with CI compared to their NH peers. Few statistically significant differences were however found in an analysis by place of articulation and for different age subgroups.

Work currently underway aims to relate findings to the duration of CI use, to the speech perception abilities of children with CI, and to explore subject variability as well as variability due to other factors including different vowel contexts.

References

Gökçe Aksoy, Abdullah Dalgıç, Tolga Kandoğan, and Levent Olgun. 2017. Evaluation of the articulatory characteristics of voice in cochlear implanted children. *ENT Updates*, 7(3):131–138.

Amalia Arvaniti. 1999. Standard modern greek. *Journal of the International Phonetic Association*, 29(2):167–172.

Amalia Arvaniti. 2007. Greek phonetics: The state of the art. *Journal of Greek linguistics*, 8(1):97–208.

Anastasia Chionidou and Katerina Nicolaidis. 2015. Voice onset time in bilingual greek-german children. In *ICPhS*.

Taehong Cho and Peter Ladefoged. 1999. Variation and universals in vot: evidence from 18 languages. *Journal of phonetics*, 27(2):207–229.

Frank G DiSimoni. 1974. Effect of vowel environment on the duration of consonants in the speech of three-, six-, and nine-year-old children. *The Journal of the Acoustical Society of America*, 55(2):360–361.

Camille C Dunn, Elizabeth A Walker, Jacob Oleson, Maura Kenworthy, Tanya Van Voorst, J Bruce Tomblin, Haihong Ji, Karen I Kirk, Bob McMurray, Marlan Hanson, et al. 2014. Longitudinal speech perception and language performance in pediatric cochlear implant users: The effect of age at implantation. *Ear and hearing*, 35(2):148.

Suco Eguchi. 1969. Development of speech sounds in children. *Acta Otolaryngol*, 257:1–51.

Marios Fourakis. 1986. A timing model for word-initial cv syllables in modern greek. *The Journal of the Acoustical Society of America*, 79(6):1982–1986.

Holly Fryauf-Bertschy, Richard S Tyler, Danielle MR Kelsay, Bruce J Gantz, and George G Woodworth. 1997. Cochlear implant use by prelingually deafened children: The influences of age at implant and length of device use. *Journal of Speech, Language, and Hearing Research*, 40(1):183–199.

Ann Geers, Chris Brenner, and Lisa Davidson. 2003. Factors associated with development of speech perception skills in children implanted by age five. *Ear and Hearing*, 24(1):24S–35S.

Mária Gósy and Catherine O Ringen. 2009. Everything you always wanted to know about vot in hungarian. In *IXth International Conference on the Structure of Hungarian*.

Pétur Helgason and Catherine Ringen. 2008. Voicing and aspiration in swedish stops. *Journal of phonetics*, 36(4):607–628.

Dennis H Klatt. 1975. Voice onset time, frication, and aspiration in word-initial consonant clusters. *Journal of Speech and Hearing Research*, 18(4):686–706.

Harlan Lane, Jane Wozniak, Melanie Matthies, Mario Svirsky, and Joseph Perkell. 1995. Phonemic resetting versus postural adjustments in the speech of cochlear implant users: An exploration of voice-onset time. *The Journal of the Acoustical Society of America*, 98(6):3096–3106.

Tatjana Lein, Tanja Kupisch, and Joost van de Weijer. 2016. Voice onset time and global foreign accent in german–french simultaneous bilinguals during adulthood. *International Journal of Bilingualism*, 20(6):732–749.

Leigh Lisker and Arthur S Abramson. 1964. A cross-language study of voicing in initial stops: Acoustical measurements. *Word*, 20(3):384–422.

Leigh Lisker and Arthur S Abramson. 1967. Some effects of context on voice onset time in english stops. *Language and speech*, 10(1):1–28.

Dale Evan Metz, Vincent J Samar, Nicholas Schiavetti, and Ronald W Sitler. 1990. Acoustic dimensions of hearing-impaired speakers intelligibility: Segmental and suprasegmental characteristics. *Journal of Speech, Language, and Hearing Research*, 33(3):476–487.

Randall B Monsen. 1976. The production of english stop consonants in the speech of deaf children. *Journal of Phonetics*, 4(1):29–41.

Randall B Monsen. 1983. The oral speech intelligibility of hearing-impaired talkers. *Journal of Speech and Hearing Disorders*, 48(3):286–296.

Richard J Morris, Christopher R McCrea, and Kaileen D Herring. 2008. Voice onset time differences between adult males and females: Isolated syllables. *Journal of Phonetics*, 36(2):308–317.

Katerina Nicolaidis. 2002. Durational variability in vowel-consonant-vowel sequences in greek: The influence of phonetic identity, context and speaker. *Selected papers on theoretical and applied linguistics*, 14:280–294.

Areti Okalidou, Kakia Petinou, Eleni Theodorou, and Eleni Karasimou. 2010. Development of voice onset time in standard-greek and cypriot-greek-speaking preschoolers. *Clinical linguistics & phonetics*, 24(7):503–519.

Andrew J Oxenham and Heather A Kreft. 2014. Speech perception in tones and noise via cochlear implants reveals influence of spectral resolution on temporal processing. *Trends in Hearing*, 18:2331216514553783.

Gordon E Peterson and Ilse Lehiste. 1960. Duration of syllable nuclei in english. *The Journal of the Acoustical Society of America*, 32(6):693–703.

Robert F Port and Rosemarie Rotunno. 1979. Relation between voice-onset time and vowel duration. *The Journal of the Acoustical Society of America*, 66(3):654–662.

Jay T Rubinstein. 2004. How cochlear implants encode speech. *Current opinion in otolaryngology & head and neck surgery*, 12(5):444–448.

Lucie Scarbel, Anne Vilain, and Hélène Loevenbruck. 2013. Phonetic characteristics of speech production by french children wearing cochlear implants.

Anna Marie Schmidt and James Emil Flege. 1996. Speaking rate effects on stops produced by spanish and english monolinguals and spanish/english bilinguals. *Phonetica*, 53(3):162–179.

Bruce L Smith. 1978. Temporal aspects of english speech production: A developmental perspective. *Journal of Phonetics*, 6(1):37–67.

Holman Tse. 2005. *The phonetics of VOT and tone interaction in Cantonese*. Ph.D. thesis, University of Chicago.

Eleni Tsiartsioni. 2011. *The Acquisition of Speech Rhythm and Stop Voicing by Greek Learners of English: A pedagogical and linguistic approach*. Ph.D. thesis, Aristotle University of Thessaloniki.

Lydia E Volaitis and Joanne L Miller. 1992. Phonetic prototypes: Influence of place of articulation and speaking rate on the internal structure of voicing categories. *The Journal of the Acoustical Society of America*, 92(2):723–735.

Sandra P Whiteside and Jeni Marshall. 2001. Developmental trends in voice onset time: Some evidence for sex differences. *Phonetica*, 58(3):196–210.

Fan-Gang Zeng, Stephen Rebscher, William Harrison, Xiaoan Sun, and Haihong Feng. 2008. Cochlear implants: system design, integration, and evaluation. *IEEE reviews in biomedical engineering*, 1:115–142.

Marsha A Zlatin and Roy A Koenigsknecht. 1976. Development of the voicing contrast: A comparison of voice onset time in stop perception and production. *Journal of Speech and Hearing Research*, 19(1):93–111.

SumSAT: Hybrid Arabic Text Summarization Based on Symbolic and Numerical Approaches

Said Moulay Lakhdar and Mohamed Amine Cheragui
Mathematics and Computer Science Department
Ahmed Draia University
Adrar, Algeria
moulaylakhdarsaid@yahoo.fr, m_cheragui@univ-adrar.dz

Abstract

The increase in number and volume of electronic documents makes the development of applications such as text summarization crucial, in order to facilitate the task for persons who want to consult their documents. The purpose of an electronic document summary is the same as that of a book abstract; it informs the reader about the subject matter. The usefulness of the summary is distinguished by the limited time devoted to its reading to synthesize all the ideas that the author wants to spend.

The objective of this paper is to present our SumSAT tool, which is an Arabic text summarization system, adopting an extraction approach. The originality of our work lies in the use of a hybrid methodology that combines three methods: contextual exploration, indicative expression, and graph method. The proposed strategy is evaluated by comparing the obtained results with human summaries using recall and precision metrics.

1   Introduction

Considered for a long time as one of the main topic of natural language processing (Luhn, 1958), Text summarization has only grown in importance since the late 90s with the proliferation of Internet use and the emergence of large amounts of information (Maâloul, 2012), which has forced researchers to make more effort to make the text summarization process more efficient. This effectiveness is linked to two (02) essential factors, on the one side reducing the size of the text and on the other side keeping the basic idea (or ideas) that are conveyed by the text.

The purpose of this paper is to present SumSAT which is a text summarization system developed for the Arabic texts. The originality of our work lies in making a contribution not only in the pre-processing phase which consists in preparing the text for the summarization process but also in the processing phase where we have chosen a hybrid strategy that showcases several techniques from different approaches.

The rest of the paper is organized as follows: Section 2 will focus on the principle of Text summarization. Section 3, briefly describes works in the literature that are related to Arabic text summarization. Section 4 presents our hybrid approach based on contextual exploration, Indicative expression and graph method. Section 5 introduces the SumSAT tool. The results of experiments on the dataset of Arabic are discussed in Section 6. Finally, a conclusion that presents the assessment of our work associated with perspectives and future work.

2   Text Summarization Between Abstraction and Extraction

There are two very divergent approaches to automatically generate summaries (Pai, 2014; Munot and Govilkar 2014; Allahyari et al., 2017). Summarization based on Abstraction and Summarization based on Extraction.; the first one (Abstraction approach) comes from the field of artificial intelligence and aims to use natural language processing techniques (such as semantic representation and modification, text understanding) to generate a new summary (with new words) that covers the main ideas found in the original text. This production process remains relatively difficult to compute, and text generation is still very imperfect (Pal and Saha 2014; Zhu et al.,2009; D'Avanzo et al., 2004).

However, in the extraction-based approach, the main purpose is to extract the most important or significant phrases in the original text and combining them to make a summary. Its objective is to produce the summary without going through deeper analysis, so the main task is to determine the relevance of these phrases according to one or more criteria (generally a statistical features) (Mohamed, 2016; Oufaidaa et al.,2014).

3 Related Work

Compared to other languages such as English, works on the Arabic language are very few due mainly to its morphological and syntactic complexity. The table below gives an indication of some tools and works done on Arabic text summarization (Douzidia and Lapalme, 2004; Sobh et al., 2006; Schlesinger et al., 2008; Mahmoud et al., 2009; Alotaiby et al., 2012; Belguith, 2014; AL-Khawaldeh and Samawi , 2015; Belkebir and Guessoum, 2015; Lagrini et al., 2017).

Tool and Work	Methodology	
LAKHAS (Douzidia and Lapalme)	Numerical	Sentence position terms frequency title words cue words
Al Sanie	Symbolic	RST (Rhetorical Structure Theory)
Sobh, Ibrahim, Nevin Darwish, and Magda Fayek	Numerical	Bayesian Genetic Programming classification
CLASSY (Schlesinger, Judith D., Dianne P. O'leary, and John M. Conroy)	Numerical	Log-likelihood
AQBTSS and ACBTSS (Mahmoud O.EI-Haj and Bassam H. Hammo)	Numerical	TF-IDF

Table 1: Summarizing reviewed Works and tools (A).

Tool and Work	Methodology	
Alotaiby, Fahad, Salah Foda, and Ibrahim Alkharashi.	Numerical	Frequency of non-stop words Machine Learning
Belghuith	Hybrid	RST Machine Learning
LCEAS (AL-Khawaldeh and Samawi)	Hybrid	Based on semantic relations Roots extraction
Belkebir and Guessoum	Numerical	Machine Learning
Samira Lagrini, Mohammed Redjimi and NabihaAzizi	Hybrid	RST machine Learning

Table 2: Summarizing reviewed Works and tools (B).

4 SumSAT's general architecture

SumSAT is a text summarization system by extraction. To generate a summary, our system operates in three main steps, which are:

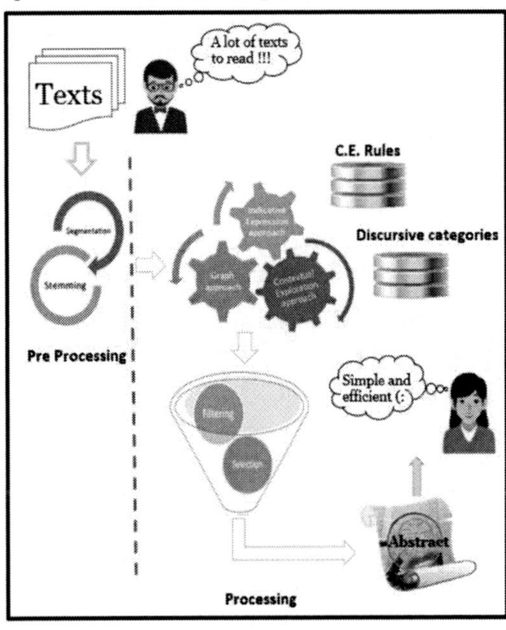

Figure 1: General architecture of SumSAT.

4.1 Step 1: Pre-processing

This phase is divided into two sub-phases:

Segmentation: Since the text summarization operation consists in selecting relevant phrases, the first task to be performed is the segmentation of the source text into phrases. The method used to divide a text is based on the contextual exploration method, where the input is a plain text in the form of a single text segment. The segmentation starts with detecting the presence of indicators, which are punctuation marks (« . », « ; », « : », « ! », « ? ».). If there is an indicator, segmentation rules will be applied to explore the contexts (before and after) to ensure that additional indicators are present and that certain conditions are met. In the case of an end of a phrase, this decision is converted into the action of segmentation of the text into two textual segments. Thus, and by repeating this operation on the resultant segments, we obtain a set of textual segments which, placed next to each other, which form the input plain text.

It is important to specify that in our segmentation the dot « . » cannot be always considered as an indicator of a sentence end; i.e., cases like : abbreviation, acronym or a number in decimal, where particular rules can be added.

Stemming: This operation consists of transforming, eventually agglutinated or inflected word into its canonical form (stem or root) (Roubia et al., 2017). In our case, we need the results of the Stemming in the graph method in order to define the most important phrases. To generate these roots, we use the Full-Text Search technique, which allows us to generate the roots of words composing the phrases and eliminate the stopwords. This technique also generates other features such as ranking (rank value) to classify the found phrases, in order to filter the relevant ones according to their scores.

4.2 Step 2: Processing

Since we adopt an extraction approach, the main task is to evaluate the phrases, select the most relevant ones, then build the summary. We adopted a hybrid approach combining three methods: the contextual exploration (main methods), the indicative expression and graph model (secondary methods). The secondary methods will scramble on the result of the principal method to give better results or provide a solution in the case that contextual exploration is not efficient.

Contextual Exploration method: This method has been chosen in order to produce a consistent summary and to offer users the possibility to choose the summary by point of view, where the information to be summarized is classified into discursive categories. The contextual exploration module receives a segmented text as input (the result of the segmentation module). The first task is to detect the presence of some linguistic indicators in each segment. Once an indicator is found, all contextual exploration rules related to that indicator will be set to find additional clues and to verify the conditions required by that rule. If all conditions are verified, an annotation action, determined by the exploration rule, is performed on the segment exactly where the linguistic indicator is placed.

For our SumSAT System, we have defined 13 discursive categories, each category has its own complementary clues (See figure 2).

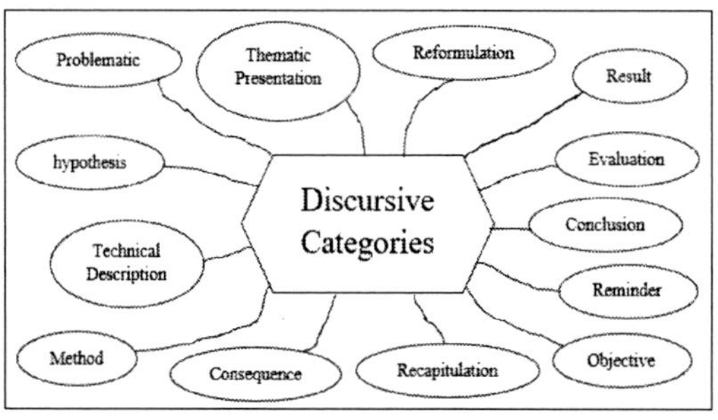

Figure 2: The discursive categories defined for SumSAT.

Example: The following example illustrates an application of our method to select sentences that contains information about the discursive category "conclusions and results". One of the rules associated with this category is as follows:

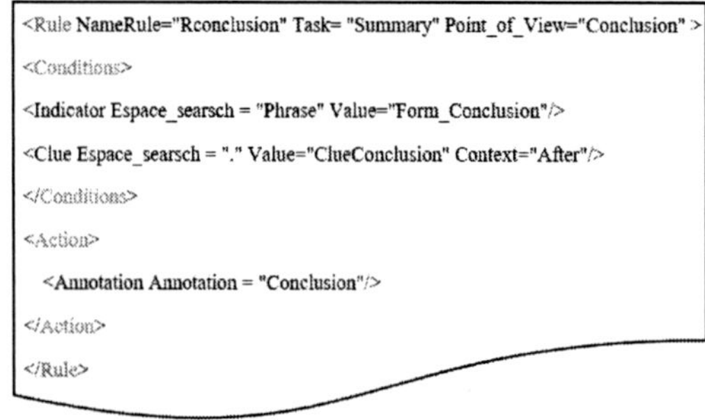

```
<Rule NameRule="Rconclusion" Task= "Summary" Point_of_View="Conclusion" >
<Conditions>
<Indicator Espace_searsch = "Phrase" Value="Form_Conclusion"/>
<Clue Espace_searsch = "." Value="ClueConclusion" Context="After"/>
</Conditions>
<Action>
  <Annotation Annotation = "Conclusion"/>
</Action>
</Rule>
```

Figure 3: Example of discursive rule.

The rule, delimited by the tag (<Rule> and </Rule>), consists of two parts :
- Condition part: delimited by (<Conditions> and </Conditions>): It groups together

information about the indicator (delimited by <Indicator and />) associated with an information category, and information about the additional clues (<clue and />) that are associated with it.

- Actions part: delimited by (<Actions> and </Actions>): Action to be done, after verifying the existence of additional clues and the required conditions.

Where:

- ✓ NameRule: the name that identifies the rule.
- ✓ Task: The task this rule performs since contextual exploration can be used for annotation and summary generation, as it can be used for segmentation.
- ✓ Point of View: Represents the category name of the information retrieved.
- ✓ Search_space: Space or context, where the additional clue is located; whether the search is done in the phrase itself or in the paragraph.
- ✓ Value: It is the name of the file where the indicators are stored, or the name of the file where the clues are stored, associated with this category of information.
- ✓ Context: Specifies whether the search for additional clues should be done before or after the indicator.

Consider the following phrase to be annotated (applying the rule mentioned above):

فعلى سبيل المثال، أظهرت الدراسات الحيوانية أنّ نبتة "روزماري" تقي من سرطان الثدي، وأن الكركم يحمي من بعض أنواع الأورام.

For example, animal studies have shown that rosemary protects against breast cancer and that turmeric protects against some types of tumours.

Figure 4: Example of a contextual exploration rule.

In this phrase, it can be said that the complementary clue (أن) is present after the indicator (أظهرت الدراسات). Therefore, the action to be taken is indicated in the actions part (delimited by <Actions> and </Actions>); so, this phrase assigned the value 'Conclusion' to indicate that it contains information concerning a result or conclusion.

Indicative expression: This method is selected to offer the possibility of generating a summary of a general order, or a specific field; sport, culture, economy, etc. This method consists of identifying phrases that contain indicators. These indicators are determined according to the field of the text to be analyzed, and its main task is to identify indicators in phrases, neglecting the additional clues. Using the following formula:

$$Score_{cue}(S) = \begin{cases} 1 & if \ \ S \ is \ an \ indicator \\ 0 & else \end{cases} \quad (01)$$

Graph method: In order to reduce the deficiencies of SumSAT's, we have used a hybrid approach that integrates a symbolic method (E.C.) and numerical methods (graph and indicative expression methods). The use of this hybrid approach allowed us to offer the user the possibility to choose a summary by point of view through contextual exploration, as well as the possibility to choose a default summary, to cover cases where the information is not present in the form of a discursive category.

The generation of the summary, using the graph method, consists of selecting the most representative phrases of the source text, since it attributes to the sentences a relevance score or similarity measure by calculating the number of intersection terms. These terms are the result of the stemming process performed in the pre-processing process.

Suppose that we have a text composed of six sentences (P1, P2, P2, ..., P6). After applying stemming for each sentence, the total number of terms shared with all the others are given in the table below:

Phrases	P1	P2	P3	P4	P5	P6
Total number of Stems (Roots) shared with all other phrases	9	8	7	3	6	5

Table 2: Phrases Weight.

Modelling this problem for the summary is like considering: The document as a graph, the phrases as nodes of this graph, the intersections of the phrases as edges of this graph, the total number of intersecting terms (stems or roots), of a phrase with all the others, as a weight of the node representing this phrase. Finally, to generate the summary we use the Greed algorithm.

	P1	P2	P3	P4	P5	P6
P1	0	0	1	1	1	1
P2	0	0	1	1	0	1
P3	1	1	0	0	1	0
P4	1	1	0	0	0	1
P5	1	0	1	0	0	1
P6	1	1	0	1	1	0

Table 3: Phrase intersection matrix

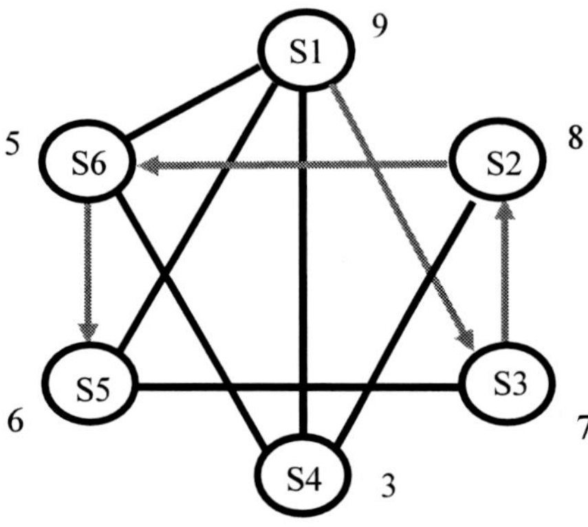

Figure 5: Pathway followed using the Greedy algorithm.

4.3 Step 3: Filtering and selection

The generation of the summary must take into consideration the user's requirements, and the compression ratio to determine the relevant phrases to be selected. The final summary is made up of all phrases that fulfill the following conditions:

- Phrases that belong to the discursive categories, or to the selected domains (chosen by the user) ;

- And/or the phrases that appear in the list of nodes visited by the graph method (the case of the default summary) ;

- The number of phrases is limited by the summary rate, introduced by the user ;

- The appearance order of the phrases in the summary must respect the order of these phrases in the source text.

In order to generate a dynamic summary, a link is established between the summary phrases and their corresponding phrases in the source text.

5 Presentation of SumSAT

SumSAT (Acronym of Summarization System for Arabic Text) is a web application system that runs at web browsers. Its execution is local to the IIS server (Internet Information Server), of Windows. The interaction between our system and Microsoft SQL Server is done by queries (T-SQL transactions). SumSAT is introduced to the user through a GUI, based on HTML5, ASP, C#, and Silverlight.

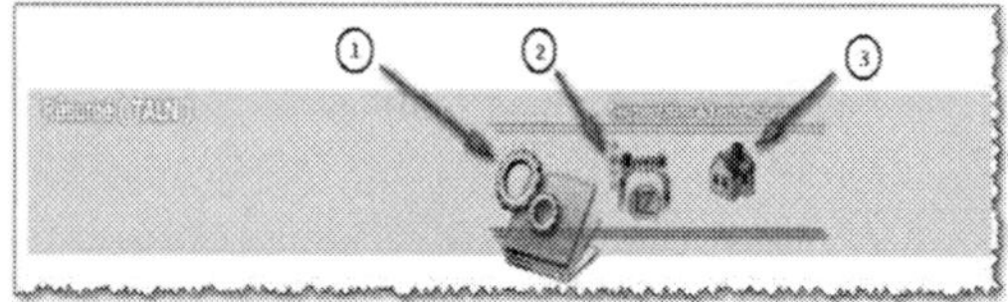

Figure 6: GUI Main Menu.

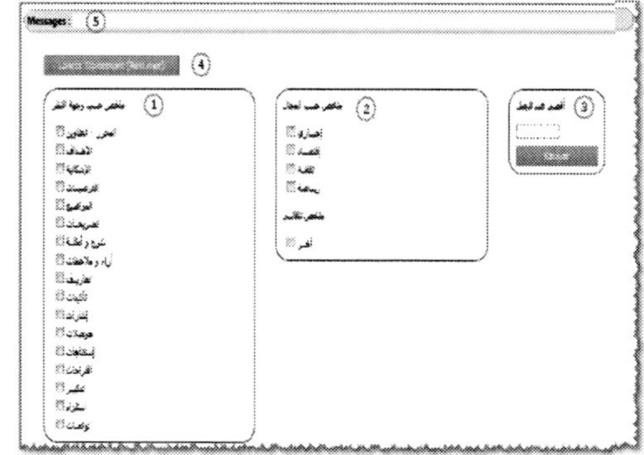

Figure 7: GUI Generation of Summary.

Figure 8: GUI of the Result (summary)

6 Experimentation and Results

SumSAT's summary generation is based on a hybrid approach where the discursive annotation constitutes its main task: the generated summary

124

is based on the concept of point of view. Therefore, the relevance of a phrase depends on the presence of surface linguistic markers characterizing (referring to) a discursive category. The evaluation of the summary generation process by point of view consists of the evaluation of the discursive annotation task made by SumSAT.

The objective of this evaluation is to know the percentage of phrases correctly annotated by the system, compared to the total number of annotated phrases, and compared to the total number of manually annotated phrases (reference summary). This can be expressed by measuring:

6.1   The precision rate

The number of correct discursive categories, detected by the system, compared to the total number of discursive categories detected by the system.

6.2   The Recall Rate

The number of correct discursive categories, detected by the system, compared to the total number of discursive categories presented in the reference summary

The precision and recall rates are calculated as follows:

$$Precision\ (\%) = \left(\frac{a}{b}\right) * 100 \qquad (02)$$

$$Recall\ (\%) = \left(\frac{a}{c}\right) * 100 \qquad (03)$$

Where :
- a : Number of automatically assigned correct annotations.

- b: Number of automatically assigned annotations.

- c: Number of manually assigned correct annotations.

For this purpose, we have set up corpora composed of twenty-five texts, and their corresponding summaries (The reference summaries are manually compiled by two experts). For each of the selected texts, we have proceeded to the generation of summaries, by discursive categories one by one. The evaluation consists of applying the metrics, in order to criticize and conclude based on the results obtained.

The results of the calculated rates, as well as the precision and recall results, are illustrated in Table 5, 6 and 7 and by representative graphs (Figure 9, 10 and 11). These results are calculated for all the selected texts in the corpora, and for each of the discursive categories adopted by SumSAT. For all categories, the precision rate is higher than 66%, except for four of them (hypothesis, Recapitulation, Reminder, Prediction), which have a precision rate between 40% and 50%. Similarly, the recall rate is higher than 66%, except for three categories that have a recall rate between 30% and 50% (Prediction, Definition and Reminder) . This shows that SumSAT has promising results which can be improved, despite the difficulties of generating coherent summaries.

- Precision rate: These results show that much more work needs to be done on refining surface markers to maximize this rate. In technical terms, it is necessary to work on two parameters. The first parameter, related to regular expressions, detects discursive markers (indicators and additional clues). The second parameter, linguistic (the good choice of these discursive markers).

- Recall rate: The results show that the work which can contribute to improving these results will be linguistic, especially the collection of discursive markers in order to enrich linguistic resources.

Note that the obtained results are influenced by the divergence of the texts from the point of view of style, discursive and argumentative strategies, and the covered topic. This means that the surface markers, for some categories, are rarely the same from one text to another. Similarly, the indicators are sometimes weak and cannot refer to a discursive category. Moreover, the additional clues are sometimes equivocal.

Category	Precision (%)	Recall (%)
Objective	73,68	82,35
hypothesis	42,03	70
Conclusion	77,78	70
Explanation	88,57	95,38
Consequence	77,27	70,83

Table 3: SumSAT evaluation using P/R (01).

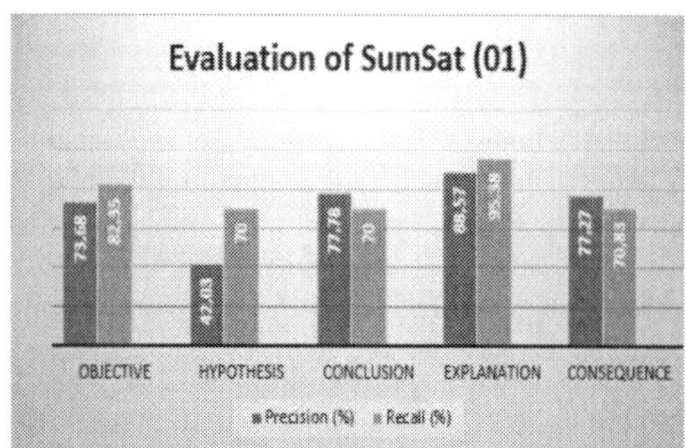

Figure 9: Graphical representation of SumSAT's evaluation results (01).

Category	Precision (%)	Recall (%)
Definition	66,67	32,67
Confirmation	97,5	82,98
Problematic	66,67	66,67
Reminder	50	44,02
Recapitulation	50	88,24

Table 4: SumSAT evaluation using P/R (02).

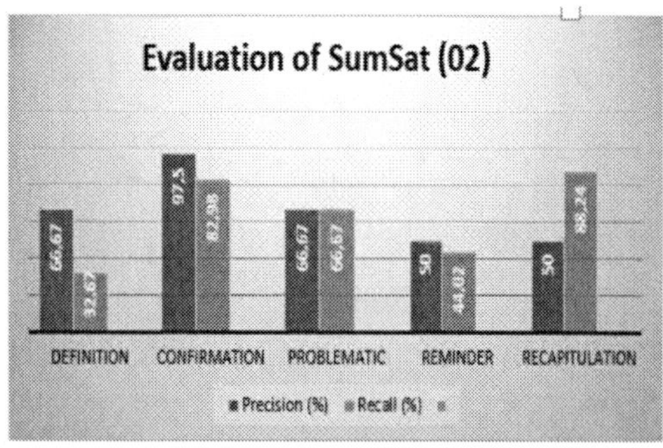

Figure 10: Graphical representation of SumSAT's evaluation results (02).

Category	Precision (%)	Recall (%)
Author, Title & Subtitle	91,94	91,94
Thematic	85,71	66,67
Prediction	50	50
Finding & opinion	90	69,26
Enunciation	94,94	91,85

Table 5: SumSAT evaluation using P/R (03).

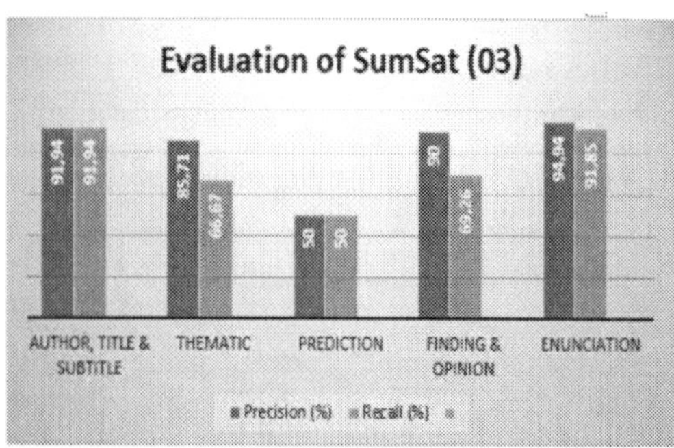

Figure 11: Graphical representation of SumSAT's evaluation results (03).

7   Conclusion and Continuing Efforts

In this paper, we have presented SumSAT which is an Arabic text summarization system that adopts a hybrid approach (i.e: contextual exploration method, indicative expression method, and graph model method) to build summary. The work we have done has given us an overview of the difficulties that we have encountered in the field of Arabic text summarization. In pre-processing, the incorrect use of punctuation marks (author's style) induces segmentation errors, and as a result, the relevance of phrases is incorrect, which gives an incoherent summary. On the processing phase, one of the difficulties met, and which influences the performance of the system, is the manual search for linguistic markers, to enrich the list of discursive categories. This task costs time and resources, which has reduced the list of the information offered by SumSAT. In addition, we found that the representative phrases with a high weight may not be selected because of the restrictions on the incrementation of the list of visited summits when the transition is made only between the adjacent ones (Graph model method).

Based on the obtained results, we propose an amelioration of the methods used to generate the summary by making a modification, such that the glutton algorithm (graph model method) gives the advantage to the representative nodes, without being limited by the transitions between the adjacent summits. Also, the integration of a tool for identifying surface linguistic markers in documents is a good way to enrich the system's linguistic resources.

References

Allahyari Mehdi , Pouriyeh Seyedamin , Assefi Mehdi, Safaei Saeid , Trippe D. Elizabeth, Gutierrez B.Juan and Kochut Krys. 2017. Text Summarization Techniques: A Brief Survey. *In Proceedings of arXiv. rXiv:1707.02268.*

Alkhawaldeh Fatima Taha and Samawi W. Venus. 2015. Lexical cohesion and entailment based segmentation for arabic text summarization (lceas). *The World of Computer Science and Information Technology Journal.* (WSCIT)5 (3): 51-60.

Alotaiby Fahad, Foda Salah and Alkharashi Ibrahim. 2012. New approaches to automatic headline generation for Arabic documents. *Journal of Engineering and Computer Innovations.* Vol. 3(1), pp. 11-25.

Belguith Lamia Hadrich. 2014. Automatic summarization. Natural Language Processing of Semitic Languages. Springer Berlin Heidelberg.371-408.

Belkebir Riadh. and Guessoum Ahmed. 2015. A supervised approach to arabic text summarization using adaboost. New Contributions in Information Systems and Technologies. Springer International Publishing. 227-236.

D'Avanzo Ernesto, Magnini Bernardo and Vallin Alessandro. 2004. Keyphrase Extraction for Summarization Purposes: The LAKE System at DUC-2004. *In Proceedings of the 2004 Document Understanding Conference (DUC2004),* Boston, MA.

Douzidia Fouad Sofiane and Lapalme Guy. 2004. Lakhas, an Arabic Summarization System. *In Proceedings of the 2004 Document Understanding Conference (DUC2004),* Boston, MA.

Lagrini Samira, Redjimi Mohamme and Azizi Nabiha. 2017. Extractive Arabic Text Summarization Approaches. *In Proceeding of the 6th International Conference, ICALP 2017,* Fez, Morocco.

Luhn Hans Peter. 1958. The automatic creation of literature abstracts. *IBM Journal of Research and Development, Volume 2 Issue 2.*

Maâloul Mohame Hedi. 2012. Approche hybride pour le résumé automatique de textes. Application à la langue arabe. *thesis doctorat,* University Aix-Marseille.

Mahmoud El hadj, Kruschwitz Udo and Fox Chris. 2009. Experimenting with automatic text summarisation for Arabic. *Language and Technology Conference.* Springer Berlin Heidelberg. 490-499.

Mohamed Ashraf Ali. 2016. Automatic summarization of the Arabic documents using NMF: A preliminary study. *In Proceedings of the 11th International Conference on Computer Engineering & Systems (ICCES).* Egypt

Munot Nikita and Govilkar S. Sharvari. 2014 . Comparative Study of Text Summarization Methods. *International Journal of Computer Applications.* Volume 102–No.12.

Oufaida Houda., Noualib Omar and Blache Philippe. 2014. Minimum redundancy and maximum relevance for single and multi-document Arabic text summarization. *Journal of King Saud University - Computer and Information Sciences,* Volume 26, Issue 4.

Pal Alok Ranjan and Saha Diganta. 2014. An Approach to Automatic Text Summarization using WordNet. *In Proceedings of the 4th Advance Computing Conference (IACC),* Page(s): 1169 – 1173. India

Pai Anusha. 2014. Text Summarizer Using Abstractive and Extractive Method. *International Journal of Engineering Research & Technology,* Vol. 3 Issue 5.

Rouibia Rima., Belhadj Imane. & Cheragui Mohamed Amine. 2017. JIDR: Towards building hybrid Arabic stemmer. *In Proceeding of the 1st IEEE International Conference on Mathematics and Information Technology (ICMIT).* Adrar. Algeria.

Schlesinger D. Judith , O'Leary P. Dianne and Conroy M. John 2008. Arabic/English multi-document summarization with CLASSY—the past and the future. *In Proceedings of the International Conference on Intelligent Text Processing and Computational Linguistics.* Springer Berlin Heidelberg. 568-581,

Sobh Ibrahim , Darwish Nevin Mahmoud , Fayek Magda B. 2006. An Optimized Dual Classification System for Arabic Extractive Generic Text Summarization. Available at: http://www.rdi-eg.com/rdi/technologies/papers.htm.

Zhu Junyan, Wang Can, He Xiaofei, Bu Jiajun, Chen Cun, Shang Shujie, Qu Mingcheng and Lu Gang. 2009. Tagoriented document summarization. *In Proceedings of the 18th International Conference on World Wide Web,* WWW '09, ACM, New York, NY, USA.

Speech Coding Combining Chaos Encryption and Error Recovery for G.722.2 Codec

Messaouda Boumaraf and Fatiha Merazka
LISIC Laboratory, Telecommunications Department
USTHB University, Algiers, Algeria
boumaraf.messa@gmail.com, fmerazka@usthb.dz

Abstract

With the evolution of network communication technology and advances in multimedia application, speech or data networks over an IP connection are vulnerable to threats. Therefore, the need to protect data attracts many researches on safe communications, especially speech secure communication. Additionally, with the large volume of unprotected speech data transmitted over the internet, Voice over Internet Protocol (VoIP) packets could be lost, and they cannot be recovered back, which would result in a degradation of speech quality. In this paper, we propose a secure speech communication approach based on chaotic cryptography combined with G.722.2 error recovery technique performed by interleaving. On the one hand, this approach uses the interleaving technique on inter-frames of G.722.2 speech in order to make a continuous packet loss becoming an isolated packets loss. On the other hand, speech will be encrypted using chaotic Lorenz system which achieves high encryption efficiency. To evaluate performance, the proposed design was evaluated through Enhanced Modified Bark Spectral Distortion (EMBSD) and Mean Opinion Score (MOS) with different packet loss rates to confirm the efficiency of our proposed scheme.

1 Introduction

Recently, with the development of network communication technology and signal processing techniques, it has become realistic to transmit speech, just like computer data, over the Internet (VoIP: Voice over Internet Protocol). However, the emergence of Internet use became very apparent; and the huge mass of data overloads the network (Mata-Díaz et al., 2014 - Labyd et al., 2014).

Networks must provide predictable, secure, measurable, and sometimes guaranteed services. Realizing the required Quality of Service (QoS) by managing the delay, delay variation (jitter), bandwidth, and packet loss parameters on a network become the secret to a successful end-to-end business solution. In real-time transmissions, IP networks are unpredictable and offer a best-effort transfer service with no QoS securities. Therefore, packets could be lost, causing an interruption in the conversation and a feeling of hatching of speech that is very annoying for the listeners. Therefore, it is fundamental to put a mechanism for concealing packet loss such as interleaving method, Forward Error Correction (FEC) (Nagano and Ito, 2013 - Shetty and Gibson, 2007).

In addition, speech data is vulnerable to corrupted or stolen by the hacker on the internet. For secure communication, it is necessary to protect data using encryption methods (Alvarez and Li, 2006).

Recently, research on chaotic cryptography increased expeditiously in order to improve chaos-based cryptosystems. In 1963, Edward Lorenz founded chaos theory, followed by the discovery of the Rössler attractor in 1976, since several chaotic systems are established (Jiang and Fu, 2008 - Kaur and Kumar, 2018). A chaotic system is a non-linear, deterministic presenting good properties such as aperiodicity, pseudo-randomness and sensitivity to changes in initial conditions, which makes it unpredictable. Because of its characteristics, the chaos was used in the encryption system (Zhang and Cao, 2011 - Moon et al. 2017).

In (Afrizal, 2018), the authors' study focus on examining a few speech codec that usually used in connectionless communication such as G.711, G.722, G.729, AMR-NB, and AMR-WB for voice over LTE application and the impact of random and burst packet loss on voice communication against the codec using Evalid and NS-3 simulator. in (Li et al, 2015) the paper describes a method of digital encryption based on Lorenz continuous chaotic system, combined with chaotic dynamics, continuous sequence of numbers generated by the Lorenz chaotic system. Discrete the continuous data through the Euler method. Image encryption as an example, verify the Lorenz chaotic system digital encryption features. In (Guo et al., 2002) authors propose a VoIP technique combining the speech data encryption and G.729 error recovery. This technique uses the chaotic data interleaving on inter-frames of voice to make situation of continuous packet loss becoming an isolated packet loss situation. Then, they propose a Periodical Parameter Re-initialization (PPR) recovery approach to reduce the signal quality degradation in the G.729 decoder due to the lost of state synchronization to the G.729 encoder. Beside the proposed VoIP technique, also uses the idea of chaotic data encryption on intra-frames of speech to scramble the data sequence within a speech frame.

In this paper, we propose a secure speech communication approach based on chaotic cryptography combined with G.722.2 error recovery technique performed by interleaving, and it is organized as follows. In Section 2, an overview of the AMR-WB G.722.2 is introduced. Section 3 gives a very brief description of the proposed technique, which has a direct relation to our contribution. Simulations and interpretation are presented in Section 4. Finally, the conclusion is provided in section 5.

2   Overview of the AMR-WB G.722.2

The adaptive Multi-Rate Wideband (AMR-WB) speech codec is based on Adaptive Multi-Rate encoding, using similar methodology as algebraic code excited linear prediction (ACELP). AMR-WB is codified as G.722.2, an ITU-T standard speech codec, then was improved by Nokia and VoiceAge and it was first defined by 3GPP.AMR-WB offers enhanced speech quality due to a larger speech bandwidth of 50–7000 Hz compared to narrowband speech coders. G.722 sample audio data at a rate of 16 kHz, it contains nine bit rates of 23.85, 23.05, 19.85, 18.25, 15.85, 14.25, 12.65, 8.85 and 6.6 kbps, these ones are presented by modes 8, 7, 6, 5, 4, 3, 2, 1 and 0 respectively. To reduce average bit rate, this codec supports the discontinuous transmission (DTX), using Voice Activity Detection (VAD) and Comfort Noise Generation (CNG) algorithms (ITU-T Standard G.722.2, 2003).

The coder works with a frame size of 20-ms and the algorithmic delay for the coder is 25-ms. The AMR-WB G722.2 uses six parameters (VAD-flag, ISP, pitch delay, LTP-filtering, algebraic code, and gain) to represent the speech and these are shown in Figure 1 for bit rate 6,60 kbps.

Headers (3bits)	B_1	B_2	....	B_{132}

Figure 1: The bitstream of the coder parameters (coder output / decoder input) for the 20-ms frame in mode 0

where B_1, B_2, ..., B_{133} represent the bit 0 (BIT-0: FF81) or the bit 1 (BIT-1: 007F) of the coder parameters which is codified on 16 bits (WORD16).

3   The proposed technique

In this study, two techniques are combined employing interleaving and encryption processes. The encoded bitstream will be reordered using the interleaving, then transmitted over lossy IP channel after encryption, channel encoding and modulation. All these steps will be reversed at receiver as depicted in Figure 2.

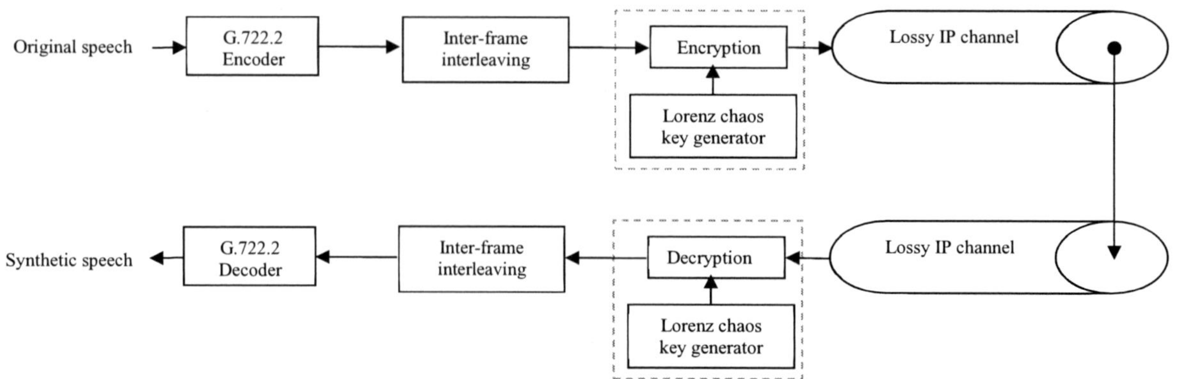

Figure 2: Proposed scheme of combined speech encryption with error recovery based on interleaving

3.1 Interleaving process

Interleaving technique is very useful when the packets contain multiple frames and the end-to-end delay is not important. Before transmission of the bitstream, the frames are re-arranged in such a way that the initially adjacent ones are separated in the transmitted bitstream and then put back in their original order at receiver level. As a result, the packet erase effects are scattered and produce situation of continuous packet loss becoming an isolated packet loss situation (Okamoto, et al., 2014).

3.2 Encryption process

Some important properties of chaos, such as the ergodicity, high sensitivity to the changes of control parameters, initial conditions and unpredictable behavior can be used in the generation of random numbers. So we use Lorenz model, the first well known dynamical system, governed by the differential equations (Lorenz, 1963):

$$\begin{cases} \dot{x} = a(y - x) & (a) \\ \dot{y} = cx - y - xz & (b) \\ \dot{z} = xy - bz & (c) \end{cases} \quad (1)$$

where x, y, z are state variables and a, b, c are real constant parameters of the system. With $a = 10$, $b = \frac{8}{3}$, $c = 28$, Lorenz system generates a chaotic behavior and its attractor is depicted in Figure 3:

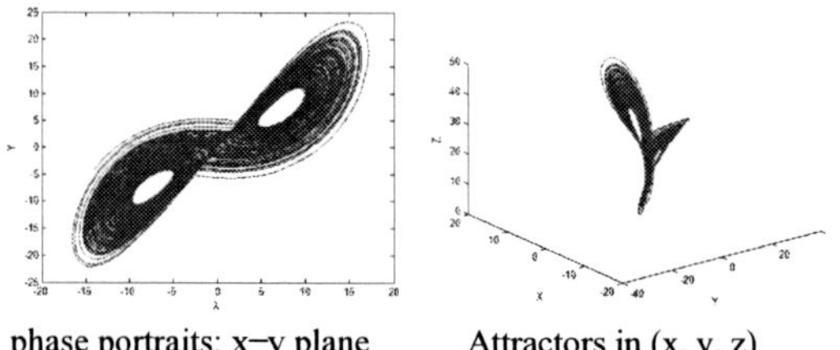

Figure 3: Phase portraits and chaotic attractors of Lorenz model

The speech encryption algorithm is done in two stages: confusion and diffusion.

Step1: In the confusion stage, the parameters of the frame are permuted by using the keys x_n of Lorenz formula (1-a). So, the values are sorted in decreasing order while safeguarding the position or the index of each key values. then, the position of data speech is changed according to indexes' keys.

Step2: In the diffusion stage, the permuted parameters of frames are substituted formula (1-b) of Lorenz equation. The obtained keys are calculated as follows:

$$key(i) = \left[y(i) - floor(y(i))\right] * 32767$$

So, the diffusion is performed using XOR operation between data and the key.

4 Simulation and discussion

In this section, we study the performance in terms of security and recovery quality of lost packets. Several experiments are carried out to test the interleaving and encryption efficiency of the presented wideband speech cryptosystem. The quality of the encrypted interleaved speech and the reconstructed signals is assessed for the standard AMR-WB G.722.2. Thus, the speech file was encoded using AMR-WB G.722.2 CS-ACELP. The resulting bit streams were rearranged employing interleaving technique and encrypted using Lorenz model. In the experiments, signal assessment in both the time and frequency domains is done to evaluate the distortion degree between the original and reconstructed speech. Therefore, the speech signal is displayed in two representations: waveform and spectrogram.

The evaluation of speech quality includes two measures: objective and subjective, Enhanced Modified Bark Spectral Distortion (EMBSD) (Yang, 1999) and Mean Opinion Score (MOS) (ITU-T, 2006) respectively. Note: for the MOS assessment, scores on the scale range from 1 to 5 (1: Unsatisfactory, 2: Poor, 3: Fair, 4: Good 5: Excellent). To demonstrate the efficiency of our proposed VoIP scheme combining G.722.2 frames with interleaving and chaos encryption, we have performed individually simulations for AMR-WBG, followed by the interleaving technique, then the chaos encryption and finally, we combine them.

4.1 Performance of AMR-WB

In our test, a speech file with 198 frames is used which is represented in Figure 4. Recall that encryption uses 9 modes, of which we opt, in our experiments, for mode 0 (6.6 kbps) and mode 7 (23.05 kbps).

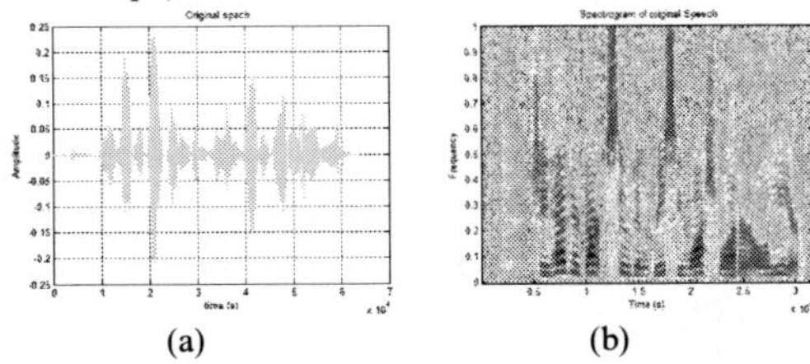

(a)   (b)

Figure 4: (a) Original speech, (b) its spectrogram

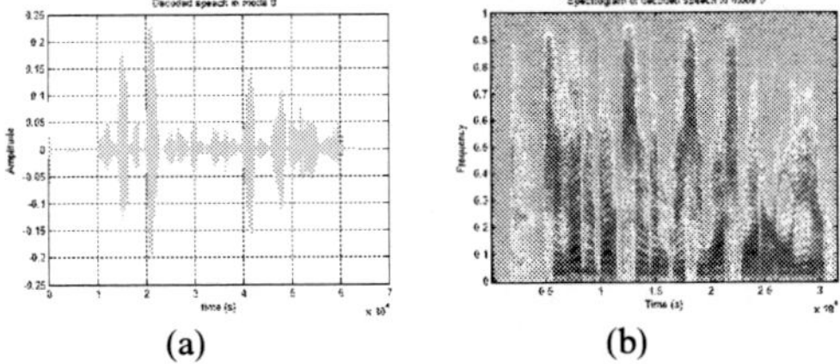

(a)   (b)

Figure 5: (a)Decoded speech in mode 0 (b) its Spectrogram

Figure 5 shows the speech decoded in mode 0.

We can see that the original and the decoded speech seem identical in waveforms (Figure 4-a and Figure 5-a) and spectrograms (Figure 4-b and Figure 5-b) representations.

The EMBSD and MOS assessments of speech quality are given in Figure 6. The values given by the two metrics show that the speech encoded in mode 7 is better than the one encoded in mode 0, while noticing that the original speech (no coding) is the best. A small difference between the original and the encoded speech is because we have a lossy codec. But generally, the encoded speech in both modes is classified good.

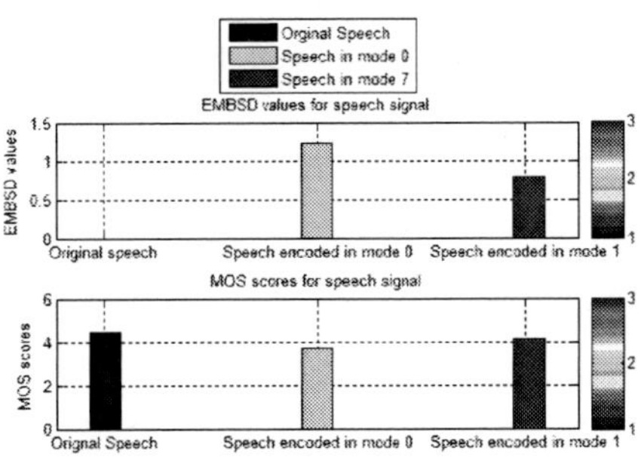

Figure 6: EMBSD and MOS scores

4.2 Interleaving tests

The encoded speech data will be scrambled using interleaving method. To simulate VoIP network losses, we use two-state Gilbert model.

Rate (%)	P	q
00	00	00
5	0,05	0,15
10	0,09	0,15
20	0,22	0,20
30	0,31	0,23
40	0.39	0.38

Table 1: shows the loss rates.

We use interleaving method to recover the lost packets during network congestion or degradation. Figures 7 and 8 give the obtained results from tests with EMBSD and MOS objective and subjective measurement tool respectively. We can see that the proposed method in both modes performs well than the original for the two losses rates 5% and 10%, contrariwise for the higher i.e more than 10%.

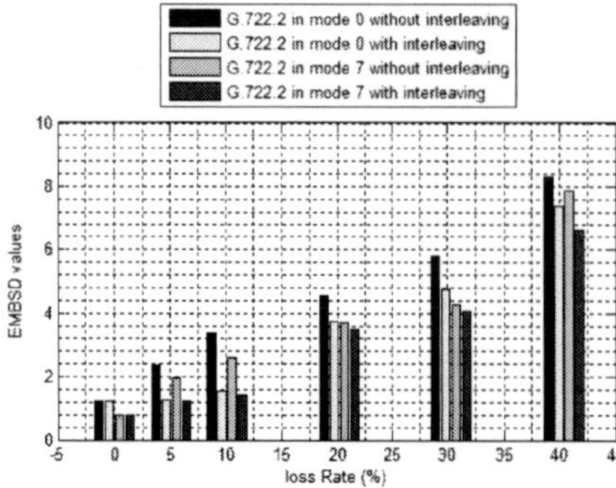

Figure 7: EMBSD values for interleaving

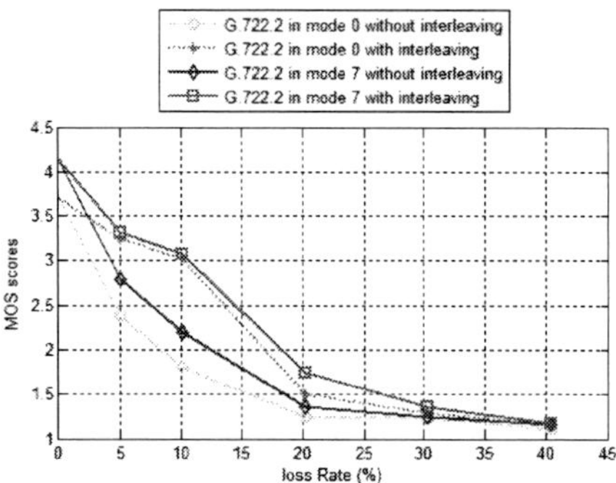

Figure 8: MOS scores for interleaving

we can confirm that by analyzing the audiograms speech slices in Figure 9.

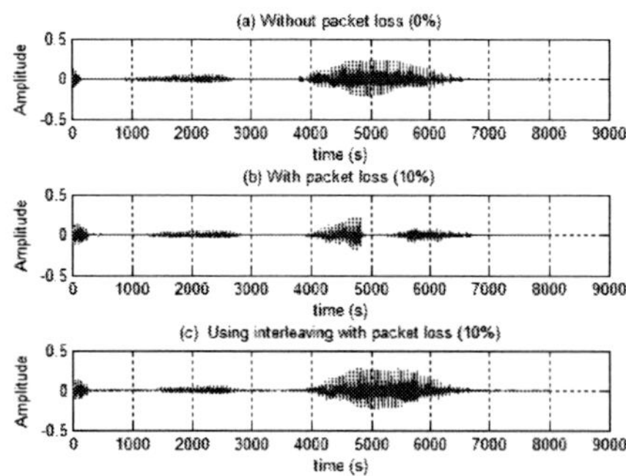

Figure 9: Portion of G.722.2 speech in mode 0: (a) original speech (b) Original speech with packet loss (10%)(c) Using interleaving with packet loss (10%)

4.3 Encryption tests

The speech file was encoded using AMR-WB G.722.2 CS-ACELP. The resulting bitstreams were encrypted using chaotic full encryption performed by both confusion & diffusion processes. Figure 10 depicts the signal inspection in both the time and frequency domains.

We can see from Figures 10-a and 10-b that the encrypted speech signals are similar to the white noise, which indicates that no residual intelligibility can be useful for eavesdroppers at the communication channel. However, the reconstructed speech signals (Figures 10-c and 10-d) using the right keys are the same as the original.

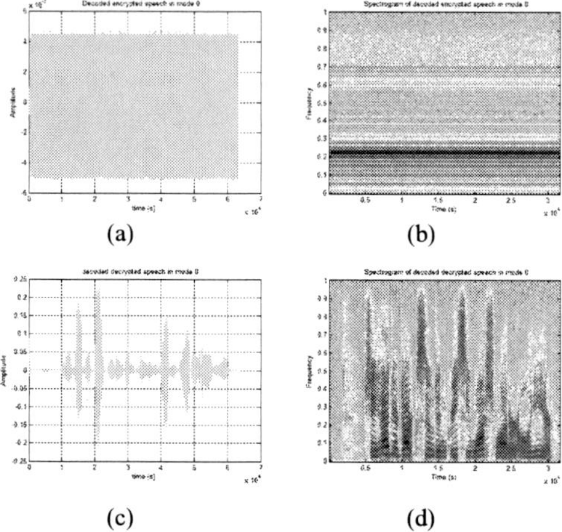

Figure 10: Full encryption using mode0 of WB-G722.2: (a) Decoded encrypted speech (b) its spectrogram (c) decoded decrypted speech (d) its spectrogram

To evaluate the efficiency of the encryption schemes, we have used the EMBSD and MOS tools. We can see that the EMBSD (Figure 11) values for the original speech coded in the modes 0 and 7 are near zero which indicates its good quality.

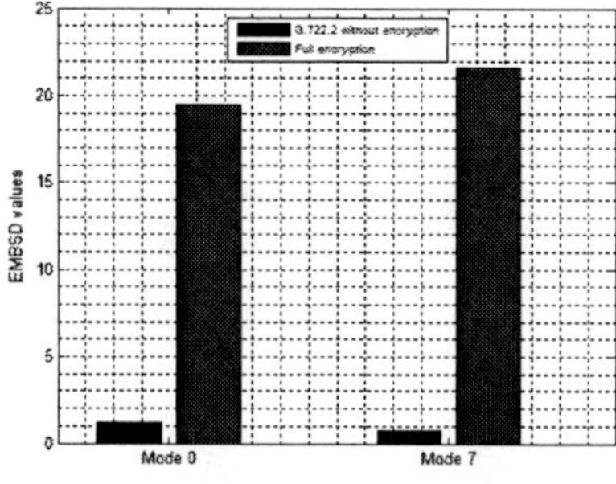

Figure 11: EMBSD values for full encryption

In return, significantly greater values increase for encrypted speech data which indicates its worse quality.

Also, the MOS evaluation in Figure 12 confirms and gives scores "Good" for the original speech and "unsatisfactory" for the encrypted one. We can also notice that the quality of the decrypted speech employing the same keys than the encrypted one give a signal quality identical to the original speech.

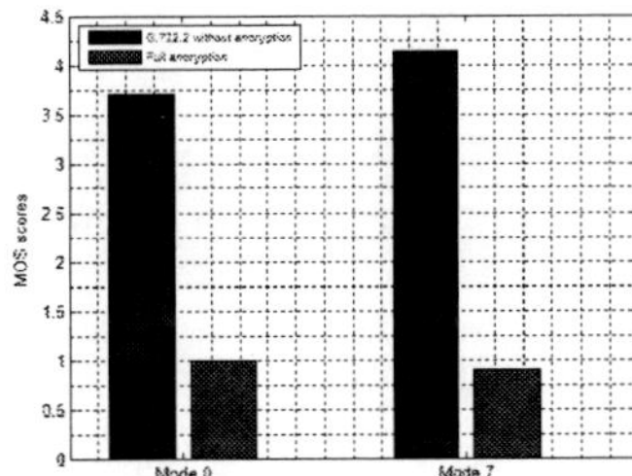

Figure 12: MOS scores for full encryption

4.4   Combined tests

The speech file will be encoded then scrambled using the interleaving process, in order to make the continuous multiple-packet loss situation to isolated packet loss situation. Next, it is encrypted by chaotic Lorenz mode. Figure 13 shows the combination of interleaving and encryption processes. We can see that, for the two losses rates, the speech data appears as a white noise.

Note: The EMBSD values and MOS scores for the interleaved and encrypted file in mode 0 or mode 7 give the same value than the only encrypted speech which indicate the efficiency of the full encryption.

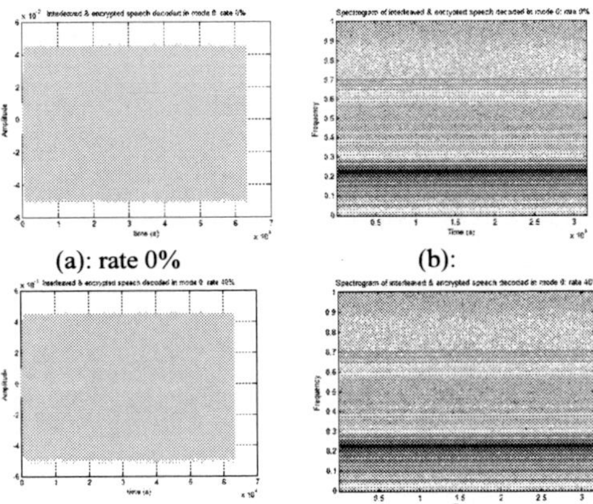

(a): rate 0%   (b):

(c): rate 40%   d):

Figure 13: Interleaved & encrypted speech decoded in mode 0

Figure 14 shows the speech audiograms of the proposed schema.

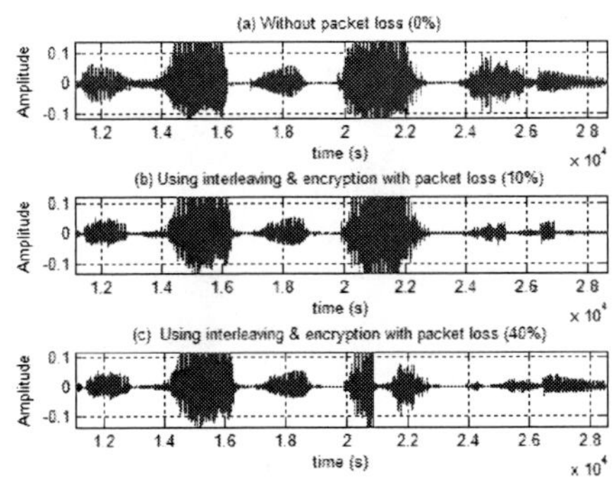

Figure 14: Portion of G.722.2 speech in mode 0: (a) original speech (b) Using interleaving & encryption with packet loss (10%) (c) Using interleaving & encryption with packet loss (10%)

5   Conclusion

In this paper, we have presented our proposed method which combines chaos encryption using the Lorenz system and error recovery based on interleaving techniques for the standard ITU-T AMR-WB G.722.2 codec. The purpose of interleaving is to improve speech quality degradation caused by packet losses. In addition, the experimental results and analysis show that the cryptosystem is efficient in terms of security which is suitable for transmission over public transmission channels.

References

Mata-Díaz, J., Alins, J., Muñoz, J. L., and Esparza, O. 2014. A simple closed-form approximation for the packet loss rate of a TCP connection over wireless links. *IEEE Communications Letters*, 18(9), 1595-1598.

Labyad, Y., MOUGHIT, M., Marzouk, A., and HAQIQ, A. 2014. Impact of Using G. 729 on the Voice over LTE Performance. *International Journal of Innovative Research in Computer and Communication Engineering*, 2(10), 5974-5981.

Labyd, Y., Moughit, M., Marzouk, A., and Haqiq, A. 2014. Performance Evaluation for Voice over LTE by using G. 711 as a Codec. *International Journal of Engineering Research and Technology*, 3(10), 758-763.

Nagano, T., and Ito, A. 2013. A Packet Loss Recovery of G. 729 speech using discriminative model and N-gram. In *2013 Ninth International Conference on Intelligent Information Hiding and Multimedia Signal Processing.*2013: 267-270.

MITTAG, Gabriel et MÖLLER, Sebastian. Single-ended packet loss rate estimation of transmitted speech signals. *In : 2018 IEEE Global Conference on Signal and Information Processing (GlobalSIP).* 2018: 226-230.

Shetty, N., and Gibson, J. D. 2007. Packet Loss Concealment for G. 722 using Side Information with Application to Voice over Wireless LANs. *Journal of Multimedia, 2*(3).

Alvarez, G., and Li, S. 2006. Some basic cryptographic requirements for chaos-based cryptosystems. *International journal of bifurcation and chaos,* 16(08): 2129-2151.

Jiang, H. Y., and Fu, C. 2008. An image encryption scheme based on Lorenz chaos system. *Fourth International Conference on Natural Computation.* 4: 600-604.

Alshammari, A. S., Sobhy, M. I., and Lee, P. 2017. Secure digital communication based on Lorenz stream cipher. *30th IEEE International System-on-Chip Conference (SOCC).*2017: 23-28.

Zhang, J. 2015. An image encryption scheme based on cat map and hyperchaotic lorenz system. *IEEE International Conference on Computational Intelligence & Communication Technology .* 78-82

Kaur, M., and Kumar, V. 2018. Efficient image encryption method based on improved Lorenz chaotic system. *Electronics Letters,* 54(9): 562-564.

Zhang, Z. X., and Cao, T. 2011. A chaos-based image encryption scheme with confusion-diffusion architecture. *In International Conference on Computer Science and Information Engineering. Springer, Berlin, Heidelberg.* 258-263.

Zhu, Z. L., Zhang, W., Wong, K. W., and Yu, H. 2011. A chaos-based symmetric image encryption scheme using a bit-level permutation. *Information Sciences,* 181(6): 1171-1186.

Wong, K. W., Kwok, B. S. H., and Law, W. S. 2008. A fast image encryption scheme based on chaotic standard map. *Physics Letters A,* 372(15): 2645-2652.

Wang, B., Xie, Y., Zhou, C., Zhou, S., and Zheng, X. 2016. Evaluating the permutation and diffusion operations used in image encryption based on chaotic maps. *Optik-International Journal for Light and Electron Optics,* 127(7): 3541-3545.

Moon, S., Han, B. S., Park, J., Seo, J. M., and Baik, J. J. 2017. Periodicity and chaos of high-order Lorenz systems. *International Journal of Bifurcation and Chaos,* 27(11): 1750176

Afrizal, G. 2018. Impact of Random and Burst Packet Loss on Voice Codec G. 711, G. 722, G. 729, AMR-NB, AMR-WB. *In 2018 4th International Conference on Wireless and Telematics (ICWT).* 2018: 1-4.

Li, W., Zhang, Q., and Ding, Q. 2015. Digital encryption method based on lorenz continuous chaotic system. *Fifth International Conference on Instrumentation and Measurement, Computer, Communication and Control (IMCCC).* 2015: 262-266.

Guo, J. I., Lin, C. C., Tsai, M. C., & Lin, S. W. 2002. An efficient voice over Internet protocol technique combining the speech data encryption and G. 729 error recovery. *In Proc. Int. Computer Symposium (ICS'2002).* 2002

ITU-T Standard G.722.2, 2003.Wideband coding of speech at around 16 kbps using Adaptive Multi-RateWideband (AMR-WB).

Okamoto, M., Nose, T., Ito, A., and Nagano, T. 2014. Subjective evaluation of packet loss recovery techniques for voice over IP. *In 2014 International Conference on Audio, Language and Image Processing.* 2014: 711-714.

Lorenz, E. N. 1963. Deterministic non periodic flow. *Journal of the atmospheric sciences,* 20(2): 130-141.

Yang, W. 1999. Enhanced Modified Bark Spectral Distortion (EMBSD): An Objective Speech Quality Measure Based on Audible Distortion and Cognitive Model. *Temple University.*

ITU-T. 2006. Mean opinion score (MOS) terminology. *Recommendation P.800.1.*

Compositional pre-training for neural semantic parsing

Amir Ziai
Department of Computer Science
Stanford University
Stanford, CA
amirziai@stanford.edu

Abstract

Semantic parsing is the process of translating natural language utterances into logical forms, which has many important applications such as question answering and instruction following. Sequence-to-sequence models have been very successful across many NLP tasks. However, a lack of task-specific prior knowledge can be detrimental to the performance of these models. Prior work has used frameworks for inducing grammars over the training examples, which capture conditional independence properties that the model can leverage. Inspired by the recent success stories such as BERT we set out to extend this augmentation framework into two stages. The first stage is to pre-train using a corpus of augmented examples in an unsupervised manner. The second stage is to fine-tune to a domain-specific task. In addition, since the pre-training stage is separate from the training on the main task we also expand the universe of possible augmentations without causing catastrophic forgetting. We also propose a novel data augmentation strategy that interchanges tokens that co-occur in similar contexts to produce new training pairs. We demonstrate that the proposed two-stage framework is beneficial for improving the parsing accuracy in a standard dataset called GeoQuery for the task of generating logical forms from a set of questions about the US geography.

1 Introduction

Semantic parsing is the task of converting natural language into machine-executable logical forms. Examples of this parsing include asking questions that are then converted to queries against a database, generating code from natural language, converting natural language instructions to an instruction set that can be followed by a system, and even converting natural language into Python (Yin and Neubig, 2017). These logical forms can be captured using notions of formal semantics in linguistic such as λ-calculus and a more compact version called lambda dependency-based compositional semantics or λ-DCS (Liang, 2013).

Traditionally this task has been tackled by a combination of heuristics and search to build up parsers from large datasets of question-answer pairs (Berant et al., 2013) or from text that is paired with knowledge base information (Berant and Liang, 2014). However, with the advent of the sequence-to-sequence (Sutskever et al., 2014) architecture, the majority of the research has shifted towards using this framework.

Many sequence-to-sequence use cases involve converting a sequence of natural language into another sequence of natural language. Semantic parsing is different in that the decoded sequence need to be constrained by what would constitute a valid logical form. This additional challenge adds extra complexity to semantic parsing systems. Similar to more conventional sequence-to-sequence tasks semantic parsing also suffers from the problem that one source sentence can have multiple valid logical forms which introduce a wrinkle in evaluation.

2 Related work

The approach used in this work is a continuation of the work by Jia et al. (Jia and Liang, 2016) where the authors proposed a sequence-to-sequence model with an attention-based copying mechanism. This supervised approach leverages the flexibility of the encoder-decoder architecture and the authors demonstrate that the model can learn very accurate parsers across three standard semantic parsing datasets. The augmentation strategy used in this work allows for injecting prior knowledge which improve the generalization power of the model.

One disadvantage of this approach is that the decoder outputs are considered unstructured and can lead to invalid logical forms. Krishnamurthy et al. propose to overcome this problem by imposing a grammar on the decoder that only generates well-typed logical forms (Krishnamurthy et al., 2017). However, this approach increases the complexity of the system, which was unwarranted in our experiments and most of the results produced by the model in our experiments were valid logical forms (with sufficient training).

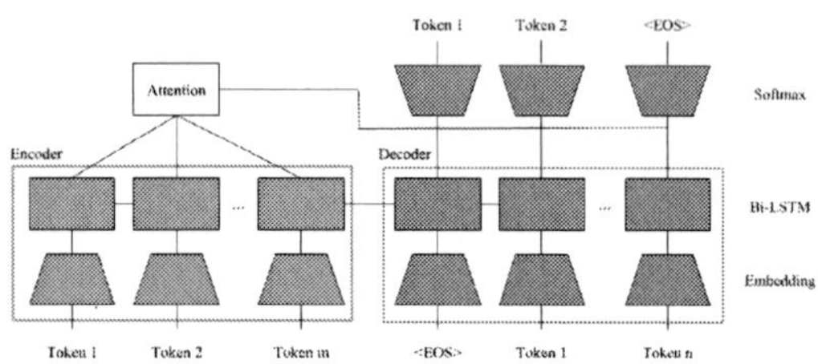

Figure 1: Seq-2-seq architecture with an attention-based copying mechanism

Moreover, building annotated semantic parsing datasets is highly labor-intensive and parsers built for one domain do not necessarily transfer across domains. Fan et al. propose a multi-task setup and demonstrate that training using this setup can improve the accuracy in domains with smaller labeled datasets (Fan et al., 2017). This approach is aligned with one of the main contributions in our research. Our proposed framework allows for pre-training the model in an unsupervised manner with data from multiple tasks that enables transfer learning.

3   Approach

A sequence-to-sequence model with an attention-based copying mechanism is used to learn logical forms from natural language utterances. Moreover, a novel data augmentation framework is used for injecting prior knowledge by inducing a synchronous context-free grammar. This novel framework, first proposed in (Jia and Liang, 2016), is called data recombination.

As depicted in Figure 1, the encoder takes the natural language utterances as a sequence of m tokens. The first step is to lookup the embedding vector for the token and then to pass it through a bidirectional LSTM. The hidden states for the forward and backward RNNs are generated and the

last hidden state is used as the initial hidden state for the decoder. At train time we run the natural language utterance through the encoder, initialize the decoder using the last hidden states, and then use teacher forcing to produce an output at each of the n steps of the decoder while using the actual token for the next step. The objective function we're optimizing at each Stochastic Gradient Descent (SGD) step is the standard negative log-likelihood computed for the softmax probability of the true token y_t summed over the sequence. The per example loss is summed over all of the training examples N to produce the total loss.

Three strategies are used for inducing a grammar over the original examples from the dataset. The first strategy simply abstracts entities in the examples with their type. Assuming that each entity has a corresponding type the authors generate two rules. For instance the example with input `what states border Texas?` and output

```
answer(NV, (state(V0), next_to(V0
, NV), const(V0, stateid(texas)))))
```

results in the following two recombinant rules:

- ROOT `-> (what states border StateId?, answer(NV, state (V0), next_to(V0, NV), const(V0, statid(StateId))`

- StateID `-> (texas, texas)`

The second strategy abstracts whole phrases and adds one or two rules to the output grammar. The first of these two rules looks for matches between input and the output and replaces both of them with the type of the entity. Afterwards, if the entire output expression is of a particular types then a new rule is generated of the form `type -> (input, output)`. Finally a k-concatenation strategy is used where $k >= 2$ is a parameter and simply creates a new rule that concatenates the sequence k times. The authors argue that the concatenation strategy has the effect of creating harder examples for the RNN to attend to, which has been shown to improve generalization.

3.1   Co-occurrence augmentation

We propose a novel augmentation strategy to be used in addition to the aforementioned strategies. This augmentation relies on the intuition that tokens which appear in similar contexts are interchangeable in both the source as well as the target sequences. For instance consider the following pair of natural language and logical form:

- What is the capital of Alaska?

- ```
  _answer(NV,(_capital(V0)
  ,_loc(V0,NV),
  _const(V0,_stateid(alaska))))
  ```

We can replace Alaska with any of the other 49 states in the US and get a valid pair. Our strategy for computing these equivalences is to look at source sentences with an equal number of tokens that only differ in a single token. These tokens are then linked together as we observe a minimum number of co-occurrences in the corpus. For example `alaska` co-occurs with the following tokens: `{alabama, arizona, arkansas, california, ...}`, which include over half of the US states.

This augmentation strategy also captures semantically similar tokens and allows for teaching these semantic invariances to the model. Consider the source sentence `what is the highest point in ohio.` An example of an augmented sentence based on this sentence is `what is the highest elevation in oklahoma.`

It should be noted that the co-occurrence strategy fails in some cases. For example the source sentence `"list the states ?"` may produce the augmented sentence `"list the california ?"`. As the tokens `states` and `california` have been linked together due to co-occurrence in similar contexts. We have allowed for these cases to be produced so long as the generated logical form is valid. Our hypothesis is that the benefit of having the model generalize better by seeing correctly augmented examples outweigh the cost of producing semantically incorrect pairs.

3.2 Pre-train and fine-tune

There's diminishing returns associated with data recombination in the original formulation. In particular, overusing data recombination can come at the cost of learning the actual task. We hypothesize that pre-training using recombinant data and subsequently fine-tuning the actual task can overcome this issue.

This framework is inspired by recent success stories such as BERT (Devlin et al., 2018). To validate this hypothesis we start by simply breaking the original paper's single-stage training approach to the aforementioned two-stage approach. However, we only use recombinant examples for the pre-train stage and use the original, non-augmented training examples for fine-tuning. This framework allows for a high level of flexibility on the data, augmentation strategies, and objective functions that can be used for each stage as summarized in Table 1. For instance we can leverage unlabeled data and train the encoder and decoder as independent Language Models (LMs) as in (Ramachandran et al., 2016). In addition, we can use less precise recombinant strategies such as the co-occurrence strategy that would've been detrimental in the previous formulation.

Table 1: Data, augmentation, and objective functions used in the two stages of the proposed framework

	Pre-train	Fine tune
Leverage unlabeled data	Yes	No
Leverage other tasks	Yes	No
Data recombination used	Yes	No

The baseline for this work is the parsing and token accuracy reported for three standard semantic parsing datasets in (Jia and Liang, 2016). Parsing accuracy is defined as the proportion of the predicted logical forms that exactly match the true logical form (Liang et al., 2013). It is possible that the same question could be captured by multiple valid logical forms and therefore a strict string match may be overly strict. Token accuracy is the proportion of the tokens in the true logical form that were present in the predicted sequence. We use parsing accuracy as a secondary metric as the model can learn to game it by producing more tokens. However, token accuracy is a useful metric for models that results in a similar parsing accuracy as well as a proxy for equally valid logical forms.

The original contribution of this work is the co-occurrence strategy as well as the proposed framework for pre-training and later fine-tuning without the recombinant strategies resulting in catastorphic interference or forgetting (Goodfellow et al., 2013). The code for the original paper was written in Theano (Bergstra et al., 2010) and the code along with a number of utilities for preparing and
  ```

evaluating the datasets and the experiments are all available in `https://worksheets.codalab.org/worksheets/0x50757a37779b485f89012e4ba03b6f4f/`. We have re-implemented the architecture and the two-stage framework in PyTorch (Paszke et al., 2017) and have used these utilities for preparation and evaluation. We have also used the OpenNMT library for experimenting with a variety of architectures such as Transformers (Klein et al.).

4 Experiments

4.1 Data

We used the GeoQuery dataset which is available at `http://www.cs.utexas.edu/users/ml/geo.html`. This dataset consists of a set of questions about US geography facts and the corresponding Prolog query which represents the logical form. We use 600 examples for training and 280 examples for testing. The task is to produce the logical form given the question.

4.2 Evaluation method

Parsing accuracy (described in an earlier section) is used for evaluation.

4.3 Details

For the first experiment we explored the co-occurrence augmentation strategy as well as the two-stage training approach. Experiments are conducted with an encoder-decoder architecture with a bidirectional LSTM encoder with 256 hidden units and an LSTM decoder with the same number of hidden units. We have used a similar attention copy mechanism that was employed in (Jia and Liang, 2016), a learning rate of 0.001, word embedding size of 64, and 1,000 epochs of training. The original implementation in Theano used Stochastic Gradient Descent (SGD). We are using an Adam optimizer and using mini-batches of size 256 for training. Training the model in mini-batches resulted in significant speedups and allowed us to conduct many more experiments. Finally we have appended the training data with an equal number of augmented examples in the cases that augmentation was used.

After establishing the best combination of augmentation strategies we conducted hyper-parameter search to explore the effects of the embedding size, RNN hidden size, and the learning rate on the parsing accuracy.

Each experiment took an average of about 30 minutes to run on an AWS EC2 instance with 64 cores and 256GB of memory. We ran up to 32 experiments in parallel.

4.4 Results

Table 2 summarizes the sequence and token accuracy for the explored augmentation and pre-training strategies.

The results suggest that pre-training can be marginally beneficial to sequence accuracy. However, the co-occurrence augmentation is leading to poorer results for this combination of hyper-parameters. One possible explanation is that this lower precision augmentation, by not enforcing a tight coupling between source and target sequences, is leading the model astray by producing semantically incorrect pairs that draw the wrong association between incompatible pairs which just happened to co-occur. We will see examples of this in the upcoming analysis section.

To gain more insight into the importance of the hyper-parameters we conducted search over the learning rate, word embedding size, and RNN hidden size. The results are summarized in Table 3.

The hyper-parameter search results suggest that a larger hidden size for the recurrent units is more beneficial while increasing the size of the embedding size has diminishing returns. This makes intuitive sense as the vocabulary size for this problem is very small and increasing the embedding size too much results in overparameterization.

We briefly experimented with using Transformers (Vaswani et al., 2017) for both the encoder and the decoder but did not manage to reproduce the same level of parsing accuracy and abandoned that line of investigation.

5 Analysis

In this section we analyze the best-performing model from the previous section. This model uses pre-training and employs all augmentation strategies except for co-occurrence. The model is trained with learning rate of 0.001, word embedding size of 64, and RNN hidden size of 256.

A useful metric for comparing the predicted and true sequences is the Intersection over Union (IoU) of the unique tokens in the two sequences:

$$IoU = \frac{True \cap Predicted}{True \cup Predicted} \quad (1)$$

Table 2: Augmentation and pre-training experiments

Augmentation	Pre-train	Sequence accuracy	Token Accuracy
nesting, entity, concat	Yes	**74.3**	87.8
nesting, entity, concat	No	73.6	**88.2**
nesting, entity, concat, co-occurrence	Yes	66.1	87.3
no augmentation	Yes	62.1	81.6
no augmentation	No	58.6	81.6
nesting, entity, concat, co-occurrence	No	56.1	81.7
co-occurrence	Yes	55.4	79.8
co-occurrence	No	51.7	80.7

Table 3: Hyper-parameter search for best augmentation and pre-train combination

Learning rate	Word embedding size RNN hidden size	32	64	128
0.001	64	0.0	2.1	11.1
	128	24.6	32.1	63.2
	256	70.4	**74.3**	71.4
0.010	64	40.7	45.4	36.1
	128	68.9	68.2	59.6
	256	66.1	55.0	69.6

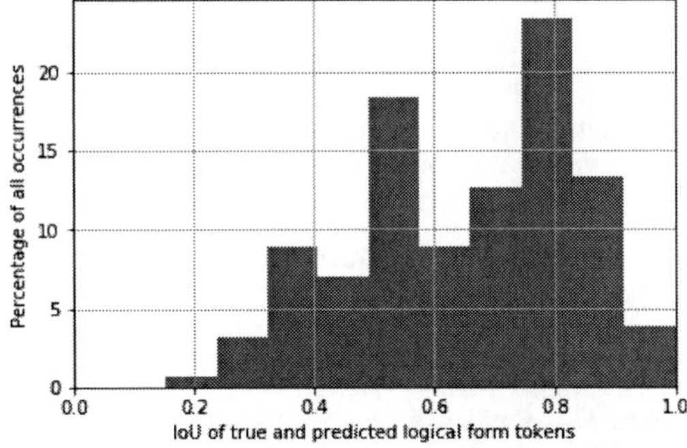

Figure 2: Distribution of the error attributable to the predicted tokens

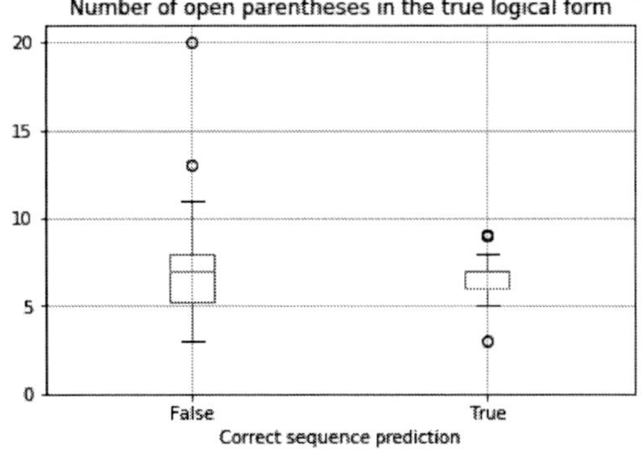

Figure 3: Effect of the logical form complexity on parsing accuracy

where True is the set of non-punctuation tokens in the true logical form and Predicted is the same set in the predicted sequence.

This metric focuses on how well the system is producing the correct tokens and disregards the order of the produced tokens and the correct nesting. For a correct parsing we get a value of 1, however an incorrect parsing can still get an IoU of 1 when the order or nesting is incorrect. Figure 2 shows the distribution of this metric for the incorrect results.

In the vast majority of the cases the model is not even producing the correct tokens. Most of these are cases where the model is confusing similar predicates such as cities, states, mountains, or rivers. For example instead of generating `_stateid(utah)` the model generates `_cityid(utah)`. These mistakes results in the generation of incorrect logical forms.

A smaller proportion of the errors made by the model can be attributed to the logical form complexity. Figure 3 depicts the parsing accuracy against the number of open parentheses used in the

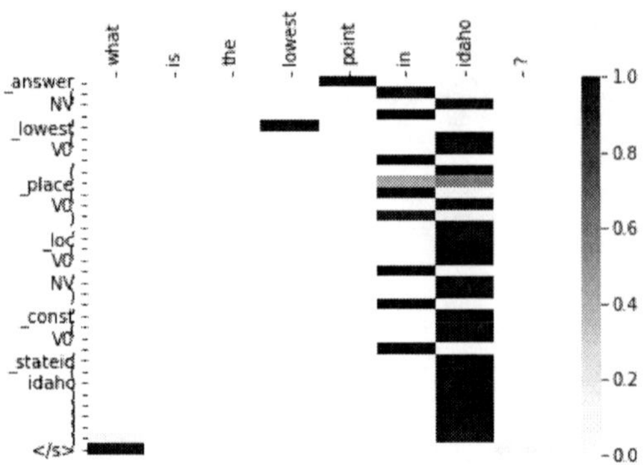

Figure 4: Attention weights for a correctly predicted example

true logical form as a measure of the logical form complexity.

Logical forms with a larger number of opening parentheses tend to be more complex and have deeper nesting which make them harder to predict correctly. We can see that the model has not been able to correctly produce a logical form with more than 10 opening parentheses. To gain more insight into this process let's visualize the attention layer for a correctly predicted example in Figure 4.

We can see that the majority of the attention tends to be focused on a small subset of tokens in the source sentence. This lack of alignment makes it difficult for the model to switch attention between tokens in deeply nested logical forms as most of the instances in the training example do not take that form and look more similar to the example in Figure 4.

6   Future work

We showed that the two-stage framework proposed in this work can improve the parsing accuracy for a semantic parsing task. We need to extend the experiments conducted in this work to more datasets in order to establish a more definitive answer to whether these gains are persistent and significant beyond the GeoQuery dataset. We also need to explore other strategies for pre-training. In this work we used the same objective function for pre-training and fine-tuning. However, we will experiment with different strategies such as pre-training the decoder and encoder separately as language models. Especially for the decoder this can have the effect of teaching the model to produce valid logical forms using a large corpus.

The co-occurrence strategy proposed in this work did not prove to be promising in its current form. As we hypothesized earlier this may be due to the fact that co-occurring tokens may be linked together by appearing in similar contexts. We strategy to overcome this problem is to restrict the augmentation to cases that do not affect any of the predicates in the logical form. This higher precision strategy may reduce the production of semantically incorrect natural language utterances while teaching the model about semantic invariances.

References

Jonathan Berant, Andrew Chou, Roy Frostig, and Percy Liang. 2013. Semantic parsing on freebase from question-answer pairs. In *Proceedings of the 2013 Conference on Empirical Methods in Natural Language Processing*, pages 1533–1544.

Jonathan Berant and Percy Liang. 2014. Semantic parsing via paraphrasing. In *Proceedings of the 52nd Annual Meeting of the Association for Computational Linguistics (Volume 1: Long Papers)*, volume 1, pages 1415–1425.

James Bergstra, Olivier Breuleux, Frédéric Bastien, Pascal Lamblin, Razvan Pascanu, Guillaume Desjardins, Joseph Turian, David Warde-Farley, and Yoshua Bengio. 2010. Theano: a cpu and gpu math expression compiler. In *Proceedings of the Python for scientific computing conference (SciPy)*, volume 4. Austin, TX.

Jacob Devlin, Ming-Wei Chang, Kenton Lee, and Kristina Toutanova. 2018. Bert: Pre-training of deep bidirectional transformers for language understanding. *arXiv preprint arXiv:1810.04805*.

Xing Fan, Emilio Monti, Lambert Mathias, and Markus Dreyer. 2017. Transfer learning for neural semantic parsing. *arXiv preprint arXiv:1706.04326*.

Ian J Goodfellow, Mehdi Mirza, Da Xiao, Aaron Courville, and Yoshua Bengio. 2013. An empirical investigation of catastrophic forgetting in gradient-based neural networks. *arXiv preprint arXiv:1312.6211*.

Robin Jia and Percy Liang. 2016. Data recombination for neural semantic parsing. *arXiv preprint arXiv:1606.03622*.

G. Klein, Y. Kim, Y. Deng, J. Senellart, and A. M. Rush. OpenNMT: Open-Source Toolkit for Neural Machine Translation. *ArXiv e-prints*.

Jayant Krishnamurthy, Pradeep Dasigi, and Matt Gardner. 2017. Neural semantic parsing with type constraints for semi-structured tables. In *Proceedings of the 2017 Conference on Empirical Methods in Natural Language Processing*, pages 1516–1526.

Percy Liang. 2013. Lambda dependency-based compositional semantics. *arXiv preprint arXiv:1309.4408*.

Percy Liang, Michael I Jordan, and Dan Klein. 2013. Learning dependency-based compositional semantics. *Computational Linguistics*, 39(2):389–446.

Adam Paszke, Sam Gross, Soumith Chintala, Gregory Chanan, Edward Yang, Zachary DeVito, Zeming Lin, Alban Desmaison, Luca Antiga, and Adam Lerer. 2017. Automatic differentiation in pytorch.

Prajit Ramachandran, Peter J Liu, and Quoc V Le. 2016. Unsupervised pretraining for sequence to sequence learning. *arXiv preprint arXiv:1611.02683*.

Ilya Sutskever, Oriol Vinyals, and Quoc V Le. 2014. Sequence to sequence learning with neural networks. In *Advances in neural information processing systems*, pages 3104–3112.

Ashish Vaswani, Noam Shazeer, Niki Parmar, Jakob Uszkoreit, Llion Jones, Aidan N. Gomez, Lukasz Kaiser, and Illia Polosukhin. 2017. Attention is all you need. *CoRR*, abs/1706.03762.

Pengcheng Yin and Graham Neubig. 2017. A syntactic neural model for general-purpose code generation. *arXiv preprint arXiv:1704.01696*.

Encoding Position Improves Recurrent Neural Text Summarizers

Apostolos Karanikolos and Ioannis Refanidis
Department of Applied Informatics
University of Macedonia
Thessaloniki, Greece
{a.karanikolos, yrefanid}@uom.edu.gr

Abstract

Modern text summarizers are big neural networks (recurrent, convolutional, or transformers) trained end-to-end under an encoder-decoder framework. These networks equipped with an attention mechanism, that maintains a memory of their source hidden states, are able to generalize well to long text sequences. In this paper, we explore how the different modules involved in an encoder-decoder structure affect the produced summary quality as measured by ROUGE score in the widely used CNN/Daily Mail and Gigaword summarization datasets. We find that encoding the position of the text tokens before feeding them to a recurrent text summarizer gives a significant, in terms of ROUGE, gain to its performance on the former but not the latter dataset.

1 Introduction

Within NLP a number of tasks involve generating text conditioned on some input information (machine translation, image caption generation, headline generation, single and multi-document summarization).

To accomplish the task of text summarization, a system needs the ability to capture the semantic content of the source text and then predict its grammatical, faithful and coherent summary. Since the structure of the system summary has to be closely related to the structure of the input text a central challenge to this task is the problem of alignment, i.e. the problem of how to relate sub-elements of the input to sub-elements of the output (Cho et al., 2015).

Similar to a human-produced summary that intuitively is as good as the clarity of her thoughts and goals, a machine-generated summary depends heavily on the quality of its internal information. For neural network summarizers that is equivalent to strong representations of the source document and of the summary generated so far, both kept as vectors, respectively, in their encoder and decoder hidden states.

Deep learning methods, employing end-to-end trained neural network models, have recently achieved significant, although not robust, ability in generating reasonable multi-sentence abstractive summaries of long news articles. Extending the sequence-to-sequence framework, already adapted in other sequence transduction tasks, these models mostly consist of three cooperating modules, whose parameters are learned jointly through gradient descent or reinforcement learning techniques.

First, an encoder mechanism that produces hidden representations of the source document; second, an attention network that selects its salient information; and third, a decoder module that produces the model summary. This decoder module is often an autoregressive[1] network that splits high dimensional data into a sequence of small pieces and then predicts each piece from those before.

For most languages, these neural models perform summarization in a left to right manner, one word at a time, until a special stop token is generated, which ends the summary. This information processing pipeline can be seen as a four step process "embed – encode – attend – predict". In the "embed" step lexical tokens are converted from indices in a vocabulary to dense vectors, encoding distributional semantics. Then, in the "encode" step information is passed through hidden neural connections (either recurrent, convolutional or feed-forward cells) building the source document matrix representation. Each row of this matrix encodes the "meaning" of each token in the context of its surrounding tokens. Next, in the "attend" step the previous matrix is reduced to a vector

---

[1] Autoregressive model is one in which the prediction for every one sample is influenced by all previous ones.

while ensuring this reduction comes with minimal information loss, reflecting the goal of the attention mechanism to select the most important element from each time step. The final "predict" step reduces this vector to a prediction of the next token in the summary.

Recently, convolutional (Gehring et al., 2017) and self-attentive purely feed-forward (Vaswani et al., 2017) networks have proven able to match the performance of recurrent neural networks (Chopra et al., 2016; Tan et al., 2017) in the role of encoder and decoder modules, replacing them on several sequence generation tasks (Xie, 2017). Used as summarizers, these models can produce not only general but also topic-aware (Wang et al., 2018), query-based (Hasselqvist et al., 2017), or user-controllable (Fan et al., 2018) summaries. However, in this work we choose to only focus on general summaries.

Creating summaries from documents, seen as a sequential decision making problem for the decoder-agent, is also amenable to reinforcement learning techniques. In this setting, the model at each step learns to make a decision of the next token to generate while optimizing a sequence–level objective, the full sequence ROUGE score (Lin, 2004). Here, arises the issue of the exploration-exploitation tradeoff, a problem but also an opportunity for the agent to generate a more diverse, hence more abstract and human-like summary (Chen and Bansal, 2018).

In the standard supervised setting, the model needs labeled summaries in the training phase to provide the appropriate learning signal. In an unsupervised setting, a model could potentially learn to summarize documents without having access to ground-truth summaries in the learning phase (Chu and Liu, 2019).

The quality of the produced system summaries can be rated both by automatic metrics (ROUGE, Meteor) and by human raters. Intuitively, a high quality summary should be a concise text that captures the salient and rejects the secondary information of the source document. It would use grammatical language structures and include a significant amount of novel words and phrases not found in the source text.

The key contribution of this work is the novel use of the token-position information in a recurrent neural text summarizer. We show that our neural network approach, while requiring fewer

Source Document

governments around the world are using the threat of terrorism -- real or perceived -- to advance executions, amnesty international alleges in its annual report on the death penalty. ...

Reference

amnesty international releases its annual review of the death penalty worldwide; much of it makes for grim reading. slayl shetti countries that use executions to deal with problems are on the wrong side of history.

Baselline Model

amnesty international releases its annual review of the death penalty worldwide. it was indicative of a trend that was starkly evident last year around the world. in pakistan, the government lifted a six-year moratorium on the execution of civilians.

Our Model

amnesty international claims governments are using the threat of terrorism to advance executions. the report, "death sentences and executions 2014, " cites the example of pakistan lifting a six-year moratorium on the execution of civilians following the horrific attack on a school in december.

Figure 1: Example of different model generated two-sentence summaries of the same input text (source document). Reference denotes the ground-truth summary. With position encoding (our model) we see more abstractive ability, while without position encoding (baseline model) we see less paraphrasing and more copying from input text.

learnable parameters than a transformer model, outperforms it on the CNN/Daily Mail dataset (Hermann et al., 2015) and performs on par with it on the Gigaword corpus (Rush et al., 2017). These results suggest we do not need the computation-heavy self-attention processing of the transformer architecture in neural text summarizers.

2 Background

We describe the standard approach for supervised abstractive summarization learning based on the attentive sequence-to-sequence framework, and the challenges it faces in text representation and generation. The goal of a model under this framework is to maximize the probability of generating correct target sequences.

2.1 Sequence-to-Sequence Framework

The sequence-to-sequence framework consists of two parts: a neural network for the encoder and another network for the decoder. The source text, reference summary data is tokenized and fed to the encoder and decoder networks respectively during training. The encoder network reads the source text and transforms it into a potentially useful vector representation which then passes to the decoder network to help in the prediction of the summary sequence on a token per token basis.

Encoder Mechanism: The encoder mechanism uses a deep neural network to convert a sequence of source words into a sequence of vectors representing its contextual meaning. This encoding is done using recurrent, convolutional or transformer neural networks. Word and positional embeddings can be used before feeding the source sequence to the deep neural encoder network.

Decoder Mechanism: The decoder network uses the vector representation coming out of the encoder network and its own internal state information to represent the state of the sequence generated so far. Essentially, the decoder mechanism combines specific vectorial knowledge about the relevant context with general knowledge about language generation in order to produce the output sequence. Analogous to the encoder, it can also use word and positional embeddings to the tokens it already generated, before feeding each new token to the deep neural decoder network.

2.2 Attention Mechanism

A mapping of the decoder state at each time step with all the encoder states into an attention vector, helps produce a context vector which is a weighted sum of the encoder states. Incorporating this context vector at each decoding time step helps improve text generation (Bahdanau et al., 2014).

Necessity for Attention: From a cognitive science perspective, attention, defined as the ability to focus on one thing and ignore others, allows for picking out salient information from noisy data and to remember one event rather than all events. Thus, attention is selective and appears to be as useful for deep learning as it is for people. From a sequence-to-sequence standpoint, attention is the action of focusing on specific parts of the input sequence. It can be stochastic and trained with reinforcement learning (hard attention) or differentiable and trained with back-propagation (soft attention). We note that attention changes over time. As the model generates each word, its attention changes to reflect the relevant parts of the input.

Self-Attention: When a sequence-to-sequence model is trying to generate the next word in the summary, this word is usually describing only a part of the input text. Using the whole representation of the input text (h) to condition the generation of each word cannot efficiently produce different words for different parts of the input. But, if we first divide the input into n parts, we can compute representations of each part $(h_1, ..., h_n)$. Then, when the model is generating a new word, its attention mechanism can focus on the relevant part of the input sequence, so that the model can only use specific parts of the input. This is the idea of self-attention.

2.3 Text generation

Greedy decoding: When using greedy decoding, the model at any time step has only one single hypothesis. Since a text sequence can be the most probable despite including tokens that are not the most probable at each time step, greedy decoding is seldom used in practice.

Beam decoding: When using beam search decoding the model iteratively expands each hypothesis one token at a time and in the end of each iteration it only keeps the beam-size best ones. Small beam sizes are able to yield good results in terms of ROUGE score while larger beam sizes can yield worse results. To make decoding efficient the decoder expands only hypotheses that look promising. Bad hypotheses should be pruned early to avoid wasting time on them, but pruning compromises optimality.

Challenges in text generation: In neural summary generation, a model error occurs when the summary with the highest score under the model is not a good summary, while a search error occurs when the decoder network cannot find the summary with the highest score under the model.

Other challenges include the generation of truncated or repetitive outputs, the production of blank or generic text, or ungrammatical gibberish. Rare or out of vocabulary (OOV) word generation, that naturally arises for languages with very large vocabularies can be mitigated in practice by the use of the copy mechanism, introduced later.

Another issue is the early summary termination. During the beam search procedure, hypotheses terminate with the "eos" token. The decoder should learn to place very low probability to this token until the summary is fully generated. However,

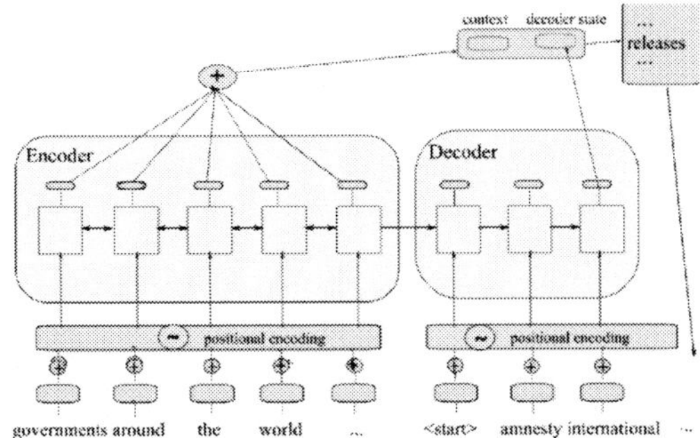

Figure 2: Model architecture. Encoder is a bi-directional 4-layer LSTM and the decoder is a uni-directional 4-layer LSTM. The vector containing encoder context and decoder state is used to compute the distribution over the output vocabulary.

sometimes "eos" does not have sufficiently low probability resulting in production of short or truncated system summaries. Length normalization, or the coverage penalty (Koehn and Knowles, 2017) technique that re-ranks these early terminating hypotheses can successfully address this issue.

Other problems for existing sequence-to-sequence neural summarizers include generation of factually incorrect summaries, and, importantly, vulnerability to adversarial information suggesting a crucial lack of semantic understanding. Finally, abstractive summaries can still be largely extractive or contain redundant information ((See et al., 2017)).

3   Model

Our model learns to generate an abstractive summary from a given source document. Based on and extending the sequence-to-sequence framework, we compute copy and coverage vectors to address redundant and repetitive generation, and positional encodings to achieve good source text representation. Figure 1 shows an example of our model generated two-sentence summary of a news article. The overall structure of our model is illustrated in Figure 2.

3.1   Copy Mechanism

As some tokens that occur in the source document are out-of-vocabulary words, a mechanism is needed to enable their generation. We use the copy mechanism, initially introduced in (Gu et al., 2016), to allow copying words from the source text thus enabling our model to produce OOV words

and not be restricted to a pre-set fixed vocabulary.

The final probability distribution from which the model makes predictions is a weighted sum of the probability of generating words from the pre-set vocabulary and the probability of copying words from the source text using the attention distribution.

To calculate the attention distribution a over the source text at decoder time step t we use the bilinear dot product of the last layer decoder output s_t and encoder output h_j as follows:

$$u_t = s_t W_c h_j$$
$$a_t^j = \exp u_t^j / \sum_k \exp u_t^k$$

Then we calculate the copy probability $g_t \in [0, 1]$ which we use to adjust the model selection between copying from the source and generating from the vocabulary.

$$g_t = sigmoid(W_g[s_t, h_j] + b_g)$$

where Wc, Wg, bg are learnable parameters. So, the final probability distribution P from which the model predicts the summary token w to generate or copy at each time step t is calculated as follows:

$$p_t(w) = (1 - g_t)P_t^{vocab}(w) + g_t \sum_i^{w_i=w} a_t^i$$

3.2   Coverage Mechanism

We compute a vector to discourage repetition in our model-generated summaries. We follow ((See et al., 2017)) and maintain a coverage vector c_t as the sum of attention distributions over all previous decoder time steps:

$$c_t = \sum_{t'=0}^{t'=t-1} a^{t'}$$

Then, we use the coverage vector c_t as an extra input to the attention mechanism to help it remember its previous decisions and avoid repeated attention to the same locations in the source text.

3.3   Positional Encodings

Sinusoidal positional encodings were developed for non-recurrent neural networks, initially for the transformer model for machine translation (Vaswani et al., 2017). We are the first to make use of this feature in a recurrent neural model.

We compute positional encodings and add them to the initial word representations as seen in Figure 2. The position computation of embedding size 512 uses sine and cosine functions of different frequencies as follows:

$$PosEnc_{(pos,2i)} = sin(pos/10000^{2i/512})$$

$$PosEnc_{(pos,2i+1)} = cos(pos/10000^{2i//512})$$

with each dimension i of the encoding corresponding to a sinusoid.

3.4 Learning Objective

We use a token level learning objective. During model training, the decoder is fed the ground-truth summary and the model parameters θ are optimized maximizing the likelihood of the training data, which is achieved by minimizing the cross entropy loss L:

$$L(\theta) = -\sum_{\tau=1}^{T} logp(yt|X, y < t; \theta)$$

In this method, also known as teacher forcing, ground truth tokens are shown to the model just before the decoder makes its next step prediction. A more time consuming approach would be to use a sequence level objective which incorporates policy gradient learning or a minimum risk training strategy to maximize the ROUGE score of generated summaries as in (Carbonell and Goldstein, 1998). A mixed objective that combines word and sequence level objectives with a fixed hyperparameter value was used in ((Paulus et al., 2017)).

4 Experiments

4.1 Datasets

We perform experiments on the CNN/Daily-Mail news articles summarization dataset ((Hermann et al., 2015)) and the Gigaword sentence summarization/headline generation corpus (Rush et al., 2017), which are both standard corpora for long and short document summarization. For the CNN/Daily-Mail train and validation splits, we truncate source text to 400 tokens and target summaries to 100 tokens, following standard practice. We limit both input and output vocabulary to the 50000 most frequent words, and replace the rest with UNK tokens. For training on the Gigaword dataset we follow the pre-processing steps of (Rush et al., 2017), replacing all digit characters

Dataset	Train	Valid	Test	DL	SL
CNN/DM	287226	13368	11490	781	56
Gigaword	3803957	189651	1951	31.4	8.3

Table 1: Dataset statistics. DL and SL denote average number of tokens in source document and summary, respectively.

with # and tokens seen less than five times with UNK. Table 1 shows the main statistics for both corpora.

4.2 Training details

We train our models with the Adam optimizer (Kingma and Ba, 2014) with $\beta1 = 0.9$ and $\beta2 = 0.998$. We increase (warm up) the learning rate linearly for the first 8000 steps and then decrease it exponentially, following the noam decay scheme. We randomly initialize and learn during training word embeddings of size 512, and apply positional encoding before feeding them to a four layer LSTM stack with 512 hidden units per layer. To regularize, we use dropout (with probability 0.2) between the stacked LSTM hidden states. At test time, we use a beam size of 3 and, for CNN/Daily Mail, set the minimum length of the generated summary to 35. We do not use the trigram repetition avoidance heuristic defined in ((Paulus et al., 2017)), because we find it results in decreased performance on both datasets. We implemented our models using PyTorch on the OpenNMT system (Klein et al., 2017). We ran the experiments on a 12GB Titan Xp GPU.

4.3 Models

Baselines: We consider two strong baseline models that do not use positional encodings, (1) a four-layer transformer model with 80,68 million parameters and (2) a four-layer recurrent model with 67,80 million parameters, with a bidirectional LSTM encoder and unidirectional LSTM decoder.

Our model: We form our model by simply including fixed, sinusoidal positional encodings to our recurrent baseline, thus keeping the same architecture settings and parameters.

4.4 Evaluation Metrics

For both CNN/DM and Gigaword datasets, we report the full length F-1 scores of the ROUGE-1, ROUGE-2 and ROUGE-L metrics and their average (R-AVG).

Model	R-1	R-2	R-L	R-AVG
LSTM 4l	37.99	16.73	35.04	29.92
Transformer	37.88	16.48	34.94	29.77
Our method	**38.60**	**17.50**	**35.81**	**30.64**
Celikyilmaz et al., (2018)	41.69	19.47	37.92	33.02

Table 2: Rouge scores on the CNN/DM test set.

Model	R-1	R-2	R-L	R-AVG
LSTM 4l	33	16.31	31.11	26.80
Transformer	33.49	16.85	31.67	27.47
Our method	**33.09**	**16.36**	**31.24**	**26.90**
Cao et al., (2018a)	37.04	19.03	34.46	30.17

Table 3: Rouge scores on the Gigaword test set.

5   Results

The main results of our neural text summarizers for the CNN/DM corpus are listed in Table 2. The two baseline models are shown in the top two lines followed by our proposed model. We observe that our position aware LSTM summarizer scores better than our two baselines, without requiring any additional model parameters or fine-tuning.

On the other hand, our small, cross-entropy trained recurrent model did not match the performance of the large recurrent model of (Celikyilmaz et al., 2018) which uses multiple communicating encoders connected to a single decoder, is trained using reinforcement learning and sets the state-of-the art performance in this dataset.

Table 3 shows experiments with the same three models trained and evaluated on the Gigaword corpus and Figure 4 shows the corresponding model summaries. We can see that the positional-encoding improvement compared to the baselines did not carry over to this dataset. Here, our proposed recurrent model, although marginally better than the recurrent baseline, does not outperform the transformer summarizer. We hypothesize this result could be due to the better language modeling ability of the transformer model compared to the LSTM models in this dataset, as shown in Figure 3 from their corresponding perplexity values.

We note that the state-of-the-art neural model (Cao et al., 2018a) in this dataset, is significantly more complex and memory demanding than our model. When generating its summaries it utilizes an information-retrieval platform to implement a

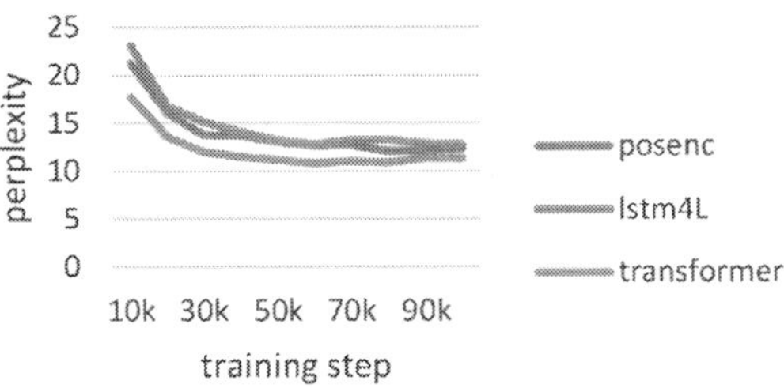

Figure 3: Perplexity scores (lower is better) of different models trained on Gigaword. Transformer scores better than both lstm and posenc (best seen in color).

template-based summarization approach and does not simply depend on the source text.

6   Related work

Early approaches to text summarization were based in first finding and then reordering (re-ranking) the most important sentences in a document based on their word frequency or some sentence-similarity metric. Then, a simple extraction of the top k highest scoring sentences from the source document could produce a grammatical correct, albeit incoherent, summary.

The need for more human-like, abstractive summary creation led to the modern sequence-to-sequence models with attention. These neural networks are able to generate any word from their vocabulary, even novel words and phrases unseen in the source document, but can also copy from it when generating an out of vocabulary word is called for.

However, problems like repetitive, generic, or ungrammatical summary generation, with limited abstraction and easily fooled by irrelevant information remained intact for the standard neural network summarizers. Several extensions to their basic encoder-decoder architecture or their end-to-end learning strategy developed accordingly.

In (Lin et al., 2018) the authors use a convolutional gated unit to help control the information flow between the encoder and decoder networks aiming to filter the secondary and preserve only the core information, while Zhou et al. (2017) design a selective gate network with the same goal. In order to avoid generating fake facts in a summary, Cao et al. (2018b) extract actual factual descriptions from the source text leveraging information retrieval techniques. A task-agnostic diverse

Source Article

india's children are getting increasingly overweight and unhealthy and the government is asking schools to ban junk food, officials said thursday.

Reference Summary

indian government ask schools to ban junk food

Model Generated Summaries

LSTM 4-layer
india's children getting unhealthy

Transformer
india askd schools to ban junk food

Our Model
indian children getting overweight

State of the Art (Cao et al., 2018a)
indian schools to ban junk food

Figure 4: Source article, reference and model generated summaries from the Gigaword test set.

beam search procedure is proposed in (Vijayakumar et al., 2018) that modifies the standard beam search algorithm in the direction of more diverse text generation.

Other works explore abstractive sentence compression with paraphrasing (Nayeem et al., 2019), different network training regimes (Ayana et al., 2016) or architectures that jointly learn summarization and semantic parsing (Fan et al., 2018). The authors in (Guo et al., 2018) propose a multitask model with parallel training of three tasks: summary generation, question generation, and entailment generation and find it provides useful guidance for summarization. While we share their motivation to make the model input richer, our work presents a much simpler approach. Another recent attempt to produce rich pre-trained encoder representations for many downstream tasks, including summarization, is BERT (Dev(Lin et al., 2018)).

7 Conclusion

The application of encoder-decoder structures has attracted growing attention in the area of longer text summarization research. Neural networks with recurrences, convolutions and transformers were developed for the task of single-document summarization. We began this work aiming to ex-

plore the causal factors with the greatest impact in final model output. In the process, we found that position aware recurrent networks can be a simpler, better performing approach than transformers in abstractive single document summarization.

Recent advances in word contextual representations hold the promise of richer, more abstractive summary generation. In this paper, we show that explicitly representing and using the positional information of source text tokens in a recurrent sequence to sequence summarizer helps improve its performance.

Relative position representations, which encode the distance between sequence elements rather than their absolute position, could also help further improve performance. This effect could take place through enabling better optimization of the information selection process in later processing steps, an hypothesis we aim to explore in future work.

Acknowledgments

This research is funded by the University of Macedonia Research Committee as part of the "Principal Research 2019" funding program. We thank the anonymous reviewers for helpful comments. The Titan Xp used for this work was donated by the NVIDIA Corporation.

References

Shiqi Shen Ayana, Zhiyuan Liu, and Maosong Sun. 2016. Neural headline generation with minimum risk training. *arXiv preprint arXiv:1604.01904*.

Dzmitry Bahdanau, Kyunghyun Cho, and Yoshua Bengio. 2014. Neural machine translation by jointly learning to align and translate. *arXiv preprint arXiv:1409.0473*.

Ziqiang Cao, Wenjie Li, Sujian Li, and Furu Wei. 2018a. Retrieve, rerank and rewrite: Soft template based neural summarization. In *Proceedings of the 56th Annual Meeting of the Association for Computational Linguistics (Volume 1: Long Papers)*, pages 152–161.

Ziqiang Cao, Furu Wei, Wenjie Li, and Sujian Li. 2018b. Faithful to the original: Fact aware neural abstractive summarization. In *Thirty-Second AAAI Conference on Artificial Intelligence*.

Jaime G Carbonell and Jade Goldstein. 1998. The use of mmr, diversity-based reranking for reordering documents and producing summaries. In *SIGIR*, volume 98, pages 335–336.

Asli Celikyilmaz, Antoine Bosselut, Xiaodong He, and Yejin Choi. 2018. Deep communicating agents for abstractive summarization. *arXiv preprint arXiv:1803.10357*.

Yen-Chun Chen and Mohit Bansal. 2018. Fast abstractive summarization with reinforce-selected sentence rewriting. *arXiv preprint arXiv:1805.11080*.

Kyunghyun Cho, Aaron Courville, and Yoshua Bengio. 2015. Describing multimedia content using attention-based encoder-decoder networks. *IEEE Transactions on Multimedia*, 17(11):1875–1886.

Sumit Chopra, Michael Auli, and Alexander M Rush. 2016. Abstractive sentence summarization with attentive recurrent neural networks. In *Proceedings of the 2016 Conference of the North American Chapter of the Association for Computational Linguistics: Human Language Technologies*, pages 93–98.

Eric Chu and Peter Liu. 2019. Meansum: a neural model for unsupervised multi-document abstractive summarization. In *International Conference on Machine Learning*, pages 1223–1232.

Lisa Fan, Dong Yu, and Lu Wang. 2018. Robust neural abstractive summarization systems and evaluation against adversarial information. *arXiv preprint arXiv:1810.06065*.

Jonas Gehring, Michael Auli, David Grangier, Denis Yarats, and Yann N Dauphin. 2017. Convolutional sequence to sequence learning. In *Proceedings of the 34th International Conference on Machine Learning-Volume 70*, pages 1243–1252. JMLR. org.

Jiatao Gu, Zhengdong Lu, Hang Li, and Victor OK Li. 2016. Incorporating copying mechanism in sequence-to-sequence learning. *arXiv preprint arXiv:1603.06393*.

Han Guo, Ramakanth Pasunuru, and Mohit Bansal. 2018. Soft layer-specific multi-task summarization with entailment and question generation. *arXiv preprint arXiv:1805.11004*.

Johan Hasselqvist, Niklas Helmertz, and Mikael Kågebäck. 2017. Query-based abstractive summarization using neural networks. *arXiv preprint arXiv:1712.06100*.

Karl Moritz Hermann, Tomas Kocisky, Edward Grefenstette, Lasse Espeholt, Will Kay, Mustafa Suleyman, and Phil Blunsom. 2015. Teaching machines to read and comprehend. In *Advances in neural information processing systems*, pages 1693–1701.

Diederik P Kingma and Jimmy Ba. 2014. Adam: A method for stochastic optimization. *arXiv preprint arXiv:1412.6980*.

Guillaume Klein, Yoon Kim, Yuntian Deng, Jean Senellart, and Alexander M Rush. 2017. Opennmt: Open-source toolkit for neural machine translation. *arXiv preprint arXiv:1701.02810*.

Philipp Koehn and Rebecca Knowles. 2017. Six challenges for neural machine translation. *arXiv preprint arXiv:1706.03872*.

Chin-Yew Lin. 2004. Rouge: A package for automatic evaluation of summaries. In *Text summarization branches out*, pages 74–81.

Junyang Lin, Xu Sun, Shuming Ma, and Qi Su. 2018. Global encoding for abstractive summarization. *arXiv preprint arXiv:1805.03989*.

Mir Tafseer Nayeem, Tanvir Ahmed Fuad, and Yllias Chali. 2019. Neural diverse abstractive sentence compression generation. In *European Conference on Information Retrieval*, pages 109–116. Springer.

Romain Paulus, Caiming Xiong, and Richard Socher. 2017. A deep reinforced model for abstractive summarization. *arXiv preprint arXiv:1705.04304*.

Alexander M Rush, SEAS Harvard, Sumit Chopra, and Jason Weston. 2017. A neural attention model for sentence summarization. In *ACLWeb. Proceedings of the 2015 Conference on Empirical Methods in Natural Language Processing*.

Abigail See, Peter J Liu, and Christopher D Manning. 2017. Get to the point: Summarization with pointer-generator networks. *arXiv preprint arXiv:1704.04368*.

Jiwei Tan, Xiaojun Wan, and Jianguo Xiao. 2017. Abstractive document summarization with a graph-based attentional neural model. In *Proceedings of the 55th Annual Meeting of the Association for Computational Linguistics (Volume 1: Long Papers)*, pages 1171–1181.

Ashish Vaswani, Noam Shazeer, Niki Parmar, Jakob Uszkoreit, Llion Jones, Aidan N Gomez, Łukasz Kaiser, and Illia Polosukhin. 2017. Attention is all you need. In *Advances in neural information processing systems*, pages 5998–6008.

Ashwin K Vijayakumar, Michael Cogswell, Ramprasaath R Selvaraju, Qing Sun, Stefan Lee, David Crandall, and Dhruv Batra. 2018. Diverse beam search for improved description of complex scenes. In *Thirty-Second AAAI Conference on Artificial Intelligence*.

Li Wang, Junlin Yao, Yunzhe Tao, Li Zhong, Wei Liu, and Qiang Du. 2018. A reinforced topic-aware convolutional sequence-to-sequence model for abstractive text summarization. *arXiv preprint arXiv:1805.03616*.

Ziang Xie. 2017. Neural text generation: A practical guide. *arXiv preprint arXiv:1711.09534*.

Qingyu Zhou, Nan Yang, Furu Wei, and Ming Zhou. 2017. Selective encoding for abstractive sentence summarization. *arXiv preprint arXiv:1704.07073*.

Association for Computational Linguistics
209 N. Eighth Street
Stroudsburg, Pennsylvania 18360

ISBN 978-1-5108-9245-3